Where the Saints Have Trod

HELEN M. GOUGAR
(1843–1907)

WHERE THE SAINTS HAVE TROD

The Life of Helen Gougar

by
Robert C. Kriebel

Purdue University Press
West Lafayette, Indiana

Photographs and line drawings are through
the courtesy of:

Tippecanoe County Historical Association
    Helen M. Gougar, John D. Gougar, Second
    Presbyterian Church, Castle Cottage, Tippecanoe
    County Courthouse, Furman E. D. McGinley,
    Lafayette in the 1890s.
Indiana State Library
    Our Herald (front pages, September and November
    1884), Zerelda G. Wallace, May Wright Sewall,
    Alexander A. Rice, Frances Wright, Benjamin
    Harrison.
Kingman Brothers' *1878 Historical Atlas of Tippecanoe
County, Indiana*
    W. DeWitt Wallace.
Lafayette Journal and Courier
    Forty Thousand Miles of World Wandering.
Purdue University Archives
    John S. Williams.

Book designed by James McCammack

Library of Congress Cataloging in Publication Data

Kriebel, Robert C., 1932–
    Where the saints have trod.

    Bibliography: p.
    Includes index.
    1. Gougar, Helen Mar Jackson, 1843–1907.
2. Feminists—United States—Biography. 3. Social
reformers—United States—Biography. 4. Lafayette (Ind.)
—History. I. Title.
HQ1413.G68K74 1985   305.4′2′0924 [B]   85–3633
ISBN 0-911198-73-3

Published 1985

Printed in the United States of America

CONTENTS

ILLUSTRATIONS

PREFACE

Like a mighty ar-my
Moves the church of God;
Brothers, we are treading
Where the saints have trod.

From "Onward, Christian Soldiers," Sabine Baring-Gould, 1864,
and Arthur S. Sullivan, 1871

The crusades for good, like the battle of the sexes, had lasted since Creation. Yet a woman's place still was mostly in the home when, in Lafayette, Indiana, on June 6, 1907, Helen Gougar died.

But this woman had been colorful and visible and audible enough in life that word of her death was front-page news in many American newspapers that day. Her place in life had been far from kitchen, hearth, and cradle. Instead she had been a soldier for reform, at times linked with the likes of Susan B. Anthony, Elizabeth Cady Stanton, Mary Livermore, and Frances Willard, as well as fellow Hoosiers May Wright Sewall, Zerelda Wallace, and Ida Harper. At other times, she dropped their causes and ridiculed their strategies to concentrate on church problems and stopping liquor or to talk about free trade, immigration, education, legislation—you name it.

Surprising things were written and said of her in death, such as these words in the *Lafayette Morning Journal*'s editorial: "Mrs. Gougar's temperament was that of the agitator; it was her mission to arouse and awaken. She thrived on antagonism, knew not the meaning of fear and had all the zeal of a martyr."

It was a woman they were writing about, do not forget, and the year was 1907; but it was all very fitting. For there was little in Mrs. Gougar's life that could be called typical of the times then—or even now. Helen Gougar was self-righteous, pushy, changeable, outspoken. Too much so for her own good. She would have been a popular guest on "Meet the Press" or "Good Morning America"—blunt as Joan Rivers, funny as Erma Bombeck, controversial as Anita Bryant, smart as Jeane Kirkpatrick, wholesome as Phyllis George. Too bad for her, and for us, that she predated radio and television, or that great experiment with prohibition, or any of the so-called world wars or Vietnam or Korea, or the Iron Curtain, or Hiroshima. Too bad she died before woman suffrage and the hullabaloo over the Equal Rights Amendment.

But maybe it is not so bad after all. Because in reading now about her life and work, one might feel the thrill of finding hidden treasure. She was the possessor of a prodigious IQ. She was a teacher, speaker, author, editor, traveler, reformer, and intellectual. She knew the law inside out but, being female, could not practice it for a living. She was a master of public affairs but, being female, could not vote on any of them. She wrote of people and spoke to millions (live and in color) but had few friends, owing surely to the controversial nature of her causes and the occasional sting of her personality.

Her remains were buried and she was rather soon forgotten. Why? Her name is hard to pronounce, for one thing. That in itself stops one from becoming a household word. (In *Gougar*, the two G's are hard, as in *gargle*, and the first syllable rhymes with *cow*.) Then, too, there already was Susan B. Anthony and Company to be sanctified. The timing was wrong for Helen Gougar to be a national leader, but her temperament was not that of a docile follower. So she acted upon what was in her own heart and mind.

It would be a great evening's entertainment to snap on a television set and listen to Helen Gougar comment on, say, the Susan B. Anthony one-dollar coin; the rise and fall of Jane Byrne, and the emergence of Geraldine Ferraro; or the true value of Billy Graham, Martin Luther King, Jr., and the Moral Majority. In light of all she wrote and said 100 years ago about similar topics, it would also be entertaining and educational to hear her orate once more on imperialism, protective tariffs, nationalizing railroads, Cuba, U.S. blundering in the Philippines, the brutal Russian government, and the sleeping giant China.

A second thought: it would make fascinating drama if one of our modern Katharine Hepburn-type actresses could rehearse the lines, make the necessary cosmetic and costume changes, and do a TV special called "An Evening with Helen Gougar" in the format in which Harry S. Truman, Mark Twain, Clarence Darrow, and others have been reincarnated. Today's woman's movement, today's ongoing fight against alcoholism and substance abuse, today's struggling church, today's diluted home life—all these causes would benefit from a booster shot right about now; and for that, we need the ideas and energy of the Helen Gougars of yesterday.

That is precisely why this book. And why now. In many an American city and town—and this is true of Helen's hometown of Lafayette—there is great effort, pride, and patting of backs associated with the preservation of historic buildings. The federal government offers aid for such preservation, and national registries list those buildings. But we are not doing enough to preserve America's historic people, especially their thinking. Therefore, this book is a piece of literary restoration work, if you will. Because of a hunch that religious fervor fueled the incredible Helen Gougar engine all those years, lines from some great hymns introduce the major phases of her life. It is eerie how the messages in the lines match her life of work and achievement. And because her life was brisk, businesslike, and without excess, a cool and chronological story-telling style, sparse in the use of adjectives and interpretations, was purposely chosen.

Never a mother in the biological sense of the word, Helen Gougar dedicated her adult life to administering motherly tongue-lashings to the world. But the sting of her lashes is felt as keenly today, to any of us endowed with brains and a century of hindsight, as they were then. Her advice about the importance of keeping home life pure and unified; her views on human weakness, hypocrisy, and slothfulness; and her concept of the world as one human family have not gathered cobwebs.

Well, it makes no difference. She was forgotten anyway. Maybe because Helen Gougar and Lafayette endured such a cold coexistence. She grew far beyond clannish Lafayette in vision and action, but Lafayette, with its typical midwestern social blinders on, kept on trying to interrupt her voice and brake her drive for reforms. To many in status-quo-Lafayette, she was an embarrassment. To some, her marriage to John Gougar, a frail, nearsighted, brilliant, leisure-loving lawyer, had been harmonious and acceptable enough. But she would not let it go at that. She had to go out and BE somebody. Thus the forty-seven-year-long affair between Helen Gougar and

Lafayette—a rough, tough, smelly, brawling, drinking, whisky-making, politics-arguing, lumber-cutting, train-whistling, wholesaling, church-going, hog-slaughtering, river-town hodgepodge of Irish, Germans, English, and American-born pioneers—was tumultuous.

So there are no monuments to Helen Gougar today save the private ones—her gray marble headstone, beside John's, just north of a dignified twelve-column piece of commemorative masonry on which the single word GOUGAR is carved—and now this book about her life and work.

This is a volume intended to inspire the modern reader by reflecting an amazing woman's long-forgotten thoughts, insights, and energies. It is a work composed of facts necessarily linked to and analyzed by a few educated guesses. But every last word of this book is crafted with love, respect, and the best of intentions and is offered as a gift to her, her town, her state, her nation, and to all—especially her embattled sisters living and dead—in the vast army of saintly people who ever have roved the earth, longing to make it better.

Robert C. Kriebel
Lafayette, Indiana
1985

I

FROM FARM TO FORUM

Take my life, and let it be
  Consecrated, Lord, to thee.
Take my moments and my days;
  Let them flow in ceaseless praise.

Take my voice and let me sing,
  Always only for my king.
Take my lips and let them be
  Filled with messages from Thee.

From "Take My Life," Frances Ridley Havergal, 1874,
and John B. Dukes, 1862

CHAPTER 1

Childhood and Beyond

*H*elen Mar Jackson Gougar's beginnings are in some respects a picture puzzle of missing, incomplete, and contradictory parts. We are dealing with life in rural Hillsdale County, Michigan, in the 1840s. We are speaking of long-demolished homes and schools, missing records, dead towns, forgotten legends, lost maps, and reminiscences or hearsay. From various sources, though, a picture can be assembled that shows Helen was born July 18, 1843, the second daughter and third child in a family of seven children of a farm couple, William and Clarissa (Dresser) Jackson. The children included one boy, Andrew, then his sisters, Mary, Helen, Edna, Etta, Lydia called "Jennie," and Adelaide called "Addie." All evidently were born in the same home near the southern Michigan town of Litchfield between about 1840 and 1855.

Helen once recalled that she was educated in the public schools until age twelve, then entered the preparatory department of nearby Hillsdale College. Forced to leave Hillsdale to help earn money to educate her younger sisters, she went to Lafayette* at the age of sixteen in May 1860, to be a schoolteacher.[1]

Editor's note: Throughout the text, notes, and bibliography of this book, towns and cities without state identification are located in Indiana. Of course, major U.S. cities also are not identified by state.

3

Why Lafayette? It appears to have been a simple case of "follow the leader." Three young uncles and school chums—Jasper, Parker, and H. H. Dresser—had moved to Lafayette to run a staple and fancy drygoods store on the south side of the courthouse square in about 1859. Next, Helen's brother, Andrew, had moved to Lafayette, perhaps to work with the Dressers.

Although Helen seemed precocious, it is not clear how she qualified to teach school at age sixteen. Over a century later, a researcher seeking an answer to that question wrote to the archivist at Hillsdale College, near Helen Jackson's birthplace, to verify reports that "Helen Jackson" had studied and, in fact, been graduated. The college's records show that "Helen Gougar" received an honorary Master of Arts degree in 1892 but do not show that she ever actually attended the college, known during her girlhood as an antislavery or abolitionist institution. The archivist did concede that a fire in 1963 had destroyed most of the early records.

But here again is a mystery. Surviving Hillsdale College records do show that a "Helen M. Jackson" was enrolled in the preparatory course of the Female Department in 1857; she returned as a student in 1858 and again in 1859. It is tempting to attach this academic record to the eventual Helen M. Jackson Gougar. But the "Helen M. Jackson" connected with these records also is listed in the college files as hailing from Loda, Illinois, and may indeed have been another Helen M. Jackson entirely.[2]

There are more contradictions. Helen Gougar's obituary in 1907 (most surely prepared by local newspapers from facts provided by her husband) reported that she had "graduated from Hillsdale College in 1858, receiving the degree of A.M.," had come to Lafayette in 1859, and had accepted a position as a teacher in the public schools.

Choose your own story. In any case, Helen Jackson clearly was a girl of superior intelligence, ability, and courage. She came to the Indiana river town, probably on a train from Michigan City, into the welcoming arms of uncles and a brother who met her at the station. In the beginning, she probably roomed and boarded with one of the Dressers or her brother. By 1860 Parker and H. H. Dresser seem to have left Lafayette while Jasper Dresser, twenty-two, had just started practicing law.

From this mixture of contradictions and fact fragments, though, emerges a generally accurate picture of Helen Jackson's beginnings. She was a brighter-than-average rural girl of hardworking, frugal, well-disciplined, Christian habits. Hers was a home in which parents, God, the Bible, learning, and work had been supreme forces. She left this childhood and arrived in the Indiana river town, surely a little bit excited, a little bit afraid, a little bit uncertain, yet soundly prepared for life "on her own" in that spring of 1860.

CHAPTER 2

Sweet Land
of Liberty

*A*merica, the nation, and Lafayette, the town, had been caught up in years of sweeping change when Helen Jackson arrived with her physical, mental, and spiritual baggage. Factories and towns springing up were changing America. The machine was replacing the horse. The National Road already was open from Baltimore across central Indiana to Vandalia, Illinois. Such new roads were busy with people, pack horses, carriages, coaches, and wagons.

To cut shipping costs, the Erie Canal had been built to link the Hudson River to Buffalo; and the Wabash and Erie Canal now connected western Indiana with Toledo and Lake Erie via the Wabash River valley through Lafayette.

Then there was the steamboat. Since the 1820s, river steamers had carried most of the products of the Mississippi Valley; and when the water was high, steamers and flatboats chugged upstream from the south to Lafayette on the Wabash, while the mule-drawn canal boats floated along serenely in the skinny channel of the Wabash and Erie Canal nearby.

Railroads soon grew out of the commercial rivalry among eastern cities in the 1830s. The completion of each new stage of the transportation system connected areas like Indiana more closely with the East. Eastern products began arriving in growing volume. Eastern factories grew. Foreign trade grew. And from all this emerged problems associated with working women, child labor, employer abuses, and efforts to organize workers into unions.

Immigration had changed towns like Lafayette. The Irish and Germans especially arrived in great numbers. The Irish came to work on the roads, canals, and railroads. Germans settled in the Midwest, took up trades, and groomed immaculate, moneymaking farms. The immigration stirred resentment among some Americans whose families had arrived at an earlier date. Sometimes riots broke out, and by the early 1850s, the Know-Nothing party had risen politically, vowing to support only American-born Protestants for public office.

People's ideas were shifting, too, and various reformers were addressing every facet of life. Women always had worked with men to build early America, but they had been regarded as inferior by nature. Tradition, religious ideas, even the law had fed this attitude. The rise of industry created a new and exploited class of women workers and led to an expanding middle class in which the ideal of the "lady" limited a woman's role to gentle enterprises in the home, such as needlework and the entertainment of guests. The teaching of school, especially Sunday school, was acceptable. But it was viewed as "unladylike" for a woman to take part in public meetings. Politics, too, was the concern of men.

In the 1830s, a few women had begun to protest their exclusion from high school and college education, the professions, and participation in public affairs, including the rising antislavery movement. Among the early leaders were Lucretia Mott, a Philadelphia Quaker, and Elizabeth Cady Stanton who, as a girl, had been troubled by the legal discrimination faced by women clients of her father, an upstate New York lawyer. Mott and Stanton had organized America's first woman's rights convention in Seneca Falls, New York, in July 1848. Another early reformer was author and philanthropist Dorothea Lynde Dix from Boston, whose efforts had led to improved conditions in prisons and institutions for the mentally ill. Susan B. Anthony of Rochester, New York, synonymous today with the cause of woman's rights, joined the movement in 1851 when she was thirty-one.

In Indiana as in the rest of the nation, workers for women's causes had appeared. State historians consider Frances Wright of New Harmony to have been the first feminist in Indiana. She cooperated with the Owen educational movement in obtaining many advantages for women in early Indiana. She was the state's first public crusader for women's property rights, the first advocate of woman suffrage, and a believer in the abolition of slavery. Largely due to her work and that of New Harmony's Robert Dale Owen, Indiana law granted property rights to women in 1838. She formed the Female Social Society as early as 1825, although an 1858 Minerva Club, also in New Harmony, was better known. (Essentially, these groups were forerunners of the "women's club," an organization not quite religious, not quite political, not quite charitable, not quite reformist, but mainly for self-improvement and intellectual growth.) "Let women stand where they may in the scale of improvement," Frances Wright declared, "their position decides that of the race."[1]

Early in Indiana's history, the woman suffrage effort centered in Zerelda G. Wallace, wife of Hoosier governor David Wallace and mother of Lew Wallace, the author of *Ben-Hur*. She gathered about her a small group of believers, and historians claim that in the early 1850s the first state suffrage organization in the United States was formed in Indiana.[2]

Still another major U.S. reform effort had opposed alcoholic beverages. It had enlisted men and women alike who saw in drunkenness a threat to religion, the home, family life, and law and order. Called the "temperance movement," it had begun on a national scale as early as 1833 after a convention in Philadelphia.

But of all the reforms from the 1820s to the 1860s, none pushed the growth of democracy more than the program for free public schools. Educator and Congressman Horace Mann of Massachusetts and editor and educator Henry Barnard of Connecticut led this movement nationally. Slowly these fighters won the struggle for free, tax-supported schools in one state after another.

At the same time, the issue of slavery had risen to divisive proportions across the American landscape. Americans had imported black slaves to work in the South since before the birth of the nation, yet even in America's early days some white Southerners as well as most Northerners had believed slavery to be morally wrong. By 1850 an antislavery or "abolition" movement had aroused controversy and opened a gulf between North and South.

To complicate things, the movement itself had split into militant and moderate sides; an underground network formed to smuggle slaves through northern states and into Canada to freedom. Lafayette was one of the many stops a freedom seeker might have used in the 1840s and 1850s. The abolitionists at the same time aroused widespread opposition both in North and South, and this often meant bloodshed.

The growing arguments over slavery and a state's right to determine its own policies over slavery and other issues rather than submit to federal domination had introduced the large, complex, and tragic theme which would lead to the Civil War within a year of Helen Jackson's arrival in Lafayette.

The controversial Missouri Compromise of 1820 had established the thirty-six-degree, thirty-minute parallel of latitude from the Mississippi River to the Rocky Mountains as the boundary between slave and free territory, Missouri being the only exception. But in 1854, the Kansas-Nebraska Act had the effect of repealing the Missouri Compromise and creating two new organized territories in the West, Kansas and Nebraska. Both were north of the thirty-six-degree, thirty-minute parallel and, therefore, closed to slavery. But the act abolished that dividing line and gave those territories freedom to form and regulate their domestic institutions in their own way.

Both major parties—the Democrats and the Whigs—had split over supporting the Kansas-Nebraska Act. Southern Democrats and Whigs backed it. Northerners from both parties opposed it. The act stimulated violent controversy over both slavery and states' rights. As one result, a new Republican party formed in Jackson, Michigan, on July 6, 1854. By 1858 Illinois had become the battleground for a preview of the presidential election of 1860.

The obscure lawyer Abraham Lincoln, who abhorred slavery and opposed opening new territories for it, challenged lawyer and Congressman Stephen A. Douglas, a supporter and drafter of the Kansas-Nebraska Act and a backer of "popular sovereignty" or states' rights. Lincoln's strong interest in preserving the Union kept him from being an abolitionist, yet he subscribed to the basic principle of the new Republican party: slavery must go no further. Douglas won that 1858 senatorial election in Illinois, but things said and done in the famous series of Lincoln-Douglas debates came back to cost him the presidential election against Lincoln two years later.

By 1860 North and South friendship had all but vanished, and four political parties were active: Republicans; Northern Democrats; Constitutional Unionists, made up of southern remnants of the old Whig party; and Southern Democrats.

Against this background of changing ways, bursting ideas, new opportunities, and rising hatreds, sixteen-year-old Helen Jackson, fair and slender and blonde, stepped off that train and appraised the sights and sounds and the people of Lafayette, who for forty-seven years would infuriate, disappoint, stimulate, nurture, and finally bury her, remembering only that she was one who "thrived on antagonism."

CHAPTER 3

Lafayette: Young and Confused

The birth and confused growth of Lafayette the city, founded in 1825 along the brushy east bank of the Wabash River's southwesterly flow, mirrored the decades of rapid change in America the nation.

Past its thirty-fifth year as a community when Helen Jackson arrived, Lafayette had developed from an obscure trading point to a seat of county government, of wholesale and retail trade, of river commerce, and of shipping and importing. The factory movement, too, had begun to manifest itself in the smoky brick stacks above recently constructed buildings that distilled whisky, made paper, fired bricks, dressed hogs, ground flour, brewed beer, or housed railroad shops.

In smaller Lafayette workshops, men and women toiled to make boots and shoes, roll cigars, nail sash doors and blinds, stitch together clothing, build carriages and wooden pumps, bake crackers and bread, and boil candy. The business places of blacksmiths, barbers, billiard-saloon keepers, coal and lime dealers, commission merchants, coopers, dentists, druggists, drygoods merchants, grocers, furniture makers, jewelers, and butchers lined the narrow, muddy streets. Painters, paperhangers, physicians and surgeons, printers and bookbinders, stationers, restaurateurs, tanners, soap and candle makers, and liquor dealers had brought their services and skills to the growing town. Three newspapers kept Lafayette informed; and M. S. Scudder, whose undertaking establishment stood on the north side of the courthouse square, ushered its citizens out of this life. Loose dogs, cats, chickens, and even a few grunting hogs scurried about, adding to the hurly-burly of the growing Hoosier town.

By 1860 transportation had developed substantially. Planked roads built in the 1840s and 1850s replaced footpaths and horse trails. The roads now linked Lafayette to Crawfordsville and Dayton, to Rensselaer and Attica, and to the Illinois line. The Wabash and Erie Canal with its plodding little mules and flatboats had run alongside the river since Irish work gangs dug it in the early 1840s southwesterly to Lafayette. A telegraph station had opened in 1849. Between 1851 and 1852, both the Lafayette and Indianapolis Company and the Lafayette and Crawfordsville Company had laid railroad tracks, and the first locomotive made a maiden run in 1852. Since the fall of 1847, a wooden toll bridge had connected Lafayette with the western bank over the canal and the Wabash River. Steamboats whistled as they approached and left the city wharf. And by June 1856, a third major railroad, the Lake Erie, Wabash, and St. Louis, connected Lafayette with Toledo and St. Louis.[1]

American pioneers from Ohio, Pennsylvania, Kentucky, and upstate New York joined hundreds of German, Irish, English, and other immigrants as Lafayette grew from year to year, from census to census. The 1860 census would show that Lafayette had upwards of twelve thousand residents. The growth rate since 1840 amounted to more than 672 percent, according to a certain piece of bragging in one local paper, the *Daily Courier*, making Lafayette "the fastest growing city in the land."

Bragging or not, fastest in the land or not, Lafayette's rapid growth was undeniable and haphazard; and with the arrival of more people, public institutions grew. A log courthouse built in 1826 was quickly replaced by a brick one in 1829, then by a bigger brick courthouse in 1845. Lafayette town government, begun with a small board and a president or mayor in the 1830s, underwent some variations in form and emerged in a mayor-council structure in the spring of 1853 under terms of the 1851 state constitution. There were a small police force and three companies of volunteer firefighters, too, by the time Helen Jackson arrived.

Lafayette reflected the nation's trend toward establishment of public schools. A man is said to have opened the first private school in a one-room log cabin near the courthouse during 1827. A "non-free public school" was reportedly begun in a house near the courthouse in 1829. There is some written mention of another "non-free" public school functioning in 1836 in the First Presbyterian Church. In December 1842, a tuition-supported public school known as the "county seminary" welcomed students, and during 1852 Lafayette's first parochial school opened.[2]

Meanwhile, Indiana's 1851 constitutional convention had begun producing widespread changes. Reorganization of city and town government and setting up public school systems were but two examples. In Lafayette and most Hoosier communities, town boards approved a deluge of ordinances dealing with fire protection, police, railroad rules, gas lighting for streets, wharf management, public health, nuisances, gas service, bridge and street repairs, water reservoir construction, and school board appointments. On September 7, 1853, the Lafayette City Council, in operation only four months, established a twenty-five-cent levy on each $100 worth of taxable property (buildings and land) for public school financing. Nearly a year earlier, five men had been named to the first public school board. With income from the new tax levy, the school board founded Lafayette's first free public school in the late summer of 1853 and arranged to build two more in time for the fall of 1854.

In 1855 a fourth schoolhouse opened, and the board appointed a man the city's first superintendent of schools. But later that year, Indiana's new and growing public school system experienced its first setback. Because of legal defects ruled to exist in the school tax levy laws, no money could be collected, and schools had to be closed. The Indiana General Assembly repaired the law, new taxes were collected, and schools reopened in February 1856. By the spring of 1857, enrollment in the Lafayette public schools was 1,000.

But in January 1858, free schools again had to be closed when public funding was successfully attacked on legal grounds. This time the schools remained closed until May 1860, when the school taxing problems were settled permanently.[3] At this point, when school boards apparently needed teachers quickly and desperately, Helen Jackson's services were welcomed.

Politically, the decades prior to 1860 also had been times of change, but there was no great change in Lafayette. Essentially, few people who came into Lafayette were intensely interested in politics. The town's first newspaper, the *Free Press and Commercial Advertiser*, appeared in September 1829. Espousal of the Whig party and antislavery doctrines was only one of the motives. The paper's first rival, the *Wabash Mercury*, appearing in the spring of 1833, was run by a Democrat.

The influence of the *Free Press* and of a large and well-publicized Whig convention in November 1835 held at the Battle of Tippecanoe battlefield seven miles away nudged Lafayette toward Whig domination at election time. In the 1836 presidential election, Tippecanoe County residents cast 1,244 votes for Whig Alexander Hamilton, compared to 1,041 for Democrat (and national winner) Martin Van Buren. Then during 1838, Lafayette attorney Albert S. White, a Whig who was serving in Congress, was chosen on the seventy-fifth ballot of a deadlocked Indiana legislature to be one of the state's U.S. senators. This gave Lafayette a new Whig political hero to the detriment of the struggling Democrats.

In the spring of 1840, a nationally famous rally at Battle Ground further enhanced Whig power in Lafayette and Tippecanoe County. There the hero of the 1811 battle, Congressman and Territorial Governor William Henry Harrison of Ohio was nominated for president, teamed with lawyer and Congressman John Tyler of Virginia for vice president. The resulting warcry "Tippecanoe and Tyler, Too!" rang in the victorious presidential campaign of 1840. Harrison took office March 4, 1841, died of pneumonia April 4, and Tyler became president!

The year 1854 was important in Lafayette's politics as well as the nation's. Bitter division over the merits of the Kansas-Nebraska Act split both Whigs and Democrats nationally and resulted in the formation of the Republican party in July. In Lafayette the proprietor of the *Daily Courier*, William R. Ellis, played a courageous political role in 1854. When he first bought the *Courier* in 1851, Ellis described the paper's course as "progressive Democrat." But his concept of progressive democracy embraced abolition of slavery, disgust with the Kansas-Nebraska Act, and a strong belief that women should have equal rights with men under the law in commerce and professions. In December 1853, a thirty-five-year-old Massachusetts farm native, now a rising advocate of abolition and a woman's rights orator, Lucy Stone, spoke in Lafayette. Afterwards Ellis wrote in his *Courier* with the touch of a deadly but admiring punster: "Stones are for cracking nuts."

By the late spring of 1854, Ellis had begun a permanent break with the Democratic party over Kansas-Nebraska. He even assailed U.S. Senator John Pettit, a Lafayette attorney and Democrat, in his "progressive Democrat" paper, an unheard-of switch.

The July national split-up of parties was reflected in Lafayette with the calling of a convention on September 2, 1854, to fill a new People's Republican party ticket. On October 9, the "old line" Democrats in Tippecanoe County were defeated by two-to-one pluralities in the county election by candidates of the new merger of old Whigs and new People's Republicans, who believed both in abolition of slavery and Union solidarity among the states.

By 1857 Lafayette Republicans also had started to reap the rewards of newspaper advantage. Young William S. Lingle had left the *Morning Journal* and bought the *Daily Courier*. Thus both papers promoted the Republican philosophy in town while the Democrats tried in vain to keep one partisan weekly mouthpiece in business.

When Helen Jackson left the train in Lafayette in the spring of 1860, she also was stepping into a town where public sentiment was divided three ways over various social issues. For example, there were people who were against, for, and indifferent toward liquor. Temperance probably had been preached in Lafayette since the first churches in the 1820s began meeting in log rooms. Barnstorming temperance speakers had visited as early as the 1830s, usually with church sponsorship. And in February 1842, a trend began toward "open" temperance meetings in local halls. But the fervor ebbed and flowed while drinking in Lafayette saloons roared on.

Also, typical of life in America, civic action in Lafayette was a world of white men. White men had founded the town; built the cabins and stores; cleared the brush and graded the streets; organized the churches and the schools; practiced the law; judged the courts; staffed the government; arranged for the elections and cast all the votes; run the newspapers, the shops, and the post office; healed the sick; and dominated the streets.

The women, then, had been secondary citizens in most ways. When Helen Jackson arrived, there were simply no accomplished women in the town and few sister heroes for women to emulate anywhere. A Lafayette city directory from that period, containing 100 pages of advertisements and listings, mentioned just seven women: six milliners and a sewing machine company agent. And if there were opportunities ahead for women, they were difficult to see in 1860.

Certainly the free public schools, supported by taxes, had created a new demand for teachers, and many a young white woman had launched a career as a "school marm." But why this one exception to the traditional passive role for women in America and in Lafayette? Probably because the smart young women would work cheaply and docilely and because an all-male school board felt that teaching the youngest children was akin to motherhood anyway. So men got the high school and college teaching jobs and the administrative positions while women coped with the beginners.

Women had few avenues to achievement. Other than teaching school, their opportunities for earning wages were limited to store clerking, typesetting, cigar-making, sewing, washing and ironing clothes, and serving as domestic help. Besides teaching, the only other significant outlet for women to improve life—and themselves—in the decade of the 1860s was the church.

When Helen Jackson came to Lafayette, she possessed what later was identifiable as a solid upbringing in a home in which her mother influenced her to learn, be proud of her sex, worship God, and abide by the laws of the Bible. Helen, even as a bewildered girl, seemed to possess an inner strength, a conviction that God oversaw all the people of the earth and the fishes of the sea; hers was a clear sense of right and wrong, a faith that right would prevail and that all people, regardless of sex, were His soldiers in the great fight for righteousness.

It is speculative, but reasonable to assume, that Helen's father was a hard-enough-working but lesser-endowed individual than her mother with respect to character and brains. There is also room to surmise that the father died an exhausted, wasted, and pathetic figure, perhaps even before Helen left home and family at sixteen.

Nearly forty years later, Helen would cryptically memorialize William Jackson in the dedication of a short book she had written about an immigrant: "To the memory of my sainted father, whose dying message to me was: 'Daughter, be kind to everybody.'"[4] It is mysterious, her use of that adjective *sainted*. Whether her father lived a saintly life or a scoundrel's hard-drinking, family-abusing existence to join the saints only in death cannot be proved. But such speculation is justified because of the intensity with which Helen fought for righteousness, urged strength of character and family life, and campaigned against liquor in later years. The blaze of her crusades would suggest a childhood that just possibly involved a patient, saintly mother putting up with and rearing seven children despite a father who was less so—a childhood of sadness or grimness that set her afire with purpose later on.

It is a matter of fact, though, that soon after her arrival in Lafayette, Helen found sustenance and strength in the 250-member Second Presbyterian Church. For such a newcomer, a church had much to offer. With its prayer meetings, worship services, and fellowship and outreach programs, it provided her with regular chances to make many new friends of similar conviction and faith. It gave her a sense of security both in spiritual and practical terms. It was an outlet for her abilities in music, writing, and teaching and had a library of sorts from which she could expand her mind in history, religion, the social sciences, and selected classics.

Years later Helen would recall that among the people she had met at Second Presbyterian were the handsome young attorney named DeWitt Wallace, who was Sunday school superintendent, and the bright, droll lawyer named John Gougar who, like Helen's young uncle, Jasper Dresser, was just beginning to practice law.[5]

CHAPTER 4

Marriage and Mission

*J*ohn Gougar was born December 10, 1836, in Circleville, Ohio, and came to Tippecanoe County, Indiana, with his parents when he was four. The Gougar family had crossed the Wabash to the western side and farmed high, level ground two miles west of the Lafayette Courthouse. When John was fourteen, his father died, and the surviving family moved into Lafayette. John eventually was sent back to Ohio for his education, and in 1856 at age nineteen, he was graduated from Heidelberg College. Returning to Lafayette, John began reading law, was admitted to the bar in 1861, and commenced practicing. John Gougar and Helen Jackson probably met during 1861, when he was twenty-four and she eighteen, in the year of turmoil over the outbreak of the Civil War. They were married on John's twenty-seventh birthday, December 10, 1863.[1]

One might surmise that the courtship centered on church life, meetings, socials, and committee work and that it was a case of intellectual chemistry at work. Both seemed to enjoy books and music and to take their religion seriously. In all likelihood, they shared the usual dreams of wealth, a fine home, travel, fame, and friends. Helen, during those years, was apparently living either in a boarding home or with friends she had met through church or school. John was presumably still living with his widowed mother and family, walking the few blocks to his office.

Helen was busy with schoolteaching and had been able to pick up extra money teaching piano. Again, no documents can prove it one way or another, but Helen clearly was an effective teacher, or the board would not have awarded her a principalship in 1863. What qualities did the board see in Helen? Again, one can but venture an educated guess or two. In light of what she achieved later, it seems sure that Helen was solidly educated and thoroughly grounded in arithmetic, reading, writing, and music. She was a most competent writer and exceptionally adept at speaking to a group of youngsters. Teaching forced her, as it does any good teacher, into thought, logic, planning, preparation, criticism, and self-analysis.

Quite obviously, Helen exhibited some take-charge traits in her early teaching, rare for young women of that day; these traits surely stemmed from her firm family background and her religious convictions about what was right and what should be said and done. Helen simply was not plagued by doubts—no wavering, no apologizing. Facts were facts. Good behavior was good behavior. Right was right. Evil was evil. Views were declared in blunt terms of black and white, without middle ground, without compromise, and probably without debate in her schoolroom.

By the winter of 1863–64, just after John Gougar and Helen Jackson were wed, they took up residence in a bare-bones boarding home. Later Helen recalled how she and John boarded for a year, then, as soon as they "felt able, went to housekeeping" in a rented apartment or home. Helen said she "did my own work" for the first six years of the marriage, except for washing and occasional help from her sisters. The house, she recalled, was "open to my relatives . . . anybody who needed a home was welcome to it."[2]

Helen apparently gave up schoolteaching after the spring of 1864 and devoted her time to housekeeping, the private teaching of music for extra income, and continuing her studies of such fields as English, literature, music, and social sciences. There is no record of why she left teaching, but reports here and there in the skimpy knowledge of Helen's early years reveal that she gave part of her teaching income to certain of her sisters to further their education. At least two, Edna and Addie, ended up living in Lafayette after about 1869.

By 1864 city directories indicate that John with Helen's uncle Jasper Dresser had formed a law partnership and a bounty and pension agency. Although most able-bodied young men in Lafayette in one way or another had been rounded up for Union Army duty in the many Indiana regiments mustered between 1861–63, John Gougar was left at home. He suffered from what might be generally described as "eye trouble" and was a sickly sort, who spent his spare time, evenings, and Sundays at home.

During those early years in their marriage, it became Helen's practice to read to John as well as look after him, to run errands of legal business for him, and in the process to learn a great deal about law and what was right, wrong, good, and evil in Lafayette. Helen later recalled that John "would sometimes be shut up in the house for months with his eyes." Helen said lawyers would come to the house to consult with John, and at other times, she would be sent with documents or messages to see other lawyers. "I assisted my husband in every way I could," she said years later, adding with obvious sarcasm "but of course being a woman and knowing nothing about the law, I could only be an errand boy."[3]

During the 1860s, John was treated by an oculist, Dr. Benjamin Ingersoll, whose office and residence was a short walk from John's sickbed. As her life unwound over the decades, Helen Gougar made few friends. Acquaintances, yes. Admirers, yes. Curiosity seekers, yes. Critics, yes. Enemies, yes. But few close friends. Apparently the closest and best friend from Helen's first months as John Gougar's bride was the eye doctor's wife, Maria Ingersoll. "I have been in Mrs. Gougar's home for the last 15 or 20 years, morning, noon or night, as freely as I would go to my own daughter's house," Maria Ingersoll said in 1883. "We have been very intimate. Any time I chose, I went to her home and she came to mine. Every time I have been there she was at home and Mr. Gougar also. Mrs. Gougar was in the habit of reading to Mr. Gougar, as his eyes were bad."[4]

Little else is known of John and Helen's early married life. But it is clear that during the decade of the 1860s, John with much help from Helen did slowly build a law practice and develop a knack for good investments, as well as a reputation for honesty and thoroughness in his work. The Gougars, however, never had children.

The Civil War notwithstanding, Lafayette progressed in the decade of the 1860s. The first steam fire engine was put into service. In a bitter city election in 1863, a Democrat was elected mayor while Republicans called his team a "Copperhead ticket"

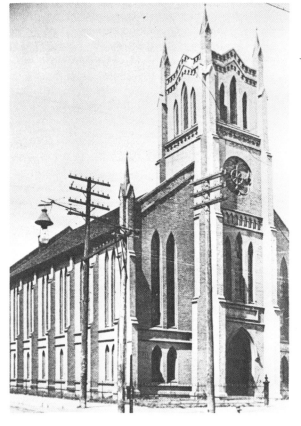

Young John Gougar and Helen Jackson first met at the Second Presbyterian Church, which stood at the southwest corner of Sixth and South streets in Lafayette. John and Helen, pictured above in their early forties, married in 1863.

and charged illegal voters had been imported from another county. A national bank began operating July 1, 1863. Robert C.
Gregory, a lawyer and a friend of the Gougars at Second
Presbyterian, was elected to the Indiana Supreme Court. Infla-
tion was a wartime problem, with many crafts demanding
twenty-five percent wage increases. Lafayette's first labor
union, Typographical Union No. 64, was formed with seventeen charter members. Lafayette High School opened in the fall
of 1864, offering Greek, Latin, mathematics, German, French,
English, and music. Late in 1864, sentiment began surfacing
through newspaper letters about the need for a good central
library. A funeral train carrying the remains of the assassinated
Abraham Lincoln rolled through town enroute to Illinois on an
April night in 1865. Nearly 4,000 men from the Lafayette area
fought in the Civil War, and 326 died. Two returned as briga-
dier generals. Ten reached the rank of colonel. A sergeant won
the Congressional Medal of Honor at age nineteen. The new
covered bridge connecting Lafayette's Main Street with the
west bank of the Wabash via a levee and with the growing town
of Chauncey was opened in the summer of 1865.

The immensely wealthy Moses Fowler started a bank. Income tax records for 1864 showed that Fowler was not the
richest man in town, though. That honor went to wholesaler
and agricultural baron Adams Earl, who paid $10,000 in taxes
on income of $103,000, and to wholesaler and manufacturer
John Purdue, who paid tax on $107,000. For a comparison,
Jasper Dresser paid on $575 in the year 1864 and John Gougar,
on $500. That was considered a fair income for beginning
lawyers.

During 1866 the legislature began weighing the land and
cash offer of John Purdue, who was lobbying to get the state's
land-grant agricultural college for Tippecanoe County. In the
fall of 1866, a building was put into short-term use as Lafayette's "opera house." Meanwhile, a development to have impact on Helen Gougar's life was the founding of a Lafayette
Young Men's Christian Association (YMCA) at a meeting of
church leaders on November 12, 1866. "Only a woman,"
Helen probably had nothing to do with the meeting, but in the
ensuing years, the YMCA became her springboard into
prominence.

One of the first projects for the new YMCA was to revive
talk of a public library. Plans for a YMCA lecture and reading
room were announced early in 1867. On February 21 at a meeting in Lafayette's Baptist Church, Clara Barton, known as the

"Florence Nightingale of the Army" because of her support work in the Civil War and who later founded the American Red Cross in 1882, spoke about her experiences.

Serious debate over woman suffrage began to surface through meetings, letters in the Lafayette papers, and street talk. Some letters were bitter and vicious; others, well reasoned. Nearly all were anonymous or signed with pseudonyms. Why the sudden public interest?

The "woman's movement," building slowly since the 1848 convention in Seneca Falls, New York, had stalled in the Civil War while women became enmeshed in war relief work and nursing. Though restless to push on, Susan B. Anthony and others helped instead to push the Thirteenth Amendment to the U.S. Constitution, abolishing slavery. Then when the war ended, woman suffrage took a back seat to the rights of freed male slaves to vote. The Fourteenth Amendment covered that, and a split began to appear in the woman's movement.

In January 1869, a convention called to discuss woman suffrage gave Elizabeth Cady Stanton a chance to push for a woman suffrage amendment to the Constitution. This divided the ranks of the old Equal Rights Association, so in May, Mrs. Stanton and Miss Anthony formed a National Woman Suffrage Association for women only. They believed the presence of men in the old leadership had betrayed women's true interests.[5] In November 1869 in Cleveland, an American Woman Suffrage Association was organized on a delegate basis with Lucy Stone and Mary Livermore as leaders. Only representatives from "recognized" suffrage organizations were seated at the conventions. Susan B. Anthony tried to work with the new association, but it would be some twenty years before unity was restored.

In this national setting on November 10–11, 1869, nearly two hundred persons attended a convention, sponsored presumably by the new American association sympathizers, in the Lafayette Opera House.[6] Helen Gougar was perhaps indifferent at first to the issue of female suffrage. Yet during these weeks at the end of 1869, one can begin to trace, with documents, her public life.

II

WAITING GAME

Once to every man and nation
   Comes the moment to decide
In the strife of truth with falsehood
   For the good or evil side.

Some great cause, God's new Messiah,
   Offering each the bloom or blight
And the choice goes on forever,
   Twixt that darkness and that light.

From "Once to Every Man and Nation," James Russell Lowell,
1845, and Thomas J. Williams, 1890

CHAPTER 5

A Modest Beginning

*H*elen Gougar remembered her emergence from obscurity:

> I first entered upon "public work" connected with temperance long before I was connected with woman's suffrage, and in those days I was opposed to suffrage.
>
> I first commenced in public life with the reading of an essay at the commencement of the YMCA and was one of the committee to arrange entertainments for that organization.
>
> I also was a member of the local Benevolent Society and if any family or person needed assistance, I did what I could.[1]

Even before Lafayette's November convention, a woman suffrage meeting had been held in Crawfordsville, in late September 1869, with a classic difference of opinion developing. One male professor from Indianapolis had sent to be read a statement saying he believed, when persons without distinction of sex or color fought their way through college and attained a classic education, they then might be entrusted with the ballot, but not before. Visiting organizer Mary Livermore climbed the rostrum to denounce the professor's views, noting that there was not a first-class college in the land that had opened its doors to women.[2]

Born Mary Ashton in Boston in 1820, she had married a Universalist minister, Rev. Daniel Livermore, in 1845. With him she had been editing a church periodical, the *New Covenant*, in Chicago since 1857. Now, about to embark on American Woman Suffrage Association crusades, she would soon move back to Boston, where she would found and edit the *Agitator*, a pro-woman-suffrage publication. Nearly forty-eight, Mrs. Livermore was seminary educated, a teacher, abolitionist, and platform speaker. Her stumping through Indiana at this time was part of a conservative, patient, state-by-state strategy the American group preferred to pursue while Miss Anthony and Mrs. Stanton's more radical National unit sought one-shot national action.

Helen Gougar may have attended the Crawfordsville convention or read of it in a Lafayette paper and may have been fascinated and inspired by Mrs. Livermore and the debate. Mary Livermore had visited in Lafayette before the convention and had done some Lafayette campaigning, so she and Helen Gougar may have met then.[3] On October 23, 1869, the *Lafayette Daily Courier* published a call for the mass meeting in Lafayette of men and women of the Seventh Congressional District to be a "calm, temperate and thorough review" of the woman suffrage question. It is significant that backers of that historic call included Second Presbyterian's minister and three other pastors, plus ten women, among them Helen Gougar's good friend, Maria Ingersoll. Mrs. Livermore; Miss Elizabeth "Lizzie" Boynton, a young activist from Crawfordsville; and Miss Lilly Peckham, a lawyer from Milwaukee, were among the featured speakers.[4]

On November 1, 1869, the *Lafayette Daily Courier* published a letter about woman suffrage, obviously written in response to an earlier letter from LEON. The response, signed with the pseudonym AGNUS, sounds curiously imbued with the logic, rhetoric, and firmly controlled command of subject and language of Helen Gougar at full power in later years. But was this Helen's letter in 1869? It can never be proven one way or the other. The letter read:

> I agree with LEON, "Woman has work enough to do in the place society has assigned her," and she does it, too, quite as willingly and as well as man does his. "Home influence" also is necessary and desirable, but can it be efficient and salutary when it proceeds from only one half of the household? Women, with but few exceptions, exert themselves to make home attractive and pleasant; if they

fail they should not be blamed, for when the "main point" falls so far short of perfection what can be expected of "side issues"? . . .

Women in married life share equally with man its cares, its duties, its responsibilities; and, therefore, are entitled to a full measure of the means necessary to its enjoyment, and this means should be given them as their right, not doled out at man's caprice. . . .

Women are well aware the ballot will bring responsibility; but whether it is a responsibility they were not intended to be burdened with is a question open to discussion. I cannot understand what right in this country an individual or a class of individuals has to say what is proper for another class. . . .

The constitution affirms equal rights and freedom to all, and yet to woman is denied the privilege of the ballot, or any part in forming laws, to which she is held strictly amenable.

The *Courier* reported in detail the November 10–11 convention and described it as orderly, shy, predictable, and almost without debate. Miss Boynton, Miss Peckham, Mrs. Livermore, *Courier* editor W. S. Lingle, and others spoke. A six-point resolution was passed, closing with the pledge that "we never will cease to urge woman to participation in the affairs of government equally with man; that justice and equality can be attained only by having the same laws for men and women; that we will not cease to agitate the subject of elective franchise and encourage its discussion upon all appropriate occasions until every state in the Union not only grants but urges women to vote."

Miss Boynton read "New Flag," a poem by writer, lecturer, reformer, composer, and woman suffrage advocate Julia Ward Howe. Mrs. Howe, a New Yorker who would be immortalized because of her patriotic song "The Battle Hymn of the Republic," published in 1862, had sent regrets that she could not attend the Lafayette meeting.

Mrs. Livermore gave conventioneers her rebuttals to the objections to woman suffrage of New York journalist and political leader Horace Greeley. Greeley had waffled over woman suffrage and in 1866 had written, among other things: "Talk of a true woman needing the ballot as an accessory of power, when she rules the world by a glance of her eye! There was sound philosophy in the remark of an Eastern monarch that his wife was sovereign of the empire, because she ruled his little ones and his little ones ruled him."[5]

The Lafayette convention passed a resolution calling for a Tippecanoe County Woman Suffrage Association. The matter was approved and an organization meeting called for the following week in the new YMCA building. The assembly named three delegates to a future American Woman Suffrage Association convention in Cleveland and adjourned in a mood of near unanimity.

Shortly before the closing, a Lafayette attorney named A. S. Embree rose to protest some of the literal terminology of those who said woman was equal to man:

> I had the misfortune to enlist in the service of the United States during the war. I was a private soldier and did my duty. I know, and so does every other man in this house that ever took part in the military service, that no woman can go through what the soldier had to do in the war against the rebellion.
>
> You speak of equal laws. Such a question as you have before this convention is the most perfect piece of foolishness in the world, and to my mind the greatest proof of your incapacity to exercise the right of suffrage if you had it.

Miss Peckham, the Milwaukee lawyer, quashed Embree's thought in a bold and sarcastic speech:

> In this country we do not believe in the divine right of kings. We only believe in the divine right of men to govern women. Women must crowd into every business. The false idea that a woman's place is at home must be given up. We demand the ballot because it will unfold to us new channels in which to work. Like all other created beings, we will be able to find our own sphere.[6]

Helen Gougar presumably was in the audience to be further inspired, stimulated, and encouraged by the dynamic women she saw and heard, but also possibly confused by and apprehensive of the gulf between the National and American associations' efforts. On November 12, Mrs. Livermore spoke at the Lafayette Baptist Church to people interested in founding a "home for the friendless."[7] Helen Gougar again may have heard the program.

On Friday evening, November 19, 1869, the new YMCA launched the first in its series of monthly literary and musical programs. These were the programs Helen Gougar helped organize. The premiere began at 7 P.M. and included an original poem, a recitation, an oration, selected readings, and music by the glee club from the city's high school.[8]

By December 1, a general meeting of "benevolent persons" was called through the newspapers to organize an association to develop the home for strangers needing "immediate relief occasioned by sickness or other causes." Twenty-five men and women signed the original constitution of the Lafayette Home Association.[9] Meanwhile, the Ladies' Benevolent Society, to which Helen Gougar belonged, also was conducting programs. Both the Lafayette Home Association and the Ladies' Benevolent Society canvassed the town for funds at the end of 1869.

But the new local woman suffrage association lay dormant. Lingle's *Lafayette Daily Courier* sniped at its inaction in a January 17, 1870, item, saying "the suffrage association in Indianapolis, unlike the Lafayette affair, is an active and aggressive institution. In the language of Seneca, it means 'biz.'"

On February 18, 1870, Helen Gougar made her first documentable public appearance. She performed in a violin and piano trio in the Baptist Church at a fund-raising dinner sponsored by the Lafayette Home Association. Helen played piano again on April 8 at one of those monthly YMCA "literary reunions," as they were called. And on May 13, she read an original essay entitled "The Occasional" at a Friday night YMCA program. On May 21, the YMCA finished its first "season" of these programs and elected standing committees for 1870–71. Helen was on the five-member unit responsible for the reading room, library, and "literary reunion" programs.

In the spring of 1870, Helen had ended her first ten years of life in Lafayette. Approaching her twenty-seventh birthday that summer, she was involved in Second Presbyterian Church, the YMCA, the Lafayette Home Association, and the Ladies' Benevolent Society. She was learning how to organize programs. She had written and delivered her first public reading. She had had time to hear and weigh the issues of social reform, temperance, woman suffrage, and equal rights. She had learned about law and economics and politics, about church affairs and church gossip. She had seen the advantages and disadvantages of organized effort; and she had met women of achievement, seeing weakness and fear and vulnerability, even hypocrisy, in some of them. From it all, she emerged with fiery views of countless deeds of reform which should be done and which she, somehow, might have to do, disunity or not, mere woman or not. If only there were acceptable ways and means.

Toward the end of May, Helen served on a Decoration Day committee composed of Lafayette "upper crust." The call had gone out to churches, Sunday schools, fraternal organizations, Masons, Odd Fellows, Red Men, Sons of Temperance, Good Templars, and public and parochial schools for ceremonial participation and for decorations for the graves of local soldiers. Groups of ladies were assigned to solicit and arrange flowers from each of the city's six wards. Such involvements, though menial and time-consuming, brought Helen into working relationships with men of business, industry, banking, education, the arts, and politics—and with their wives.

In the summer of 1870, the crusade for woman suffrage remained dormant in Lafayette. The annual meeting of the Indiana Woman Suffrage Association—aligned with the older, more radical National Association—was held in Indianapolis on June 8. Such familiar figures as Susan B. Anthony (on a long lecture tour) and Lucy Stone from the East attended, as did Indiana figures such as Lizzie Boynton from Crawfordsville and Zerelda Wallace. Lafayette, however, warmer toward the American Association's strategies, evidently sent not one spectator.

By November 2, 1870, the YMCA literary reunions resumed in Lafayette. The same day, the Lafayette Home Association elected officers after a year of progress. On September 15, its home for the friendless had opened. Interestingly, the association named two men as president and treasurer, then filled the offices of vice president, secretary, and corresponding secretary with women. The new board consisted of seven men and nineteen women.

On Friday night, November 11, Helen Gougar again performed in a piano and violin trio for the YMCA. In December Lingle's *Lafayette Daily Courier* editorially commented that "Lafayette, in the absence of an opera house, and bereft of all hope of a course of lectures, owes much to the YMCA for their charming entertainments."[10] The YMCA's reading rooms were now open seven hours a day and had added many daily newspapers to the usual fare of literary and religious books and periodicals.

Lafayette's churches sent fifty-one delegates to the Indiana Temperance Alliance Convention in Indianapolis on February 2, 1871. The convention elected Rev. A. W. Bruce, a Universalist minister from Lafayette, as vice president.

Three weeks later, Helen Gougar performed in an instrumental duet at a Second Presbyterian social. On February 27, the *Courier* reported that an American who had lived in Syria for twenty years would lecture at the Lafayette YMCA. Undoubtedly, Helen helped arrange it and learned much about lecturing and travelogues. The travelogue was one of many genres she would master in years to come.

In April and May 1871, two touring woman suffrage speakers visited Lafayette, again with Helen Gougar's probable involvement. Susan B. Anthony, now fifty-one, spoke at the YMCA the night of April 7. She had been lecturing in Michigan, Illinois, Kansas, Nebraska, Iowa, and Ohio, taking trains at midnight and at daybreak, waiting four hours in one little station, and sleeping "scarcely two nights in the same bed for over three months."[11] The *Courier* gave the event one cordial paragraph, calling it a "large and highly intelligent audience" and saying Miss Anthony "took high grounds on the rights of her sex, and presented her views in an eloquent and forcible manner."[12] Then near the end of May, a native Ohioan who had run a ladies' academy in Baton Rouge, Louisiana, lectured on "Woman's Rights and Woman's Duties" at the YMCA. Through the spring and summer, there were temperance lectures in local churches. By fall Lafayette had chalked up considerable civic progress.

On August 9, ground was broken for the first building at Purdue University. Horace Greeley spoke at the Tippecanoe County Fair on September 5. The community, rallied by church and courthouse meetings, rounded up food, clothing, and monetary support for victims of the great Chicago fire of October 8–9.

On Friday night, December 15, Helen Gougar appeared again in one of the monthly YMCA literary reunions as musician and speaker. The *Courier* told of her playing in a piano duet and said "Mrs. John Gougar's essay on 'Shirks' was an admirable production."[13] "Shirks," one may surmise, attacked weak-spined people who shirked their duty to God, family, fellowman, and self, creating the need for social reforms and help agencies like the Lafayette Home, the YMCA, and all the benevolent, temperance, and suffrage societies.

CHAPTER 6

Patience Rewarded

Now there began a period in Helen Gougar's life when she seemed to waver between the wife-of-a-prominent-lawyer existence that was hers for the taking and the life of public involvement. Her activities remained quiet, safe, and sometimes invisible for several years. Nationally, too, the woman's movement limped, weakened by disunity, shifting goals, and bewildering layers of organizations, committees, and strategies.

In 1872 there are but skimpy trails of Helen Gougar's involvement in public affairs. She did arrange a February 26 travelogue for the YMCA, featuring a former attaché of the U.S. consulate in Cairo. And that fall she was on a committee serving fund-raising suppers for the Lafayette Home. November had been the traditional opening of the YMCA literary reunions series, but in 1872 that practice was dropped because of the impending opening of an ornate new grand opera house.

On the night of December 30, 1872, John Gougar, presumably accompanied by Helen, attended one of the annual art exhibits and "distributions" of paintings by local artist George Winter. These end-of-the-year raffles included a guest speaker and a panel of three citizens who conducted the drawing on stage from a box of tickets bought by patrons.

Winter specialized in Lafayette and Wabash Valley landscapes, Indian life, and a few local portraits. He painted soft, muted canvases of many sizes, including pocket-sized renderings he called "little gems." Some five hundred tickets had been sold for that night, probably at one dollar apiece, for the sale of twenty-six paintings, seven of which were untitled "little gems" lettered A through G. To the full-sized paintings, Winter had assigned such titles as "Upper Wabash," "The Prairie," or "The Shadowed Creek." John Gougar's name was drawn twice—for "Little Gem B" and a full painting called "Mississinewa River."[1]

The anecdote reveals much about John and Helen Gougar's marriage, now entering its tenth year. They apparently took great pride in their home, in decorating it, furnishing it, and collecting souvenirs and mementos for it. They were enjoying John's profitable law practice and investments, too, by buying quality clothing and taking spring and summer trips. The Gougars, moreover, were emerging as modest society figures. The night after the art drawing, Helen and four other women assisted Mrs. DeWitt Wallace, the lawyer's wife, in a New Year's Eve open house.

The new year 1873 was memorable for the people of Lafayette. On January 23, a fifteen-inch snowstorm stopped trains and piled up in drifts four feet deep. The glittering new opera house opened the night of February 17 with the play *Enoch Arden* performed by a traveling company. A new "Sunday law," strictly limiting Sabbath activities such as fishing, took effect March 9. Police arrested thirty-three violators the first day: twenty-four railroad workers, two bakers, a milkman, and six employees of the *Morning Journal* newspaper. Stiffer "Baxter Law" temperance legislation also was enacted by the 1873 legislature. It replaced 1853 laws defeated in court by liquor and saloon interests. Indignant people began calling meetings to oppose the Sunday and the temperance laws almost immediately. In a city election soaked in temperance issues, Democrat F. E. D. McGinley, who opposed the tougher laws, was elected mayor with 1,537 votes, while Republican and independent candidates received fewer than 1,400 between them. Through much of 1873, the Sunday and liquor laws were debated, with many church people pressing for strict enforcement, but enforcement was largely ignored by summer. Nor did the woman suffrage movement, now four years old in Lafayette, show any life in 1873.

These realities may indeed have dulled Helen Gougar's activism with disappointment or disgust, even discouragement. As sympathetic as she might have felt toward temperance work, she also found Lafayette's temperance movement to be sluggish and totally dominated by church and by men. Typical was a July 23 "temperance meeting" to raise money for hiring lawyers to prosecute offenders and enforce the new temperance laws meant to control the sixty-eight Tippecanoe County saloons. The meeting resulted in a resolution that a committee of five men be named to select a committee of ladies to do the work![2]

In the late summer of 1873, a yellow fever epidemic struck down people in several southern states, centering in Memphis and Shreveport. Communities in many states formed relief committees. In Lafayette, such a committee, chaired by men, formed a task force of twenty-four women to do the work of canvassing door-to-door. Helen Gougar and the wife of a justice of the peace dutifully collected from a sixteen-block district. The committee sent nearly a thousand dollars in two installments to the stricken areas a few days later.[3]

In early November 1873, both Helen Gougar and her sister Addie served on a committee with six other ladies to plan and serve a series of Monday night benefit dinners for the Lafayette Home.

On January 13, 1874, the Purdue University trustees approved twenty-eight courses of study and decided to open the first semester on March 2. In 1874, meanwhile, women suddenly marched into prominence in temperance work, but with no documentable support from Helen Gougar. Still lacking either unanimity or unity, some women had begun organizing their own temperance clubs in the East with backing from churches, husbands, and other men. And some in the Midwest had begun to gain national attention by boldly conducting prayer meetings in the noise and jeers of saloons.

On December 23, 1873, a group of women in Hillsboro, Ohio, inspired by a temperance speaker named Dio Lewis, discouraged and dismayed at the havoc created by liquor, and disgusted with indifferent authorities, decided on prayer as their weapon. They conducted "services" in saloons and reported that within a few months there was visible improvement. Women in Shelbyville stumbled onto the same strategy at about the same time. Enraged by the arrest of two young boys in a house of ill fame, they began visiting saloons on January 21, 1874, after a "mothers' meeting" that decided whisky was the real cause of demoralization.[4]

Word spread, and in Indianapolis, after meetings in four churches, a Women's Christian Temperance Union (WCTU) was organized on March 3. The WCTU canvassed wards to prevent signatures to petitions that would, under the Baxter Law, support applications for liquor licenses. This action was followed by saloon visits and by putting watchers at the doors of saloons. Temperance meetings were held almost daily, and spectators were urged to sign a pledge. But the strain was too great to last long. The liquor lobby won repeal of the Baxter Law in 1875. A hundred-member WCTU crowd stood watch on the legislature to implore that the law stand. The leader who emerged was Zerelda Wallace, already active in woman suffrage work.

Born in 1817, Zerelda became the second wife, at age nineteen, of then Lieutenant Governor David Wallace. She was described as "a thoroughly domestic woman and exemplary in her devotion to her family," as testified to by her stepson, General Lew Wallace, who is said to have drawn his character of the mother of Ben-Hur from her.[5] She took no public action until the women's crusade, then shyly began to make speeches and organize action. She was soon at ease as a leader and was elected the first president of the WCTU of Indiana.

Meanwhile on February 13, 1874, Lafayette's male-dominated chapter of the Order of Good Templars passed a resolution opposing the United States Liquor Dealers Association's threat to vote against any men who opposed their views and who were not in favor of the repeal of all temperance and "unreasonable" Sunday laws. In the next paragraph, the Good Templars said they "hail with pleasure the efforts put forth by the Christian women of Ohio and Shelbyville in this state."[6] Thus some women, at least, seemed eager to combine their drives for suffrage and equal rights with temperance activism, as though to win male approval for all three.

On March 2 at a Lafayette temperance meeting in the Ninth Street Methodist Church, attendees pledged to renew the efforts for liquor law enforcement in Tippecanoe County. Almost as an aside, in a resolution, its members said they "endorse and approve the action of the Christian women in the different parts of the country."[7]

An organization of Lafayette Christian women was formed the afternoon of March 5, at a meeting that consisted of prayer and debate about holding saloon meetings. On March 12, the new Women's Temperance League of Lafayette, with about sixty members, petitioned Congress to pass stronger antiliquor laws and to force all public officials to sign a pledge to abstain from alcohol while in office. The ladies also vowed to circulate pledges among Lafayette's doctors and druggists, urging no prescriptions containing liquor except "where the necessity of the case imperiously demands it" and no liquor sales whatever unless prescribed by a physician.[8]

The women met March 21 and 23 in Lafayette churches to decide whether to take their crusade of hymns and prayers into the saloons. The consensus was yes. So on Friday, March 27, the crusaders visited four saloons and on the next day, six. The women, probably twenty to thirty of them, moved as a group. When allowed in, they calmly discussed their views with the saloon proprietor, invited him to close, then preached of the evils of drink and the waste of man's talent and income on it. Finally they prayed and sang "Nearer My God to Thee" before departing. When they were refused entrance, they simply held the "services" on the sidewalk just outside the saloon. After the Friday visits, the ladies received a written reminder from the mayor, via the chief of police, to keep sidewalks clear for normal passage during "services."[9]

The *Lafayette Daily Courier* of W. S. Lingle, himself a temperance officer and speaker, devoted generous space to accounts of these saloon meetings. Lingle was a Methodist and a temperance and woman suffrage proponent, but he was a newspaperman first. He viewed these controversial subjects as good reading which would sell papers.

On March 30, the *Courier* printed a recapitulation of the saloon crusade, with messages of thanks from the president of the Women's Temperance League and assurances that victory had been won. But just as swiftly as the league had zoomed into view, it vanished. By summer it had all but disbanded, while other organizations, such as a businessman's temperance prayer meeting, momentarily surfaced. Through it all, Helen Gougar's fervor must have been held back, for in late July, the *Courier* reported under "Personals" that she and John were leaving for a trip to the northern lakes.

Zerelda Wallace, whose husband now was governor, was elected president of the nation's first state WCTU organization at a September meeting in an Indianapolis Baptist church. In November, in response to a call from Ohio and Illinois women, the first national WCTU convention was held in Cleveland. Officers included Mrs. Annie Wittenmeyer of Pennsylvania as president and Frances Willard from Illinois as secretary and nominal leader and organizer. Mrs. Wallace as a state president automatically became a national vice president. The WCTU's goals were simple: the protection of the home, the abolition of liquor traffic, and the triumph of Christ's Golden Rule in custom and law.[10]

In mid-October the sheepish remnants of the Woman's Temperance League of Lafayette regrouped. This time, reflecting the trend, they voted to form one of the new branches of "that glorious institution known as the Women's Christian Temperance Union," to use the words of their secretary.[11] A temperance convention scheduled for the following week in First Presbyterian was disappointingly attended, according to the *Courier*. But the new WCTU chapter, on November 4, 1874, pressed on to organize an auxiliary in every township of Tippecanoe County.

Where was Helen Gougar? There is no way to tell where she went, what she did, or what she thought about those saloon prayer meetings. But on November 6, 1874, the *Courier* did report that she helped on a committee serving another dinner for the Lafayette Home, and her involvement in WCTU did date to 1874.

There is some cause to believe, meanwhile, that John Gougar's delicate health may have kept Helen close to home and removed from many of her former involvements. An item in the *Courier* on September 7, 1874, said John was confined to his home with an acute eye inflammation. For much of the winter of 1874–75, John again must have been ill, perhaps with influenza, colds, or cold-weather sinus infections. The *Courier* noted on April 15, 1875, that Helen had left for Nashville, Tennessee, to meet John on his return from the South, adding that "he is in improved health."

In the summer of 1875, Helen's name again began to appear in the papers in connection with bland "do-good" projects. She spoke at a convention held in the opera house by members of the Indiana State Sunday School Union on June 1 and noted admiringly how Catholics had begun building a hospital for Lafayette.

On July 1, 1875, Helen was the only woman named to the committee to revive the literary reunions series for the YMCA. On September 13, she was named treasurer, no less, of a committee from Indiana's Seventh Congressional District to help the U.S. Centennial Celebration Committee. The nation would mark that centennial July 4, 1876.

On March 24, 1876, the literary reunions began to be conducted in the opera house, with a small admission charge to benefit the YMCA reading rooms. Helen Gougar delivered an oration based on an essay she had written called "Pimples."

Earlier in the program, her friend the lawyer DeWitt Wallace, had read his poem about catching a pike on the Kankakee River. The *Lafayette Daily Courier* reported the next day:

> Mrs. John Gougar discussed "Pimples," but instead of confining her attention to pimples in a personal and practical way, she chose to consider them in a merely illustrative way, and laid down the proposition that the life of the individual is the type of national life; from which point of view she proceeded to treat of the moral principles which betoken an impure condition of the nation's life blood.
>
> The speaker concluded with a minute diagnosis of the several "pimples" which her piercing eye discerned upon the body politic.

One can guess that the pimples discerned by Helen Gougar's eye had to do with weak enforcement of temperance laws, politicians who double-talked about liquor licensing, wobbling churchgoers, individual sloth, irresponsibility, atheism, the glaring need for woman suffrage, and equal rights for women. It was a carefully documented and expertly written essay which contained some heavy religious, political, and social thought. Perhaps it was a bit too heavy for the average YMCA literary show, but Helen Gougar was learning to speak out and was testing the water among a group of friends she could trust, looking for acceptable ways to influence society.

John Gougar's health, though, continued to slow Helen's efforts. He left March 28, 1876, for another one-month boil in Hot Springs, Arkansas, returning April 26 in a "much improved" condition.

Lafayette's "municipal health" improved, too, in 1876. On January 3, Saint Mary's Hospital had opened under Catholic auspices in a small house, while a few blocks away excavating was under way for a permanent brick and stone building.

Lafayette celebrated the nation's centennial July 4 with sermons, a parade, fireworks, speeches, meetings, and other ceremonial pomp and sobriety. But those not so sober rioted. A man was killed, a carriage driver was stabbed, and a wounded Civil War veteran lost an eye and an arm in a premature cannon blast. A man attempting a balloon ascension broke both legs when the rising airship grazed the courthouse wall, burst, drifted east, crashed, and burned.[12]

On August 2, 1876, John and Helen Gougar left to visit the U.S. Centennial celebration in Philadelphia. In the fall, Helen's church work took her to West Point for a meeting called by the Tippecanoe County Sunday School Union. DeWitt Wallace, her lawyer friend, presided, and Helen was listed in the November 25 *Lafayette Daily Courier* as having taken part in the discussions.

It was during 1876 that a new wave of temperance fervor began to rise. The central figure was a forty-year-old Irishman named Francis Murphy, a Civil War veteran and organizer of temperance clubs in Maine as early as 1870. By 1876 his movement, made visible in an especially large Pittsburgh rally, had induced thousands to take the pledge against alcohol and to pin on a blue ribbon as a signal to others. The Murphy Movement, also called the "Blue Ribbon movement," spread over the entire nation and is said to have influenced ten million people to sign the pledge.[13]

Concurrently, women's clubs, especially of the literary sort, proliferated all across Indiana. These evolved into federations of many clubs and councils of clubs and established a new network from which the crusades for woman's rights, woman suffrage, and temperance would draw help, ideas, and leadership for years to come.

From the scores of ladies involved, May Wright Sewall emerged as the strongest, most imaginative, and versatile. Her affiliations with educational suffrage and cultural movements were many, including the first presidency of the Indianapolis Propylaeum. She was a president of the Indianapolis Woman's Club, founded in 1875, and ran the Girls Classical School that was a training place for young suffragists.[14] Mrs. Sewall also headed the state Equal Suffrage Society for many years and was credited with the concept of what grew to be the Indiana Council of Women and, later, the National Council of Women.

By late May 1877, a series of these new-format "temperance revivals" began to stimulate fresh interest in the issue in Indiana. Blue Ribbon and Red Ribbon temperance clubs were formed, and people who signed the pledge to abstain from alcohol wore the ribbons. On August 6, 1877, Jack Warburton, a self-educated former alcoholic from Wisconsin who traveled as a Murphy Movement revivalist, spoke in the Lafayette courthouse yard. He may have impressed Helen Gougar with his eloquence and earthy humor and shown her ways to stir a crowd into a frenzy.

That September, Helen and John Gougar helped start a group which met monthly in private homes on Friday evenings and was called the Parlor Club. Later she recalled it was "entirely private and composed of 20 active and 20 inactive members. . . . it was a literary club devoted to self-culture. President

Emerson E. White [of Purdue University] was the first president. DeWitt Wallace was the first vice president . . . and I was the secretary and treasurer."[15] A Parlor Club committee, she said, was formed to arrange a program for the year, which was to be published and sent to members. Each evening, members prepared and read an essay for discussion. Music sometimes was added to the program. The Parlor Club provided Helen Gougar with new outlets for her writing, thought, and speechmaking. It is significant, too, that she—a woman—was a founder and was entrusted with the jobs of secretary and treasurer of such a prestigious gathering. It meant that by 1877 she was recognized as a leader with character and intelligence, ability at managing things, good ideas, and the power to think clearly, write persuasively, and speak influentially. By 1877, too, she had shed some of her simpler apprenticeships in the WCTU, the YMCA, the Ladies' Benevolent Society, and the Lafayette Home Association.

As 1878 arrived, Helen Gougar truly began to emerge as a soldier for reform. A *Courier* item on January 16, 1878, said Will Carleton, a poet, author, and lecturer from rural Michigan, in town to appear in the opera house, would be the guest of the Gougars. William McKendree Carleton and Helen had been friends from Hillsdale College days. No doubt Helen asked Carleton all about the pros and cons and ins and outs of being a traveling platform speaker. By now Helen was being urged by friends to make more speeches about her beliefs on religion, schools, temperance, and suffrage. And the idea appealed to her.

That spring, Helen became involved in planning a series of temperance revivals conducted by two touring Murphy Movement laymen named Lafayette Hughes and Milo Ward. She had been active in the Blue Ribbon Temperance Club, probably since the Jack Warburton rally; and now the Hughes and Ward meetings may have appealed to her for other reasons. They were more grassroots in nature, with ordained ministers and prominent local men in the background.

In her first big break into public life, Helen accepted an invitation to speak at one of the Blue Ribbon rallies in the opera house, on stage with Hughes himself, her Parlor Club friends Emerson E. White and DeWitt Wallace, and visiting speakers from Chicago and Fort Wayne. The *Courier* estimated the crowd at fifteen hundred including two hundred on the stage the night of April 28, 1878. A choir sang "Hold the Fort for I Am Coming" and "He Signals Still," and about three hundred persons, swept up in the fervor of the speeches, signed the temperance pledge and went off wearing blue ribbons.[16] There is no record of what Helen Gougar said that night, but it must have been powerful because it launched her permanently as a public figure. The Hughes and Ward revivals ended May 31 with rallies on the Methodist campgrounds at Battle Ground. At the grand finale, more than five hundred persons reportedly signed the pledge.

The Blue Ribbon temperance wave employed several new approaches. The church appeared at the edge of the limelight, while laymen were at its center—especially reformed drinkers such as the homespun Warburton. The common man and woman were on the stage, for they were really the target of the moves to reform, anyway. A month-long, or sometimes summer-long, series of outdoor revival meetings had also replaced the stiff, old, dress-up, night meetings in churches. The little red and blue ribbons themselves had given people something more tangible than theory and philosophy, and the establishment of clubs and furnishing of headquarters and halls had given temperance a new permanence.

On June 25, 1878, Helen Gougar began a four-week rest in Indiana's lake country near Warsaw and a visit to her sister Etta Cosgrove. Helen was surely both surprised and pleased to be asked to speak at a temperance meeting in Warsaw on July 5!

On July 22, just after her thirty-fifth birthday, Helen was elected an honorary member of the new Illinois Social Sciences Association in Chicago. It probably resulted from her long friendship with Lizzie Boynton of Crawfordsville. Lizzie in 1870 had married an attorney who practiced in Evanston, Illinois. Now as Elizabeth Boynton Harbert, she was an effective activist for woman's rights, suffrage, temperance, and other social reforms and was woman's department editor of a socially conscious Chicago newspaper, *Inter-Ocean*. One branch of the woman's movement was establishing "social sciences associations" in most states to lobby for reforms. Helen Gougar and Mrs. Harbert, no doubt, had remained in touch through letters and press clippings over the years. It also may be that Helen visited Mrs. Harbert in Chicago for the Illinois association's convention before returning to Lafayette on August 2. During Helen's stay, Mrs. Harbert may have encouraged her to continue writing, to start an association in Indiana, and perhaps to engage in newspaper work herself, an acceptable new way for women to be heard by masses of people.

Back in Lafayette, Blue Ribbon Club affairs continued to

monopolize Helen's time. In the middle of August, at the annual meeting of the Tippecanoe County Sunday School Union, she lectured about the relationship between church, Sunday school, and temperance. It was an honor to be asked. This time the setting was Clarks Hill, near Lafayette, and her friend DeWitt Wallace, still a leader in Sunday school work, surely booked her for the keynote talk.

Just what was so impressive about Helen Gougar, the blossoming public speaker, at Clarks Hill? This anonymous letter to Lingle's *Lafayette Daily Courier* on August 26, 1878, explains:

> She spoke without notes or manuscript and from the beginning to the end of the lecture had the fixed attention of the vast audience.
>
> The directness and earnestness with which she spoke, and the courage displayed in some of her utterances, marked her as a strong and independent thinker, and made a profound impression upon her audience.
>
> Occasional flashes of wit and sallies of genuine humor enlivened the whole, and added greatly to the effect.
>
> Her voice was clear and distinct, and her manner easy and graceful. The lecture itself is written in sprightly, vigorous style, and abounds in strong points and happy hits.
>
> At the conclusion she was invited to repeat the lecture at several different places.

On September 15, 1878, Helen and Lafayette attorney Alexander A. Rice spoke about temperance at a basket picnic at Dayton, east of Lafayette. On September 20, Helen delivered an afternoon temperance speech at Rossville, then buggied home amid goldenrod and mellow sky to entertain the Parlor Club that night with John.

Mrs. Harbert praised Helen in the September 30 issue of *Inter-Ocean* for her essay-writing and public-speaking prowess. Privately, Mrs. Harbert may have invited Helen to contribute articles to *Inter-Ocean* and to attend the Social Sciences Association meetings coming soon in Chicago. But Indiana's new Social Sciences Association came first, and on October 1, Helen was elected as one of its vice presidents at the convention in Indianapolis.

The Blue Ribbon Club, meanwhile, had acquired its own Lafayette meeting hall in August, and by October Helen had agreed to serve on a committee to plan a course of lectures for it. On the committee were the *Lafayette Daily Courier* proprietor W. S. Lingle and the ever-present DeWitt Wallace.

It may have been a result of this contact with Lingle that Helen Gougar decided to try newspapering. For on Saturday, November 2, 1878, without fanfare or previous announcement, her weekly column called "Bric-a-Brac" made its debut on page two of the *Courier*.

III

RISE OF A FEMALE FANATIC

O teach me, Lord, that I may teach
The precious things Thou dost impart:
And wing my words, that they may reach
The hidden depths of many a heart.

From "Lord, Speak to Me," Frances R. Havergal, 1872,
and Robert Schumann, 1839

CHAPTER 7

As a Writer: More than Bric-a-Brac

*B*ric-a-Brac" enables one to read and examine Helen Gougar's writing in detail, to see the logic, the motivations, the viewpoints, and the wit mentioned by her friendly critic at Clarks Hill. In the quiet privacy of her home, Helen wrote the column from her thoughts, her books, her experiences, items in other papers, and letters from friends like Elizabeth Boynton Harbert. Often, sister Edna, a budding poet and journalist, helped. Soon women readers began sending Helen items. She would sometimes print their letters or their poems. Other times she would reprint entire speeches and essays by others. Many of the "Bric-a-Brac" passages, reworked, showed up again in Helen's lectures, and vice versa.

John Gougar's position with respect to "Bric-a-Brac" is unknown. But in the body of Helen's writing, we find bits about him that invariably imply he was continuously supportive, loving, nurturing, generous, and most importantly, encouraging—rather like a smiling prince, one step to the side and one step behind the queen.

Nor can one guess editor Lingle's motives for entrusting such generous and valuable space in his *Courier* to the city's—

and perhaps Indiana's—first woman columnist. Lingle was indeed a good newspaperman. From 1857, when he acquired the *Courier*, until a heart attack struck him dead at age fifty-one in September 1884, he was a local giant. His *Courier* built strong readership and advertising support. The paper, like Lingle, was staunch Republican, pro-Lincoln, antislavery, pro-Union. It was for law enforcement, generous in its coverage of churches and such issues as temperance, woman suffrage, and equal rights. Yet Lingle, always the professional and businessman, quite possibly gave Helen Gougar columnist status more out of a sense that the novelty would sell *Couriers*, especially to women, than from any urgent feelings about social reform. It is unclear whether Helen Gougar persuaded Lingle or Lingle persuaded Helen Gougar to launch the column. Nor is it clear how the title "Bric-a-Brac," a frilly description of shallow little decorations, came to be chosen. Surely the readers soon learned, though, that Helen Gougar's strong pen was far more than decoration.

Between November 1878 and September 1880, nearly one hundred of the columns were published. Some exceeded three thousand words, so in that twenty-two-month period, Helen published the equivalent of half a dozen books. The columns, subtitled "Literature, Sciences, Art and Topics of the Day," were bylined "By H. M. G." for a few installments, then "By Helen M. Gougar." In her inaugural column, Helen commented about an article on China and India and bitingly criticized the Rev. Henry Ward Beecher, a noted preacher, writer, and woman suffrage sympathizer. The pastor of a Congregational church in Brooklyn, New York, powerful and convincing as a speaker of wide influence in the country, Beecher had fallen upon tough times. Charged in 1874 with the crime of adultery, he had endured a six-month trial in 1875 that resulted in a hung jury, but the scandal overshadowed his last years. Now Helen Gougar—who would taste the bitterness of public trial in 1883—called Reverend Beecher "Mr. Sensation" in her first column. "One of the most patent causes for the churches being looked upon with no more respect," she wrote, "is the fact of so much sensationalism from the pulpit. The churches that are in the hands of quiet, earnest, working ministers, whose works, not strategies, do praise them, are the ones whose influences in a community are for lasting good."

She continued with an item about how the Illinois Social Sciences Association had voted to admit men to full membership, commenting that "this is as it should be." Helen wrote briefly about the new Indiana Social Sciences Association's discussions on dependent and delinquent children, contending that "it is far better that the state should devote a share of its revenue to the prevention rather than punishment of crime. And in no way can it show its wisdom better than to look with affectionate concern after the training of these waifs of society that are found in large numbers in every county in the state."[1]

By the end of 1878, Helen Gougar's "Bric-a-Brac" contained these memorable excerpts:

> Parents, not "the times," are responsible for much of this outgrowth of wickedness. Purify and beautify the simple home life, and our jails and reformatories will not be peopled with young criminals. (Nov. 9, 1878)

> Women have considered themselves for so long a time to be the decorative part of the human family that they accept the thought as an axiom. They do not stop to consider the different tints of light and shade in their characters, but quietly take it as a fact pertaining to their female selves.

> We take issue with the long accepted notion. We admit that to become such is possible with women, but that by far the majority are, like the caterpillar, in the chrysalis state, and before they can assume the most beautiful tints of womanhood they must emerge from the shell that folds their wings and live in a more exalted atmosphere.

> Nurtured in the care and freedom of our American homes, many have grown out of the chrysalis state and put on wings of angelic mould, bearing the tints of beautiful souls, made beautiful by the skillful touch of refined intellect and broad views of mind and matter.

> Whatever the American women have demanded has been accorded them, with grace, gallantry and promptness. If women have not enjoyed the full benefits of freedom, it is because they have not had the strength of character and purpose to make their wants known, and therefore the denial rests upon their own want of personality. (Nov. 23, 1878)

In the closing months of 1878, Helen Gougar again received compliments in *Inter-Ocean* for her social science work. And the mid-November state suffrage convention, featuring the conservative American Woman Suffrage Association leader, Lucy Stone, as guest speaker, commanded her time.

In her first "Bric-a-Brac" for 1879, Helen rated formation of the Indiana Social Sciences Association as one of the most significant developments of 1878. The work of social science, she said, "is the devising of methods for setting good influences in motion, and for counteracting the bad. Many are of the impression that this is an association for the promotion of woman suffrage, and the advancement of women alone. There can be no greater misapprehension. Although it is officered by women, many of the most prominent men in the state are members" (Jan. 4, 1879).

Association work required Helen to travel to Indianapolis about once a month during the first half of 1879. Meanwhile, she kept up the steady pace of "Bric-a-Brac" writing. Some highlights:

> Our taxpayers are taxed for the support of the poor, for the administration of laws and justice, for the support of schools, reformatories and asylums; but over against all these they license, yes they actually throw the sanction of law around, the rum traffic which is the principal agent in making necessary all this heavy taxation for the support of the poorhouses, reformatories and asylums, as well as most of the expense in maintaining the courts of justice. Where is the wisdom in building costly schoolhouses and in their very shadow licensing 10 times as many saloons? (Jan. 25, 1879)

> The first thing a woman must do, if she has ambition and opportunity to do much else than wash dishes, tend babies and gossip, is to encase her sensitive nature in an alligator skin, metaphorically speaking. Unless she possess philosophy and judgment enough to do this, she will either settle down to a life of inaction, or she will spend more time in senseless grieving than in earnest thought and work.

> If the "eating of the apple" ever brought one curse upon woman greater than all others, it is the curse of this element of female nature called sensitiveness; though more justly it should be named weakness. This it is that has kept women of every age and country chained to the chariot wheels of ignorance and slavery.

> This sensitivity must give place to common sense, this cringing fear to ambition and justice. Till then no woman can be a true friend of herself or her sex. True dignity of thought and action lies not in what others say we should do, but what we know we ought to do . . . a thought as applicable to women as to men. (Feb. 8, 1879)

Evidence is strong that a poor Lafayette family's tragedy late in 1878, in what Helen Gougar described as a "miserable cottage," finally ignited her to a life of flaming indignation toward alcoholism, woman suffrage foes, public apathy, weakness of character, neutral churches, and spineless politicians and political parties. Her "Bric-a-Brac" for the *Lafayette Daily Courier* of January 25, 1879, told of two tragic events: the suicide of a drunkard which left small children homeless and the death of a careworn mother "laid away in the grave only a few months ago, a victim of a drunken husband." Less than four years later, Helen wrote of the 1878 scene again in words most eloquent. The *Daily Courier* of December 2, 1882, reprinted it:

> Standing beside a dead mother in a miserable hovel in the south part of the city, hearing the sobs and cries of four worse-than-orphaned little girls as they tried to cry "mama" back to life, and in the presence of a drunken father who had murdered this mother by driving her from her bed into the storm before his drunken fury, we consecrated a life of ease to one of eternal war against the licensed curse that makes such scenes possible.
>
> That scene of orphanage, that drunken father and dead mother moved me into the championing of temperance work. I had been a member of a small temperance society, and had been adding a little, day by day, to my public work. When I first became a temperance worker, I believed in praying away the evil. But I became convinced that the best way was to vote it away!
>
> After I really investigated the matter of woman suffrage, I became a fanatic on both subjects. And I am proud to say I am a fanatic.

The May 6, 1879, election was one of several developments in Lafayette that spring. The Democratic attorney, Temperance man, and former mayor, John S. Williams, founded a sprightly, gossipy, new weekly newspaper, the *Sunday Times*, in April. The election gave Helen Gougar an occasion to preach this sermon in "Bric-a-Brac" three days before the balloting:

> We had the audacity to ask an intelligent workman the following questions: What is your rule for casting your ballot? Do you vote for the man who represents certain principles, or because he is a personal friend, or because he is of your party?
>
> He replied frankly: "Well, we are generally mixed. If we aspire to office we vote a strict party vote; if not, we pick out the man who is the most sociable, good-hearted fellow. We don't care much about the particular principles he advocates or represents."

And this, we have concluded, is the motive that in-
spires the majority of voters. This is the kind of patriotism
that elects to office men who are naught but demagogues;
men who, for place and power, make successful cajolers
instead of representatives of the best principles and the
higher interests of those they wish to serve. It is the kind of
patriotism that requires money with the enormous ex-
penditures of investigating committees and election
contests.

It is the kind of patriotism that elects the man who has
spent a good share of his life associating with the bummer
element of society, and "reforms" just in time to secure the
sympathy and votes of the better class of men. A man who
has successfully reached this happy mean is far more apt to
succeed as a candidate than one who has always been up-
right in his daily walk and conversation. He passes for the
"good-hearted fellow" and he is elected because he has
successfully played fast and loose through a series of years.
This is the kind of patriotism that is unworthy of the voter
who keeps himself posted through the daily press, of the
doings of such men while in council.

If such are overtaxed and misruled they have none to
blame but their own lack of judgment and principle. Until
the men who deposit the ballot make the principles that
each candidate possesses and represents the basis of this act
of voting, then demagoguism and political corruption
will, in the lower as well as the higher positions of prefer-
ment, threaten the best interests and life of this free
republic. (May 3, 1879)

In mid-May, the *Lafayette Sunday Times* profiled the Parlor
Club, which, it said, "numbers among its members most of the
literati of the city." [2] On May 17, 1879, "Bric-a-Brac" began
with a poem entitled "Success" signed by "A Friend." Years
later it came to light that the poem was a tribute to Helen
Gougar's courage and ambition, written by her male colleague
in Sunday school, Parlor Club, and temperance work, the attorney DeWitt Wallace. Here is what the poem said:

Think not to reach ambition's height sublime
On nerveless wing, or in brief moment's time.
Heaven crowns not those who, sleeping, wish to rise.
Each soul who wears must, struggling, win the prize.
Long time, with care, Appellees plied his art
Ere glowing life would from his canvas start.
Nor could Demosthenes, untrained, at will
Make Phillip tremble and all Athens thrill.

Genius, though bright, in full orbed splendor shines
Only when art with energy combines.
Unworthy they, who grieve that honor waits;
Go thou straight on, and fearless storm the gates.
Adhere but close to nature's plain decree:
Rewarding Time shall give a crown to thee.

In her June 28, 1879, column, Helen Gougar devoted about seven hundred fifty words to the damage and injustice that can be caused by slander and the passing along of unfounded rumor or unchecked facts. To people who thoughtlessly pass along such gossip, she advised: "Inform yourself perfectly before you be guilty of betraying so great a trust as the good name of an individual. Remember it is something too precious to be used as a football by thoughtless and unjust gossipers." It was a literary sermon of great irony, for in 1882 enemies of Helen Gougar and DeWitt Wallace would slander them and force them into a three-month ordeal of public trial which would, literally, turn Helen's hair white!

For Helen the summer of 1879 was a busy one. On July 2, she broke in a new lecture at a Blue Ribbon Club program. It was based on an essay called "Home Influences," which she reworked two weeks later for "Bric-a-Brac." Its theme was that the temperance work of the press, pulpit, and Blue Ribbon volunteers "cannot always be kept up to this point of fever heat. The work must be taken up and perfected in the silent influences of the home. Philosophical historians are pleased to tell us that the nation is the type of the individual, but a search in our department of thought teaches us conclusively that the home is the type of the nation. If we would be patriotic, this patriotism must be nursed in the cradle of the home" (July 12, 1879).

On July 26, "Bric-a-Brac" took up the question of whether women were hypocrites and the answer was essentially yes. "We hope to see the time," Helen wrote, "when personal worth shall be paramount to foibles."

On August 2, "Bric-a-Brac" attacked the French actress Sarah Bernhardt, saying "we cannot afford to cast a slur upon the estimation in which we hold the record of these [other great] men and women by receiving with open arms this brilliant but decidedly immoral woman."

The August 9 column lit into Sabbath-breakers and noted: "Unimpeachable statistics show that insanity is already alarmingly on the increase in our land, and is it to be wondered at if

we take no rest and no thought for the morrow? Our responsibility to the future generations is very great, and we cannot
begin to consider this too soon. 'The fathers have eaten sour
grapes and the children's teeth are set on edge therefore,' may
be said of us as of those of old.'' Helen Gougar signed off the
August 9 column by saying "we expect to be rolling over the
fertile fields and alkali deserts of Colorado, and hope to write
our next on top of Pike's Peak, or as near there as possible.''

The Colorado trip took between two and three weeks,
with frequent stopovers. John and Helen joined others on a
press excursion train from Indianapolis. The group returned
August 24. Just four days later in a party at the Gougar home
Helen's Sunday school class from Second Presbyterian, which
she had taught now for seventeen years, gave her a gold breast
pin as a memento. The "Bric-a-Brac" columns for August 23
and 30 and for September 6, 1879, all were based on sights,
anecdotes, and thoughts from the western trip.

On September 6, the *Lafayette Daily Courier* proudly reprinted three paragraphs from exchange newspapers in other
Indiana cities, containing complimentary remarks about "Bric-
a-Brac.'' The praise, it seemed, happily added fuel to Helen's
editorial fire in subsequent columns:

> We are not opposed to card-playing. We make this
> statement in self-defense, lest we be denominated an "old
> fogy.'' We confess that our education in this department
> has been neglected and with the single exception of "pig
> euchre'' we know not one game from another. [But we do
> know that] one of the most difficult things to accomplish
> in this life is temperance; that is, temperance in all things.
> (Sept. 13, 1879)

> Liberty does not mean license. The liberty to walk the
> public promenade in a decorous and ladylike manner does
> not include the license to frequent those places that attract
> the attention of all passersby, by loud talking and laughing
> and bantering along for the express purpose of being
> observed.
> It is a fact patent to anyone who frequents any of our
> public streets in the evening that groups of young girls,
> scarcely in their teens, are in the habit of going in twos and
> fours, arm in arm, evening after evening, for no other
> purpose but that of attracting attention of the opposite sex.
> This they soon succeed in doing, and the street-loafer
> secures an acquaintance that must finally result in being his
> victim. It is a painful fact, too, that these same girls belong

to respectable households, and that their parents would be shocked beyond thought could they observe some of the conduct. (Oct. 4, 1879)

American women are not the monstrosities some would make them, neither are they nonentities. They are living, moving, thinking beings willing to be taught, to walk in the right path when they find it.

Let each daughter be taught to be cleanly, and do only those things that are in unison with high moral conception. She may wear frizzes, love bonnets, etc., but she will not neglect her home for her mission, nor will she adopt those fashions which are injurious to health, that may in time lead to deformities of the physical nature. (Oct. 11, 1879)

CHAPTER 8

As a Speaker: 'Eloquent and Logical'

T he arrival of autumn colors and cool nights signaled the end of an eventful summer of 1879 for Lafayette. Between July and September, the first telephones were hooked up. Between July 26 and August 15, a visiting showman named William Lake walked around the courthouse 2,000 times, a distance of 500 miles, in 500 hours. He was interrupted by snapping dogs, drunks, kids throwing stones, and even a fire in the courthouse cupola.

On September 18, as another means of building a crowd for downtown trade, promoters of a trade convention arranged for a demonstration of the new incandescent electric light, run from a generating machine kept at Purdue University. Later in October, Harvey Wiley, the colorful and athletic young chemistry professor from Purdue, already notorious for boyish behavior and for playing baseball with the school team, began pedaling about the campus and the town of Chauncey on a big-wheeled bicycle, one of the first ever seen in the community.[1]

For Helen Gougar, though, the fall would not be fun and games. She left Lafayette for Indianapolis on October 11 to lead the preparations for the First Annual Conference of the Social Sciences Association of Indiana, scheduled for the fifteenth. She had been writing and rehearsing a thirty-minute address for the convention, called "What Can Social Science Do for Indiana?" The talk—at least half of it—was a success, gaining praise from a Shelbyville newspaper and the honor of being reprinted in its entirety in the *Indianapolis Sentinel.* Helen was acclaimed for being "sprightly" and "vivacious," her writing for being "elegant" and "forceful."[2]

But there was an ugly side to the convention, described in detail in the *Sunday Times* in Lafayette on October 26: "In the opinion of some [association] members, Mrs. Gougar had been assuming altogether too dictatorial a position and it was therefore thought necessary to take her down a peg." So a woman named Mary B. Hussey of Indianapolis gave a talk on "What Can Social Science Do for Indiana?" first. Then, on a motion from the floor, some debate, and a vote, further "discussion" was limited to fifteen minutes, cutting Helen's time in half.

Helen, at least in the *Sunday Times* version, "acted with great forbearance, discretion and courtesy," in the eye of criticism for some sort of "misrepresentations" that were never made clear. "Mrs. Gougar," the *Sunday Times* concluded, "is intellectually, morally and socially the peer of any lady of the Social Sciences Association, and they but throw a suspicion upon their culture and refinement when they descend to such action."

For Helen, embarrassing as the moment may have been, it was an experience that helped her grow an "alligator skin" often useful in contacts with critics and foes. In her October 18 "Bric-a-Brac," in a disguised context, she seemed to rate the convention insults somewhere between "injustice" and "pure cussedness" on the part of certain women.

The first anniversary installment of "Bric-a-Brac" was expanded on November 1 to fill nearly three and one-half columns with items, articles, poems, and a congratulatory letter in rhyme from Helen's sister Etta Cosgrove in Warsaw. Helen closed the column with thanks to the Lafayette press for its "unstinted kindness" toward her history-making, first woman-written column.

The concluding paragraph was a mystery, though: "And now as we take leave of our first year of 'Bric-a-Brac' we say to our friends, one and all, if you miss us, we shall sorely miss the pleasure we have derived from your kind words and companionship, during our short editorial career." This surely sounded like the end. But without explanation, "Bric-a-Brac" was back as usual the following week and would last another ten months.

The November 15, 1879, installment hinted that more critics of Helen were beginning to appear here and there. Their identities and reasons, however, were not gone into. Critics notwithstanding, Helen was ready for another remarkably bold step. The *Sunday Times* described it in detail in the November 23 and November 30 editions.

Helen, it was reported, on a ride in the country in late summer with her good friend, Maria Ingersoll, chanced to pass and visit the county poor farm opened in 1876 north of Chauncey. "There," Helen told the *Sunday Times*, "I saw for the first time these poor unfortunates confined in dark, ill-ventilated cells day after day with no occupation except that of looking out upon the corridors, without attendants or skillful medical knowledge.

"I resolved in my own mind that if anything could be done to alleviate their sufferings, I would try to do it. When at Indianapolis I was a guest at the opening of the new state asylum building. The superintendent promised cooperation so far as was in his power."

Using the legal training she had learned from John and from doing so much of John's reading, research, and legwork over the years, Helen prepared the necessary papers to have nineteen women and fourteen men transferred from the county poor farm to the state asylum. Helen was hailed by the *Sunday Times* as a "true philanthropist," but it was not clear whether she donated money or merely her time and mental powers.[3]

In early December 1879, both the *Courier* and *Sunday Times* printed stories to the effect that Helen was entering the "lecture field," commencing with an appearance in Fowler, twenty miles northwest of Lafayette, on Tuesday, December 10. Rain and muddy roads unfortunately postponed that speech until the following February.

The December 20, 1879, "Bric-a-Brac" contained one of Helen Gougar's more memorable essays, quoted in part:

> Women have been told long enough that they are angels by nature. They will never see themselves in the true light until they cease hearing and teaching such twaddle.
>
> First, we would like to know by what reasoning woman is better than man. Born of the same parents,

Indiana women contributed to nineteenth-century crusades for change: May Wright Sewall (top left), an Indianapolis educator of suffragists; Zerelda G. Wallace (top right), the key figure in the state's early woman suffrage effort; and Frances Wright (left) of New Harmony, the state's first feminist. Lafayette's Helen Gougar (above third from left with her mother, sisters, and nephew) complemented the work of these forward-looking women of Indiana.

brought up with the same surroundings, each reaches the age of responsibility with a pretty well balanced account of good and hateful acts.

When once a woman and a man, custom pushes the man out into the rush and whirl and temptations of the world, and he may be guilty of larger crimes than the sister, who is still kept under the protection of home life, and in a narrow sphere of action. Give her the same room and the same temptation, as the brother, and we feel safe in saying that she will be equal to the task of keeping even with him in going against the laws of right; inherent goodness is no more natural to one than to the other, and if it were so, we would be sad, on account of the extra responsibility she would be obliged to assume.

Again, one hears her religious sentiments are of much higher and purer order than his, etc. Why? Not by nature, most certainly, but because her life has been so narrow that she revolves, like a satellite, within the orbit of the religious sentiment.

It is high time that this spirit of "reform" cast off the garment of self-righteousness, and put on that of justice and self examination, and thereby learn that as there is no sex in heaven, so there is no sex in good or evil, but all are equal before God, whether male or female.

Helen Gougar spent the short gray days and long howling nights of January 1880 writing. She turned out five installments of "Bric-a-Brac," kept up with a mounting pile of correspondence and reading, and finished writing two lectures which she called "Vashti, or the Royal Feast" and "Woman in the Home and in the State."

Then on January 24, 1880, she shocked "Bric-a-Brac" readers with an enterprising piece of investigative journalism she headlined "A Day among the Poor of the City." She had persuaded a township trustee to let her accompany him on one of his tours of the homes of the poor. Then she wrote: "In this list of families there are no less than 300 girls and boys coming up to manhood and womanhood. These are not morally depraved, but are poverty deprived; and if left to grow up with no interest taken in them by people who are better circumstanced in life, what will be the result? A large majority will become criminals and paupers from the necessity of the case." The column brought a letter to the *Lafayette Daily Courier* from a children's home superintendent in Cincinnati, challenging the Lafayette area's Christian homes to open their doors and adopt children in need.[4]

On January 31, the *Courier* reported Helen also had contributed three articles to the Warsaw *Northern Indianian* and would present her weather-delayed lecture in Fowler on February 4. A weekly paper known as the *Fowler Era* praised the lecture, based on the legend of a Persian queen named Vashti and containing strong woman's rights and suffrage messages. "The lecture was interesting and instructive, full of historical truth and replete with gems of thoughts that sparkled like diamonds," the *Era* said. "It is a lecture to which every woman of the land should listen, and be profited thereby."[5] On March 7, 1880, the *Sunday Times* said Helen would present "Vashti" to an audience in Warsaw later in the month. She also was invited a few days later to give the lecture to the Parlor Club, to the Blue Ribbon Club, and to the WCTU membership.

But Helen and the *Sunday Times* ended their early cordiality with that same March 7 issue. On another page of the *Times*, an item related that Judge David Vinton of Tippecanoe Circuit Court had ruled that $286 in fees should be paid the county clerk, physician, and two justices of the peace for their work in transferring county asylum inmates to the state institution in December at Helen's behest. The fees were for processing those thirty-three men and women for whom Helen had filed applications, even though only twelve were finally accepted at Indianapolis. The *Sunday Times* editorially attacked the "ignorant somebody" who filed the defective papers and cost county taxpayers so much money. Helen Gougar shot back a reply, printed in the March 21 *Sunday Times*:

> As I am the somebody . . . I am personally responsible for this act of 'ignorance' and I hold myself financially, legally and intellectually accountable. If the laws of Indiana are defective, if fees are exorbitant, then, being a woman, I am not responsible for such ignorant legislation as no woman has a voice, as yet, in making these laws.

Helen said that sending even the twelve to the state asylum was saving county taxpayers money and that she would press for getting the twenty-one "rejects" accepted sooner or later. Then, answering charges of "fanaticism" on her part: "If some of the political demagogues who rave about fanaticism in this matter will step over to the poor farm and occupy the apartments vacated by these patients for a night and a day, they would be thankful that somebody was 'fanatical' enough to liberate them."[6]

In mid-March 1880, Helen broke in the second new lecture, "Woman in the Home and in the State," to a Lafayette audience. It was based on her belief that women should have equal rights with men regarding affairs of state. "Many objections raised against such equality were forcibly and bravely answered" at the lecture, the *Courier* reported the next afternoon.

On the second anniversary of the 1878 Hughes and Ward temperance meetings, Helen Gougar delivered remarks as part of a long program in Blue Ribbon Hall on March 31. Her April 14 rendering of "Vashti" ended up, after a series of switched arrangements, being given before a joint meeting of Blue Ribbon Club, WCTU members, and the general public in Blue Ribbon Hall. Her friend DeWitt Wallace made the introduction, recalling how Helen had come to Lafayette "over 20 years ago as a young girl whose fortune entirely consisted of an education and good natural endowments." He also pointed out that she was the "first lady journalist and lecturer which our city has produced."[7] Helen's lecture, as usual, was delivered without manuscript or notes in a clear, distinct voice and in an easy, graceful manner. The refusal of Vashti to appear before the king when he was carousing with the drunken princes of the realm was the text for the discussion of woman's rights.

Meanwhile, a newspaper "side trip" was taking Helen's time and thought. A fireman on the Lake Erie Railroad named Joseph T. Landrey had launched in May 1879 a semimonthly Lafayette paper called the *Temperance Herald*. Using the *nom de plume* "Harry Burton," he promised the paper would not be fanatical but would "show the quiet confidence of a man who knows he is in the right and the defender of a good cause."

Sweet as that all sounded, "Harry Burton" found himself the defendant in a libel suit filed in late March 1880 by a liquor and cigar wholesaler.[8] "Burton" had written in the *Temperance Herald* that upstairs in the wholesaler's establishment "animal delectation could be obtained on accommodating terms." The man denied the charge, taking "animal delectation" to mean prostitution. The libel case was filed in a justice of the peace court, and Landrey was jailed until he could post $200 bond. The matter reached Tippecanoe Circuit Court. In her April 10, 1880, "Bric-a-Brac," Helen Gougar gave "Harry Burton" advice:

> No good can come to the temperance cause in this city by upholding the publication of a sheet done in the spirit of the *Herald*. Its language needs to be toned down somewhat in order to receive the support of the best temperance people.

>We sincerely hope that the earnest editor thereof will see to it that his zealous articles be couched in more refined expressions, and that the *Herald* be made a means of doing good instead of harm to the cause it so earnestly advocates.

In mid-April 1880, Helen judged a state oratorical contest at Indianapolis sponsored by the Indiana Equal Suffrage Association, which was allied with the conservative American Woman Suffrage Association. On April 27, she spoke at the convention of the state organization held in Crawfordsville.

During May Helen delivered to a Parlor Club audience a study of Pedro Calderon de la Barca, seventeenth-century Spanish dramatist and poet. She entertained Elizabeth Boynton Harbert in her home May 23–25, then both left for the more radical National Woman Suffrage Association's convention in Indianapolis. Helen at this point was on good terms with both the National and the American groups.

In "Bric-a-Brac," meanwhile, Helen reported that she and five other WCTU women had petitioned Lafayette Mayor Furman E. D. McGinley to prevent "the exhibition of variety and other immoral shows within our city . . . which exert immoral influences upon men old and young . . . and tend to debase those engaged in them as well as those who witness them."[9] Nothing came of it.

Through the spring of 1880, Susan B. Anthony lectured tirelessly and planned a series of major woman suffrage conventions in locales such as Chicago and Cincinnati. The scheme was a show of strength that would influence the Republican and Democratic parties to adopt woman's rights and woman suffrage planks in their summer presidential conventions. The first in the series of suffrage conventions, which took place in Indianapolis, coincided with the eleventh anniversary of the founding of the National Woman Suffrage Association by Miss Anthony and Elizabeth Cady Stanton. The convention was held in the Park Theater, Miss Anthony presiding, and "all arrangements had been made and all expenses assumed by the local suffrage society under the leadership of Mrs. [May Wright] Sewall."[10] (On June 1, the Chicago convention drew 3,000 and Elizabeth Boynton Harbert gave the welcoming address.)

The Indianapolis convention was significant because it brought Helen Gougar and Susan B. Anthony together again and introduced Helen to many other fellow warriors: Belva Ann Lockwood, a Washington, D.C., lawyer and first woman admitted to U.S. Supreme Court practice in 1879; Lillie Devereux Blake, a suffrage activist from New York; Rachel Foster

Avery, a lawyer from Philadelphia; Phoebe Couzins, reputed to be the first woman ever admitted to practice law in the United States; and Rev. Olympia Brown from Wisconsin, one of the first woman ministers. Helen Gougar also met leaders of the woman's movement from Missouri, Kentucky, and South Carolina.

The convention routinely re-elected Mrs. Stanton as president (she was absent, recovering from pneumonia) and Miss Anthony as vice president.[11] But more importantly, Helen Gougar returned home to Lafayette with new friends, new inspiration and encouragement, new invitations to write and speak, and the responsibility for organizing a "mass equal suffrage convention," which would be held June 16–17 in Lafayette's opera house. On the stage, seated in a semicircle were delegates from other cities and states, as well as Lafayette citizens and suffrage workers. Helen Gougar presided and gave the welcoming address. Miss Anthony was among the speakers. Many of the visiting dignitaries were put up in hotels or homes, but John and Helen Gougar landed the prize—Miss Anthony—as their personal house guest.[12]

The relationship between Helen Gougar and Susan B. Anthony was essentially cordial, though as the years passed major differences would develop between them as to priorities, strategies, and methods. In the monumental career of Miss Anthony, neither Helen nor Lafayette was especially significant. From Helen's viewpoint, Miss Anthony's visions were not broad enough. Woman suffrage alone was too narrow a goal. The whole world needed improvement.

On Sunday, July 4, Helen delivered the Independence Day oration for celebrants at West Lebanon. For a woman to be asked was a rare honor. Helen's theme was to glorify the mothers as well as fathers of the American republic.

In midsummer the various temperance forces announced they would organize a boycott of the Tippecanoe County Fair because the fair board continued to permit the operation of a saloon there. On August 23, Helen again teamed with the pro-temperance lawyer Alexander A. Rice for a rural Tippecanoe County address at a meeting in Stockwell; then Helen alone traveled a few miles to Romney for a talk on the twenty-fourth.

Also in August, the Blue Ribbon Temperance Club refitted Lafayette's old Baptist church and opened it as the Blue Ribbon Temperance Club House with meeting and recreational rooms and a library containing about a thousand volumes. Lafayette

Hughes and Milo Ward, of the 1878 Hughes and Ward revival meeting fame, revisited Lafayette for the dedication program.

In mid-October at a WCTU meeting in Blue Ribbon Hall, Helen read a chautauqua speech of some note, delivered during the summer by a minister. Earlier, the *Courier* said, Helen had spoken at an old soldiers' reunion at Remington.

The late summer of 1880 inexplicably marked the end of "Bric-a-Brac." The columns had, indeed, become shorter and repetitive, surely owing to Helen's other ventures. But she felt she needed to say a few final philosophical thoughts:

> Instead of wishing the temperance cause success, and at the same time sitting at home fanning off flies or mosquitoes and chatting away hours in useless and frivolous conversations, if the good women of this county and city would put on the armor of work, would attend the business and public meetings held in the interest of sobriety and a high morality, would speak, sing, pray, listen, devise ways and means with which to destroy this curse of intemperance, then would such crimes as those be less frequent and consequently, more startling. . . .[13]
>
> We have been, and always expect to be, a Republican; but in our own official capacity we shall instruct all suffragists to get a declaration from all men in the state seeking legislative honors, Democratic or Republican, upon the question at issue, and the man who is in favor of the cause of equal rights, regardless of party, will be the man for whom instructions will be given to work.[14]

Helen stayed busy even without the weekly column-writing chores; besides, she had easy access to the columns of *Inter-Ocean*, her brother-in-law A. P. Cosgrove's Warsaw *Northern Indianian*, "Harry Burton's" *Temperance Herald*, and other publications when and if she felt the urge to write.

On November 7, 1880, Helen introduced as guest speaker Mary E. Haggart, a rising WCTU leader from Indianapolis, at a program in Blue Ribbon Hall. Helen lectured at Thorntown on November 8 and 9. On the tenth, she went to Indianapolis for the Indiana WCTU convention and stayed over for a meeting of the executive committee of the Equal Suffrage Association on the twelfth.

Helen was one of seven speakers at a meeting on November 29 in Lafayette's Blue Ribbon Hall where the club membership voted to become an auxiliary of the state and national WCTU. On December 2, the new Blue Ribbon Temperance

Union announced a course of lectures. The lineup included Helen and her friend and supporter DeWitt Wallace. Helen dusted off her "Woman in the Home and in the State" lecture for the series.[15]

On Sunday evening, December 12, 1880, Helen was a featured speaker at a weekly Blue Ribbon Union meeting, unveiling a new and well-aimed blast at "Our City Government," which stepped on a few toes. In it she assailed Lafayette City Marshal Felix Connolly for his dealings with saloonkeepers and errant women. She asked why gambling dens were allowed in the city, why the houses of prostitution went unmolested, and why saloons could sell liquor in open violation of law daily.

"Mrs. Gougar," the *Courier* noted in its December 13 account of the meeting, "is not in the habit of mincing matters very much, nor is she afraid to call a thing by its right name." Later in the meeting, when Blue Ribbon Union members were being put on committees, Helen agreed to serve on the one dealing with the literary programs and the reading room.

A month later, she found a measure of acclaim as a speaker. The annual convention of the National Woman Suffrage Association was held on January 18, 1881, in Washington's Lincoln Hall. Elizabeth Cady Stanton presided; and speakers such as Susan B. Anthony and Indiana's May Wright Sewall and Phoebe Couzins memorialized Lucretia Mott, who had died the previous November 11. The convention tried to get a standing committee on the rights of women added to the list in Congress but failed. Helen was but one of many convention session speakers and panelists, yet a description of her appeared in the *National Republican*, detailing her looks, manners, and strengths as a platform speaker:

> Helen M. Gougar, of Indiana, is a young and handsome lady, doubtless as fascinating and charming in social as she certainly is eloquent and logical in public life.
>
> She is a decided blonde, with luxuriant masses of light brown hair frizzled up in front upon a full magnificent forehead and shading deep blue eyes that flash and sparkle with each humorous idea, or burn and glow with steady radiance under the spell of deeper and stronger thought.
>
> Her face indicates her character—intense, intellectual. She wore a black velvet hat with appropriate trimmings, a crimson bow at her throat rested upon a mass of snow white lace, the one bit of color that relieved the white, clear-cut face, from which all color had fled to settle in the scarlet lips; a black silk dress, a black silk coat trimmed with fur, a gold watch at her girdle, and No. 2 kid boots.

Her voice is a clear soprano, distinct, well modulated, with not a little melody in its pure, soft tones.[16]

The actual content of this talk, though, was a well-used one: answers to Horace Greeley's opposition to woman suffrage.

IV

SPOILING FOR A FIGHT

Stand up, stand up for Jesus,
The trumpet call obey;
Forth to the mighty conflict,
In this His glorious day;
Ye that are men now serve Him
Against unnumbered foes;
Let courage rise with danger,
And strength to strength oppose.

From "Stand Up, Stand Up for Jesus," George Duffield,
1858, and George J. Webb, 1837

CHAPTER 9

Our Herald;
Political War and
Personal Bloodshed

By the decade of the 1880s, Lafayette had grown considerably. Purdue University was growing with it. The Lafayette Car Works employed hundreds of men making railroad cars and wheels. Serious talk about building a new courthouse began, and though drenched in political and legal controversy, a three-story, domed limestone building was finished in 1885.

The wonders of the electric light and telephone became commonplace. The public library opened at last—with a woman librarian. Women were making visible progress in business, too. A city directory for 1881 showed scores of women now listed as milliners, dressmakers, tailoresses, and as operators of boardinghouses, rooming houses, hotels, and saloons. There were three women doctors and three insurance agents.

Helen Gougar, who had rung out the old in 1880 with a smashing attack on city government, rang in the new in 1881 with a lawsuit against the Western Union Telegraph Company. She had been irritated when a wire she had sent to Frankfort on November 27, 1880, had been delayed by a number of more "important looking" messages sent by men. With two attorneys giving advice—husband John and close friend DeWitt Wallace—she sought monetary damages but wanted the true victory to be the principle that women's messages were as important as men's. Judge David Vinton weighed the matter in Tippecanoe Circuit Court.

On January 27, 1881, Helen invited friends to a tea in her home honoring sixty-year-old Mary Livermore still touring as a speaker. Then in early February she spent most of a week in Indianapolis outside the chambers of the Indiana General Assembly, talking up woman suffrage, prohibition, and Purdue University funding. In the prosuffrage talks, Helen teamed with Mary Haggart of the Indianapolis WCTU. Haggart adopted a realistic, coldly legal approach to the all-male lawmakers. But Helen used wit and logic and appealed to their sense of ethics and fair play, too, as excerpts from her address of February 15, 1881, show:

> Be assured we appreciate gallantry, but we appreciate justice more than gallantry. The time has passed when the women of Indiana will be satisfied with gallantry.
>
> Today we want not only gallantry, but justice. We are not here alone by our own convictions, but we are here upon the invitation and appointment of a large and powerful constituency, and not by the appointment of the vicious, unwashed men and women of this state. We are here by the invitation and appointment of educated, thinking, cultured and patriotic men and women—women engaged in the different professions, trades, arts, sciences and literature, who are demanding increased power—that the ballot may be given them that they may use it on behalf of justice and virtue.
>
> I have been asked on this occasion to answer what is usually called some of the popular objections against enfranchising women. One gentleman said to me, "Women do not want it." This I deny most emphatically. Anyone with the facility of seeing and knowing, as I do, the ladies of this state will agree with me in saying that nine-tenths of the women with brains above an oyster demand the ballot. There is a class of women who dance all night and sleep all day, who study nothing more elevated than a fashion-plate or the latest novel, and they are the ones who say they do not want it. Two hundred thousand women petition for the right of citizenship in Ohio, and 180,000 in Illinois. At the same time the gentleman decided "they do not want it." . . .
>
> The time has come when every man has his say-so in the government of the nation, and I hope that not many years hence the same right will be extended to woman.[1]

As it turned out, the 1881 legislature passed amendments to the state constitution on both woman suffrage and prohibition. In order for them to take effect, though, they would need to be passed by a second session of the legislature in 1883, then submitted to a popular vote. Thus it was essential that a sympathetic Republican majority be retained in the 1883 legislature in the election of November 1882.

On March 21, Helen and John entertained Elizabeth Boynton Harbert while she was in Lafayette for her Blue Ribbon Temperance Union lecture, and on the thirty-first, Judge Vinton awarded Helen $100 damages in her Western Union suit. On April 17, 1881, Helen spoke on temperance in Sheldon, Illinois, where, two days later, a local option vote to not issue liquor licenses carried by twenty-one votes.

In May and June, Helen spoke at Crawfordsville, Greencastle, and Lafayette, host city for the state WCTU convention in Blue Ribbon Hall. Helen was elected one of ten delegates to represent Indiana at the national WCTU convention in Saratoga, New York. She lectured in Frankfort and Michigantown, where she and "Harry Burton" of the *Temperance Herald* were the stars of a temperance basket picnic that drew 7,000 people, some via excursion train, from Frankfort and Kokomo. On July 4, Helen delivered the Independence Day oration in Colfax.

A tax list printed in the *Lafayette Daily Courier* on July 25, 1881, showed John Gougar had paid taxes on property valued at $1,557. That was a modest amount compared to the *Courier*'s W. S. Lingle with $2,870, but ahead of DeWitt Wallace's $1,005. Those figures mean little today beyond the fact that John was accumulating wealth, property, reputation, and clientele. At the same time, Helen was beginning to make substantial income of her own by lecturing. Her travel and lodging expenses customarily were paid by the inviting program committee, and the lecture fee might range from twenty-five to one hundred dollars, depending to some extent upon Helen's desire to give a bargain or take a windfall.

The July 25 *Courier*, meanwhile, said "Harry Burton" had sold the *Temperance Herald* to new proprietors, identified only as the Herald Company. Then on July 30, the *Courier* "scooped" all the other local papers with the intelligence that Helen Gougar had, in fact, bought the *Temperance Herald* from "Harry Burton," that she was "the Herald Company," and that the first issue under her editorship would appear in August. The word *bought* may have been erroneous. Helen calmly went about the business of getting the paper ready, interrupted it for a suffrage talk August 2 in Rossville, then introduced *Our Herald* on Saturday, August 13.

For the next three and one-half years, Helen Gougar was the proprietor—if not owner—of her very own newspaper "devoted to the best interest of home and nation." Her true role cannot be documented. The weekly contained four to six pages and under the front-page masthead was the slogan "Freedom and Law Know No Sex." Helen seems to have accepted the position of editor-in-chief of the old *Temperance Herald* with John C. Dobelbower, owner of the pro-Democrat *Lafayette Dispatch*, as the hidden owner and business manager. But Dobelbower apparently found it awkward to own papers that both supported and opposed prohibition and woman suffrage and temperance, so on February 17, 1883, he evidently sold *Our Herald* to Helen's brother-in-law A. P. Cosgrove, who served as owner until August 1883, when Helen assumed both ownership and editorship.

Supported by advertising and subscription sales and claiming a circulation of 4,000, *Our Herald* was editorially an extension of what Helen Gougar had done with "Bric-a-Brac." The paper set out to achieve several things, among them to serve as the "official organ of the WCTU." Its articles and editorials intensely covered temperance, woman suffrage and woman's rights, the law, politics, literature, religion, sociology, and advice. Book reviews and some biting political cartoons appeared on its pages. Helen's personal articles, often referring to "us" and "we," were signed "H. M. G." For the first two years, *Our Herald* resembled a tabloid newspaper; but on August 11, 1883, Helen, now full owner, announced it would become a monthly magazine printed on high quality paper, running twenty pages per issue. Circulation then may have reached a larger national or, at least, midwestern subscriber list. The editorial work was done almost solely in the privacy of Helen Gougar's home. Her brother-in-law A. P. Cosgrove, business manager of the *Fort Wayne Journal* since 1879, also was *Our Herald*'s business manager in 1883–84. Lingle's *Lafayette Daily Courier* welcomed the first issue of *Our Herald*: "It is a marvel of typographical neatness in makeup and its columns fairly glow with good, spicy reading matter and items of news, speaking not of local matters but on general topics of the hour. The masterly abilities of the editress are well known, and the first copy of *Our Herald* displays them most thoroughly."[2]

On August 15, 1881, John and Helen Gougar and the DeWitt Wallaces drove a team ten miles south to Romney for tea at a rural home, and that evening Helen spoke on "The Two Amendments" in the Romney church. The talk had to do with the proposed state constitutional amendments providing for woman suffrage and prohibition of sale and use of alcoholic beverages. Helen traveled to Darlington for afternoon and night addresses on August 18.

By the end of August, she and Maria Ingersoll, as cochairwomen, were busy preparing for a national WCTU convention in Lafayette on September 8–11. The WCTU convention sessions shuttled back and forth from Lafayette's Blue Ribbon Hall to the opera house. There were ceremonies, election of officers, committee reports, and speeches on topics such as "Juvenile Temperance Work." More than a thousand persons attended. One report estimated that there were now forty-three hundred "working" unions in the United States with a total membership of 525,000. The Republican governor of Kansas from 1879–83, John Pierce St. John, was elected national president. Lafayette's "Harry Burton" was named corresponding secretary. On the final day, Helen Gougar was one of six speakers in a panel discussion of "temperance literature." When the convention adjourned, Helen was applauded for her expert job of arranging the convention.

In late October 1881, Helen delivered an address at the American Woman Suffrage Association's annual session in Louisville, Kentucky. The *Louisville Courier Journal* reported:

> Editor Helen Gougar is a blonde. She is thoroughly conversant with the current topics of the day and can talk politics like a stalwart.
>
> She wore an elegant Parisian walking dress of maroon velvet satin de Lyon, with point lace collar, white linen cuffs and handsome gold ornaments.
>
> She is a tall, rather slender woman with a pleasing, expressive face and remarkably fine style of delivery. Her voice is full and rich and penetrated with ease every part of the house.[3]

On November 15 and 16 in Fowler, Helen spoke on temperance, discussed "Prohibition Amendments" for an evening audience, and visited school children to talk about "the effects of alcohol on the body and brain," closing the evening session of the second day with a talk on "Our Suffrage Amendment."

She spent November 23–25 in Jeffersonville. There she presided over a meeting of the Indiana Woman Suffrage Association, speaking on suffrage on the twenty-third and on "The

Sufferings or Wrongs of Woman" on the afternoon of the twenty-fourth. That night she delivered a public address on suffrage. "Mrs. Gougar is a woman of brains and is certainly one of the best lady speakers upon the platform," said the *Jeffersonville Times*. "She made her points in sharp, decisive, convincing manner and won new converts to the cause of equal suffrage."[4] Earlier in the day, she had visited the southern state penitentiary near Jeffersonville and addressed inmates.

On December 12, an Irish-American newspaper from Indianapolis, the *Western Citizen*, speculated that if woman suffrage were enacted in Indiana by passing the 1883 legislature and a referendum, then Helen Gougar would be a candidate for governor! On December 23, the *Tipton Times* speculated further. It said Helen would be a candidate for president of the United States in 1884 and referred to her, perhaps with affection (or maybe with sarcasm), as "General Gougar."[5] Helen closed 1881 by speaking at a small meeting in Goodland.

In early January 1882, *Our Herald* and the *Kokomo Gazette* engaged in an editorial spat. The *Gazette* criticized people like Helen, and her paper, for coupling the questions of prohibition and equal suffrage in speeches, articles, campaigns, and amendments, because "they have no logical connection." Helen inveighed against the "beardless editor of the Gazette" in her paper, and the exchange was soon forgotten.[6] Besides, Helen had bigger matters on her mind.

On January 17, 1882, she and John left for Washington and Philadelphia, where Helen addressed a Pennsylvania suffrage association convention, then traveled on to New York City to address that state's suffrage society convention.

In Washington Helen was again a speaker at the National Woman Suffrage Association convention and was even mentioned as a possible successor to the veteran Republican congressman from Lafayette, Godlove S. Orth.[7]

"Our legislators," Helen Gougar said in Washington, "tell us how pure, how beautiful and how angelic we [women] are, but they seem to be very much afraid of the angel in government. Many say, 'Don't you know you wield a wonderful silent influence?' However, I don't hear the married men say much about the silent influence business, it's only the single men who talk that way."[8]

The effort to get a congressional committee on woman suffrage which had failed in the Forty-sixth Congress was successful in the Forty-seventh, and a number of congressmen sympathetic to the idea were among the convention speakers in

1882. Indiana's Representative Orth was among them and, with Helen Gougar, two other women, and two other men, was introduced at the convention as being "all new on the National platform," since the last convention.[9]

Accounts in the *New York Sun* and *New York Herald* indicate Helen drew the biggest crowds at the state's suffrage convention on February 1. The *Herald* described her: "She wore a tightly fitting dress of garnet velvet, a cloud of white linen lace about her neck, and a white flower in her corsage. A pair of eyeglasses dangled over her right shoulder. She was trim in figure and employed graceful gestures. She said that for her part, if there was any fun going on in the world, she wanted her share of it"[10]

The Gougars returned from the eastern trip on February 10, having perhaps added some sightseeing, vacationing, or visiting days to the itinerary. In Indianapolis on the fifteenth, Helen spoke at a sixty-second birthday reception honoring Susan B. Anthony *in absentia* and was back again on the twenty-fourth making arrangements for a state temperance convention. On March 12, 1882, she introduced a new twist to her temperance speech in Linden: illustrated charts purporting to show the effect of alcoholic drink on the stomach.

In early April, a WCTU convention was held in Frankfort, where Helen and Mrs. Septimius Vater, wife of the proprietor of the *Lafayette Journal*, were speaking delegates. The *Frankfort Banner* on April 11, though, accused Helen both of abusing the people of Frankfort for being so restless during her two-hour speech that lasted until 10 P.M. and of converting a temperance convention into a suffrage harangue. "If she only knew how many joyous 'amens' were uttered when she quit talking she would never attempt another harangue," the *Banner* said. "If she would leave the big I's out of her addresses, they would be of reasonable length."[11]

Ever since May 1881, Lafayette's city government had been a strange creature of compromise. The jaunty little Democrat F. E. D. McGinley was elected mayor, but the voters had given Republicans a majority on the city council. Now, in May 1882, McGinley appointed a barber and former saloonkeeper named Henry Mandler to be the chief of police. Mandler was of German descent, spoke with a bit of an accent, and was in his early thirties. Broad-shouldered, with mustache and neatly trimmed goatee, soft-spoken, and polite, he was generally well liked. He went about his policing duties in a quiet enough way and was on a first-name basis with most of the downtown bums, saloon men, railroadmen, and workingmen. To them he was just a genial Dutch barber. Whether Helen Gougar still cared enough about local politics to oppose Mandler's appointment to a law enforcement job, considering his saloon pedigree, is unknown. But they would certainly get acquainted later!

Helen gave a ninety-minute temperance talk in Blue Ribbon Hall Sunday night, June 4, and journeyed to Plymouth for another the following Friday. But at home, she became enmeshed in new controversy, this time through her effort to influence the Tippecanoe County Republican convention to adopt a woman suffrage resolution. The resolution was adopted, and the *Sunday Times* instantly leaped on it as a sign that "Mrs. Gougar is the authorized spokesman for the Republican party, and the party is responsible for what she says."

Helen's Parlor Club friend Septimius Vater blasted the *Sunday Times* analysis in his own *Weekly Journal* on June 16, saying, in part:

> It would be much nearer the truth to say she represents the Democratic Party, the proprietor of the Democratic Party organ, the *Dispatch*, and the proprietor of the paper which Mrs. Gougar edits.
>
> Mrs. Gougar has written many true and excellent things. She has said some things which it has been a pleasure to endorse. She has said a great many other things which we entirely disapprove of.
>
> The [managers of] local Democratic politics are taking great pains to give out the impression that Mrs. Gougar is the Republican Party, and the Republican Party is Mrs. Gougar. This is highly complimentary to the lady but, without any discourtesy to her we may say, is rather hard on the Republican Party.

Vater insisted the resolution was authored by others, with no influence from Helen Gougar. Helen maintained silence. On July 4, she delivered the Independence Day oration at Anderson, apparently giving a talk mixing patriotism with an appeal for woman suffrage. The *Anderson Review* reported:

> The orator was fashionably attired and had her front hair 'banged' in the highest style of the art. The lady is an eloquent speaker, full of snap and vim. Even those opposed to her doctrine were willing to admit that Mrs. Gougar is an excellent speaker.[12]

In late July, Helen was one of six speakers at a suffrage "camp meeting" near the community of Acton, ten miles southeast of Indianapolis. On August 2, she boldly stepped to the platform at the Democratic state convention in Indianapolis and urged adoption of the constitutional amendment providing for a prohibition referendum. It was a message from the WCTU. The Democrats essentially laughed at the whole thing and passed a resolution which Helen later branded a "delusion and snare, too transparent to deceive either the temperance people or satisfy the whisky ring."[13]

On August 11, 1882, the *Lafayette Morning Journal* reported that Helen would leave in September to campaign in Nebraska for a woman suffrage amendment. She would visit both major party conventions and speak in numerous cities and towns with local workers as a field representative of the National Woman Suffrage Association. Before she left, though, she assailed the *Journal* and the Republicans for a "namby pamby course" over Indiana's proposed amendments on prohibition and woman suffrage.[14]

Nearly a month after the Indiana Democratic convention had adjourned, the rehash continued over whether Helen had blundered or had outsmarted the Democrats. The *Indianapolis Journal* said "it appears that she fully comprehended the Democrats' mood, and her remarks at the convention were in the spirit of the keenest satire. It was the convention that was simple-minded, not Mrs. Gougar." But a letter to the *New Albany Public Press* said:

> The Equal Suffrage Society ought to lay in a supply of sackcloth and ashes and appoint a day to be occupied in mourning after its unfortunate exponent, Helen Gougar, made a colossal blunder in her speech before the Democratic State Convention. If her sarcasm is so subtle as to be imperceptible to the vast democratic intellects of our state, she is an unsafe individual to be roaming at large.
>
> Away to Nebraska, Helen, and hide your diminished head.[15]

Away to Nebraska, Kansas, Iowa, and Illinois she did go, but hide her head she did not. The *Lincoln Journal* (Nebraska) reported in early September that she gave an outdoor suffrage speech lasting over an hour to an audience of about three hundred, and "her voice was as clear as a bell and every word could be distinctly heard by those present."[16]

On September 12–13, Helen attended the annual meeting of the American Woman Suffrage Association in Omaha and was elected a vice president representing Indiana.

Ever since 1878, Helen had been a leader in organizing the temperance people, mostly women, against licensing beer and gambling at the Tippecanoe County fairs. That first year, the county agricultural association had paid little attention, stating that the petitioning was too late and that women not contributing to the industries of the community should not have a say in the beer and gambling matter. In 1879 the women had petitioned earlier but again were rebuffed. The association argued that the beer ensured financial success of the fair. The license for beer alone, they claimed, provided $1,000 in revenue. But Helen, irritated by this argument, next led a special appeal from the rostrum for pledges to boycott the fair while liquor and gambling were allowed. The campaign secured 5,000 pledges which, at an admission of fifty cents, would amount to several times more than the beer license revenue. The agricultural association, after battling the temperance women yet another year, finally relented in 1882.

With a "dry" fair now going in early September, the *Lafayette Daily Courier* told of a game booth where little images were set on a cross beam to be knocked off by balls thrown by players. The images were of U. S. Grant, President Chester Arthur, Lafayette Postmaster (and *Courier* proprietor) W. S. Lingle, the *Journal* proprietor Septimius Vater, and Helen Gougar.[17]

By mid-September 1882, the political campaign began to heat up, and the *Lafayette Sunday Times* editorialized:

> Deacon Dobelbower, of the *Dispatch*, is the owner, publisher and manager of *Our Herald*. That weekly teems with the most virulent abuse of the Democrats and is especially violent in its denunciation of the Democratic platform on the subject of prohibition. Mrs. Gougar, a woman of brains and ability, is hired and paid by Dobelbower to do work while he hides behind her petticoats. And this is the man who, with his jackanapes, was engaged last week in the columns of the *Dispatch* in reading Democrats out of the party.[18]

To which Septimius Vater's pro-Republican *Lafayette Morning Journal* retorted:

> The sting of reproach is in its truth. This is true. The *Dispatch* on the one hand is waging war on Captain Wallace on a false issue touching woman suffrage and prohibition while on the other hand *Our Herald*, printed and owned by the wily Deacon, is sandpapering the Democracy on the other side.[19]

The reference to "Captain Wallace" was to attorney De-Witt Wallace's 1882 candidacy for election to the Indiana Senate from Tippecanoe County. Wallace was on a Republican ticket which, for county voters, included Godlove S. Orth for re-election to Congress and David P. Vinton for re-election as circuit court judge.

The county had almost always voted Republican, but this year there were national and local issues at stake, not to mention the state amendment questions over prohibition and woman suffrage. Wallace's opponent was Democrat Francis Johnson, a German native who ran a book and stationery store and edited a German-language newspaper, the *German-American*, for Lafayette's sizeable German-speaking population. Johnson was a quiet scholar who wrote books and national magazine pieces and lived as a bachelor with his aged mother.

Wallace caught it from the Democrats because he was a Republican and from anyone else who might disagree with his belief that prohibition and woman suffrage both should be subjects of referenda, a position that Helen Gougar supported. In campaign talks during October, though, Wallace often side-stepped both issues while he promoted Purdue University as the "apple of our eye" and pledged to support its financing in the state senate if he were elected for the 1883 session.

Helen Gougar returned late in September from her suffrage campaign work in Nebraska, Kansas, Iowa, and Illinois to many concerns at home. In early October, the Nebraska woman suffrage amendment was defeated 57,000 to 23,000. *Our Herald* continued to draw editorial fire. A *Lafayette Weekly Journal* article charged that Helen worked for Dobelbower for fifteen dollars per week and had given at least one speech that had helped the Democrats. Dobelbower denied it in his *Lafayette Dispatch*.

In the meantime, the Tippecanoe County WCTU was planning a series of "nonpartisan" meetings between October 5 and 15 to acquaint those who would vote in November with the importance of the prohibition amendment and of supporting protemperance candidates. Helen Gougar and her occasional teammate Mary Haggart of Indianapolis would be the speaker tandem. The meetings were booked for Battle Ground, Octagon, Montmorenci, Romney, Odell's Corner, West Point, Stockwell, Dayton, Monitor, and Transitville and would close October 15 in Lafayette's opera house.

Helen Gougar had her first experience in state politics when the American Woman Suffrage Association at its Washington convention in 1880 urged that the elective franchise be secured through state activity. She returned from the convention and suggested that Dr. Mary F. Thomas, a Richmond physician, social reformer, and state suffrage leader, obtain the opinion of DeWitt Wallace on the constitutionality of extending the vote to women in Indiana. Wallace answered that the legislature had the power to determine presidential electors and need not be limited or controlled by a state constitution restricting the vote to white male citizens. Wallace's opinion encouraged Helen Gougar to campaign for state legislative action. About five thousand copies of Wallace's opinion were then printed and distributed throughout the state.

During the regular session of the 1881 legislature, Helen Gougar, Mary Haggart, and other women had lobbied and addressed the committee on women's claim and both houses on behalf of suffrage. In April of that year, the legislators passed both the suffrage amendment and the prohibition amendment. Consequently by the 1882 campaign, women like Helen Gougar had become prominent figures in the state campaigning for repassage of woman suffrage and prohibition amendments in the 1883 legislative session so that the issues then could go to referendum.

So now, for the November election of 1882, WCTU stalwart Mary Haggart canvassed Tippecanoe County for temperance and woman suffrage advocate Helen for DeWitt Wallace. Helen was enthusiastic and optimistic as to the role Indiana women would play in the campaign. "The recent campaign found women more forward and active than ever in political matters," she wrote in *Our Herald*. "Their growth of influence has been marvelous and is well worthy of attention from all who would take courage from the signs of the times."[20]

Unsure how women would react to party planks on prohibition and suffrage, Indiana party leaders consulted leading women, and the women agreed to work for the party that declared to submit the questions of prohibition and suffrage at a special election to the people. The Democrats and Liquor League declared for submission at a general election, while the Republicans declared for submission at a special election. Through the state, women then worked for the Republicans. This support was met with mixed reactions. The state central committee and the local central committees were divided on allowing women to stump for Republicans. Many feared women would offend the "liquor vote"; others believed women were necessary to awaken moral sentiment. Reviewing in *Our Herald* the 1882 campaign by women, Helen remained hopeful:

> The recent campaign has shown women to be less tenacious of party than principle, shown that she cannot be turned aside from duty by threats or entreaties, and that men cannot call upon her to carry out their whims and serve only to be driven back and called out when he stumbles into the pit that he has dug about him.
>
> Women's influence in the campaign demonstrates her patriotism and power and her determination to be a factor in the political future of this republic in whose life she is more interested than man because in an unequal government, woman is always the greatest sufferer.[21]

Campaigning for the Indiana Senate in 1882, DeWitt Wallace supported sending the temperance and suffrage questions to the people and took positions for compulsory education and against convict labor. The *Lafayette Daily Courier* described Wallace: "A manly man, with the courage of his convictions, and with the ability to make himself felt in the senate, he will reflect honor on the county of Tippecanoe." The *Courier* predicted that Wallace would run well ahead of the ticket because he "combines in an eminent degree the best qualifications for the place."[22]

The submission of the temperance amendment, however, was the principal issue in the campaign. Wallace made about thirty speeches around Tippecanoe County, which generally produced a Republican plurality of four hundred to six hundred votes. Helen Gougar presented fifteen talks, while Mary Haggart gave eleven. Wallace felt the women could not harm his chances and accepted their help. He frequently consulted them on their views and activities. For the most part, Wallace was absent from the women's public appearances, but Helen Gougar's work certainly did not go unnoticed. Her campaign for Wallace stirred the anger of opposing Democrats, the liquor interests, and even some Republicans. She later contended that Democratic politicians had coaxed, threatened, and bribed her to cancel her political speeches.

Probably through fear of her possible influence on the election and hatred of her political views on suffrage and temperance, opponents viciously attacked Helen Gougar's character. During the last days of the campaign, rumors spread that Wallace and Helen had perhaps a too-familiar relationship. Unfortunately, Helen and Wallace could not locate the source of the rumors during the campaign.

In early November, Democrat-inspired handbills appeared all over the county, denouncing Wallace's woman suffrage position. And when the November 7 votes were counted, the "whiskey Democrats" claimed some big and historic victories in Tippecanoe County. Republican Judge Vinton won re-election by an incredible 8,377 to 133 tally; but Democrat Francis Johnson defeated DeWitt Wallace for state senator 4,233 to 4,190.

There followed some days of numbed Republican silence and licking of campaign wounds, but then the earthquake began to rumble in Helen Gougar's life.

CHAPTER 10

The Gougar-Mandler Trial

T he Democrats were not content with just the upset defeat of DeWitt Wallace. A few nights after the election, they paraded the streets of Lafayette with a huge painted cartoon in which Wallace lay prostrate, Francis Johnson stood with his foot on Wallace's throat, and Helen Gougar, half-dressed, pointed to Wallace and said, "I did it." Drunkards bellowed publicly things that had only been whispered in low circles, and Helen's name was bandied about the streets as if she were a common adventuress.

She reacted with an angry speech against the Democratic mayor, Furman E. D. McGinley, and all connected with city government and with a reckless article in *Our Herald* on politicians who opposed Wallace and temperance. Then a new rumor surfaced that on Sunday, November 19, 1882, Wallace and Helen Gougar had been seen entering Wallace's law office at 8 P.M. where they stayed until nearly midnight. The irate Wallace was able to trace the rumor to Police Chief Henry Mandler and Charles Poock, a downtown barber.

Peculiar to Indiana law was the statute that a man could not demand justification; only a woman could bring charges of slander. So on Tuesday, November 28, Helen Gougar filed a $10,000 damage suit against Mandler.

Frequently referred to in subsequent *Our Herald* columns as the "Dutch barber," Mandler had lived for nine years in Cincinnati where he had learned the barber trade. He had served in the Union Army during the Civil War. At one time, his commander was Judge John Gould of the Carroll County Circuit Court in Delphi, twenty miles northeast of Lafayette. During his army days, Mandler had moved to Lafayette; and after the war, he was alternately employed in the saloon and barber professions.

Judge Gould came down from Delphi to preside as special judge in the trial, held in a second-floor room because the county's new courthouse still was being built a block away on the square. After the preliminaries of seating the jury on January 21, 1883, the first major argument concerned whether the defense could enter evidence of rumor and general reputation on the conduct of Wallace and Helen Gougar during the previous few years. The defense wanted to prove that Helen possessed "a depraved and adulterous disposition."[1]

The judge ruled for the defense while denying Helen permission to enter testimony proving conspiracy. The defense, for the most part, then presented evidence of prior acts and associations rather than events of November 19, 1882. The defense called many witnesses to testify that Helen and Wallace had been frequently seen on train trips, that Helen had visited Wallace's law office, and that Wallace was a frequent visitor to Helen's home. The main testimony, though, rested upon seven propositions.

First the defense charged that in a specific week in December 1880, in early evening, Helen and Wallace had met indiscreetly on the public streets of Lafayette, gone to Wallace's law office, and remained there for some time. But Helen countered with a denial and provided witnesses and public announcements of various activities that she had attended that week.

The defense charged that Wallace and Helen Gougar had been seen together at the Republican National Convention in Chicago in 1880. But Mr. and Mrs. Harbert of Evanston, Illinois, testified that Helen had been their houseguest and that they could account for every hour of her stay.

The defense produced a saloonkeeper who testified that he had seen Helen on the afternoon of September 7, 1880, although a card on the door stated that Wallace was out, enter Wallace's law office, put down the windows, and remain about an hour. After she left, the saloonkeeper said, he saw that the windows were up. But Helen denied that she had been there that day, and

Lawyer W. DeWitt Wallace backed prohibition and woman suffrage and befriended Helen Gougar—a combination which led to involvement in a slander trial in 1882.

Shown here in lecture attire about 1900, Helen had reduced slightly her speaking and writing schedule. At about the same time, a strain of disillusionment began to appear in her work.

Wallace's sister testified that she herself had visited the office that day for family advice. The saloonkeeper admitted that he did not know Helen Gougar well, and Wallace's sister did fit his description of the visitor.

The defense presented a witness who testified that Helen, while visiting her sister Addie Sherry's farm in July 1882, had lain down beside a young man on a comfort spread in the yard and told a risqué story. But her sister Edna Jackson, present that afternoon as Helen rested between speeches, denied the incident.

Then Mary Simms, a former hired girl of Helen Gougar's, testified that on April 27, 1882, while John Gougar was away, Wallace had spent the night at the Gougar home. Miss Simms testified that from her window she had seen Wallace leave. But Addie Sherry and Edna Jackson claimed they also had spent that evening with Helen, and President White of Purdue University swore that he had been with Wallace in Indianapolis that day. An engineer also testified that Mary Simms would have had to lean out her window five feet and eight inches to see anyone leave the home.

Another witness for Mandler and Poock recalled seeing Wallace and Helen Gougar returning together on a train from Acton after the camp meeting July 25, 1882. Part of the time Helen's head had rested on Wallace's arm on the back of the train seat, he said. Witnesses for Helen, though, swore that there had been no improprieties.

Finally the defense produced witnesses who said they had seen Wallace and Helen strolling in the brush away from the crowd at a Battle Ground temperance meeting. But John Gougar testified that Wallace and Helen had been only a few feet away from him at the meeting and he had heard every word of their conversation.

The purpose of all this testimony was to substantiate the main charge. Mandler and Poock testified they had seen Helen and Wallace enter Wallace's law office on November 19, 1882, about 8 P.M. and remain there without lights on until midnight. But Helen's mother and sisters testified that she had spent that evening with them until 10 P.M. and then had gone home where she was met by John. And Wallace's mother, his wife, and a housekeeper, Hanna Johnson, all said Wallace had been home all evening on November 19 except for a short walk to the telegraph office.

The testimony was often delivered with histrionics. Tempers flared frequently on both sides, and at times orderly court procedure was ignored. Receiving the most sensational publicity were the outbursts of Helen and Wallace themselves.

On March 5, during cross-examination of witnesses to Helen's chastity and reputation, the defense asked: "Has not her character been smirched during the last year or two?" Before the answer came, Helen hissed loud and long. She was quieted, but then announced: "I can't stay in the courtroom!" She took her cloak and left the room. From the hall she was heard to scream, and there was a stampede from the courtroom. The bailiffs quieted the crowd inside the courtroom while a physician attended Helen in the city clerk's office. She wept bitterly in the office and was taken home by John.[2]

Another time the defense asked the lawyer Alexander A. Rice, formerly Wallace's partner, if in March 1882, he had not proposed that a church committee speak to Helen and Wallace about their conduct. The defense asked Rice if he had said that Wallace drove out to Rossville to meet Helen at a speaking engagement and then drove her to Frankfort to spend the night in the Coulter House. Wallace rose excitedly at this point, clapped his hands, and cried: "I pronounce it false!" Wallace, Helen Gougar, and the defense all began haggling. Before the confusion was settled, Wallace rushed out of the courtroom to confront the next witness. He shook his fist in the old man's face and shouted: "Do you mean to say I was at the Coulter House with Mrs. Gougar? If you do I'll shoot you! I'll shoot you! I'll shoot you!"[3]

As the all-male jury reviewed the evidence, the general public scrutinized every activity and character in the courtroom, with Helen Gougar attracting the most attention and interest. Before the trial even began, Susan B. Anthony and the National Woman Suffrage Association wired Helen expressions of sympathy and faith; Miss Anthony believed there was "no cause in fact for the charge, that it emanates from malice and downright meanness."[4]

Not all women leaders, however, viewed Helen Gougar's plight with sympathy. Mary Livermore, allied with the more conservative American Woman Suffrage Association, came through Lafayette from Boston enroute to a speaking date in Templeton, fifteen miles from Lafayette. In an interview, she told the *Lafayette Daily Courier* she believed the trial to be "insane folly" but she did regard Helen Gougar as rather a "coarse woman."[5] And some of her friends in the Indiana Equal Suffrage Association considered Helen "detrimental" to the cause of female suffrage because of the scandal.

Then, as countless newspaper editorials debated the virtue of Helen Gougar, a frequent thought emerged about women in public life. "The moral of Mrs. Gougar's case is already evident," one paper said. "It is that women and men as well cannot be too careful to avoid even the appearance of evil. When a woman enters the field of debate where she feels called upon to condemn and to remedy wrongs, it is incumbent on her to exercise the utmost circumspection, to wear the amulet of prudence, and to show that native modesty with which she was endowed by nature."[6] Another paper opined: "Women cannot be too careful in their daily walk among men. They should avoid even the appearance of evil. To fly in the face of public opinion and bid defiance to the long established rules of intercourse between men and women is as unwise as it is dangerous."[7]

After eleven weeks, the trial ended. A total of 260 witnesses had been called, 133 for Mandler and Poock and 127 for Helen Gougar. After so many weeks of testimony and such contradiction, though, jury deliberation surprisingly took only seven and one-half hours. On the first ballot in the evening of April 10, 1883, the jury voted ten to two for Helen Gougar. On the next ballot, the twelve men all voted for her. Nine more ballots determined the damages. After additional instructions about exemplary damages from Judge Gould in mid-morning the next day, the jury awarded Helen $5,000.

Wallace said he was satisfied and that he and Mrs. Gougar both felt completely vindicated. Mandler commented: "Of course, I feel hurt over it. It was unexpected, and nine-tenths of the people think the same. I had a hard fight against a man and a woman, and the man, who really fought the battle, was a witness, an attorney and her alleged paramour. That Wallace would screen himself behind the petticoat of a woman is not elevating to him."[8]

Helen Gougar said she felt vindicated. Later, in *Our Herald*, she lashed out at those she believed were her true attackers: the "saloon interests" of the city and state, the Democratic and Republican "whisky politicians," the enemies of woman suffrage and temperance, and those against women in public works. She seemed neither humbled by the trial nor deterred from her course, but more determined than ever in her work. "Thank God we have come out of this battle unconquered, bearing in one hand the palm of victory, and grasping in the other, more firmly than ever, the sword of battle," she wrote. "While life shall last we shall wield it in the cause of temperance and equal rights, and shall strike right and left, regardless of the social, political, financial or religious status of the enemy. We forgive those who have so despitefully used us, and move steadily forward in a work that is dearer to us than life itself."[9]

Trial testimony produced some detailed biographical material about Helen Gougar:

• Helen had delivered about 200 lectures for pay since the middle of 1881 and had saved an estimated $5,000 from the fees.

• The marriage of Helen and John, though certainly different, was fundamentally sound. In *Our Herald*, Helen wrote: "Feeling secure in the love and confidence of a pure and noble husband, it only nerved us to work for the most purifying aspects of society."

• Helen wore a bonnet through most of the trial, and her attire was on the "flashy" side, often drawing comment in the papers. On January 24, for example, she reportedly wore a bottle-green velvet hat with ostrich plume and a bottle-green walking suit, which had a close fitting waist, with velvet front, antique bronze buttons, tight sleeves, and velvet cuffs; an overskirt with a festoon gathered behind at the waist with a double bow; and an underskirt flounced around the lower edge with a parallel flounce for five inches above.

• On January 26 after a day of embarrassing testimony, Helen was overheard to declare: "Male gossips take the cake, the bakery, and the wheat in the field!"

Soon after the courtroom victory, though, Helen began to feel waves of criticism. The *New Albany Public Press* commented: "Mrs. Gougar for some time has been a noisy, meddlesome, disagreeable partisan politician in petticoats. She has obtruded herself upon political conventions of all parties, invaded precincts of secret caucuses and private committees until, by common consent, she has been considered an impertinent bore."[10]

The *Delphi Journal* said: "The hour of bitter battle has not demonstrated Mrs. Gougar's fitness to lead the women of Indiana. We have but little admiration for a life consecrated to 'cussing' everybody who don't like it."[11] The *Chicago Herald*, too, blasted Helen for having "brass-mounted" cheek, and said "it must be apparent that this unsexed, unscrupulous and diabolical bulldozer has had but one aim—to coin money out of her shame and, like the bearded woman, exhibit for a price. She never delivered a lecture that she did not lift a collection, or blackmail her victimized hearers into a subscription to *Our Herald*—never—not one!"[12]

John and Helen Gougar spent about $2,000 to prosecute the slander suit. Tippecanoe Circuit Court records show the $5,000 damage award never was paid by Henry Mandler. The Sunday evening after the end of the trial, the WCTU had a sort of victory party for Helen Gougar.

V

GAINING STRENGTH AND MONEY

Work, for the night is coming,
  Work through the morning hours;
Work while the dew is sparkling,
  Work 'mid springing flowers;
Work when the day grows brighter,
  Work in the glowing sun;
Work, for the night is coming,
  When man's work is done.

From "Work, for the Night Is Coming," Anna L. Coghill,
1860, and Lowell Mason, 1864

CHAPTER 11

Travel and the Lecturing Life

*F*or three months after the slander trial, Helen's lecture work came to a standstill. Either the notoriety of the trial prevented her getting invitations, or perhaps she simply turned them down until she could regain her concentration and composure. She apparently spent May, June, and July of 1883 mapping plans to revamp *Our Herald* into a monthly magazine more national in scope. On July 3, she was back on the platform, lecturing to an audience in Hoopeston, Illinois. And on July 13, she was up to her neck in controversy again.

She had been booked for a temperance talk in Anderson at the Presbyterian Church, but certain members of the church board, presumably disapproving of her reputation in light of the slander trial testimony, voided the agreement on short notice. Helen instead gave her speech on the courthouse lawn, where she denounced the church board as "whisky drinkers who pander to the bummer element and are licentious men."[1] Within days the *Terre Haute Journal*, clear across the state from Anderson, commented: "There should be temperance in the tongue as well as in the appetite." The *Indianapolis News* noted that: "The church [in Anderson] did not seem backward in taking hold of a much-needed reform when it refused to allow her a place to abuse everybody who does not look upon liquor traffic as she does." The *Richmond Palladium* expressed the opinion that "Mrs. Gougar is doing herself no good."[2]

On August 5, Helen spoke against liquor licensing at a Sunday night meeting in Lafayette's Pythian Hall. One new idea for control of liquor was an exorbitantly high license fee. The subject of "high license," then, became a frequent one for temperance speakers to attack.

On August 11, Helen announced the changing format for *Our Herald* but failed to disclose what may have been permanent strife with her brother-in-law A. P. Cosgrove, who had been the paper's business manager. On November 2, 1883, the *Lafayette Morning Journal* printed a four-paragraph story saying Cosgrove wished it to be known in Lafayette that he had transacted no business for *Our Herald* since August and was in no way responsible for any of the "vagaries, inaccuracies or statements" in the paper.

On Saturday night, September 15, Helen Gougar appeared with Lafayette Hughes and Milo Ward and others at a temperance meeting in Lafayette, but the Blue Ribbon movement seemed to be losing crowds. The next day she spoke in a church near Stockwell. Interestingly, on September 12, the *Lafayette Daily Courier* reported a real estate transaction in which John and Helen as co-owners sold two lots for $2,325. That was the approximate cost of prosecuting the slander suit.

Helen's unnerving year was completed back on the rostrum. On Sunday night, October 28, she spoke on "Prohibition in Kansas" for a Pythian Hall audience in Lafayette. She and John quietly marked their twentieth wedding anniversary and his forty-seventh birthday on December 10 with a small party at home. During Christmas week, the *Lafayette Morning Journal* mentioned that Helen was in Chicago but would be back to entertain the Parlor Club January 4, 1884, and to present an essay on "The Misanthrope."

If 1883 was a year of setbacks for Helen Gougar, 1884 was a "lost year." She is absent from the pages of Lafayette's daily papers. One can only speculate as to why. Perhaps she went into a year of retreat from public life because of the 1883 traumas. Or perhaps she was *persona non grata* with people, places, and organizations that had once welcomed her— including the newspapers—so her inactivity was forced.

The *Lafayette Daily Courier* did mention that in early July Helen's speech was part of a program dedicating a WCTU room in the basement of the opera house. But, in general, it appeared to be a year when both Helen and her causes were under heavy criticism, and she felt more useful simply lying low. A little item in the *Crawfordsville Argus* in March reflects that atmosphere: "Lafayette has a Henry Mandler, a Helen Gougar, an artesian well that scents the air for miles around, a woman suffrage newspaper, a tremendous debt, and to add to its other difficulties a home talent minstrel company has been organized. Lafayette will stand anything!"[3]

In late July, the *Lafayette Daily Courier* printed an excerpt from the recently published posthumous letters of the female French novelist who wrote under the pseudonym George Sand. Her words seemed to predict the women's movement backlash mood prevailing in some sectors of 1884 America:

> Women who pretend that they would have time to be deputies and to educate their children have not educated themselves; otherwise they would know that it is impossible. Many excellent women, good mothers besides, are obliged for the sake of their work to confide their little ones to strangers; but this is a vice of a social state which at every moment misapprehends and contradicts nature.
>
> A woman may well, at a given time, by a sort of inspiration, fill a social and political part; but she cannot permanently accept a function which deprives her of her natural mission, which is domestic love.
>
> People have often said I am backward in my ideal of progress, and it is quite true that in the matter of progress imagination can admit everything; but will the heart ever change? I do not think so. I see woman forever the slave of her own heart. I have often written this, and I persist in thinking it.[4]

Helen Gougar also must surely have felt hurt and disillusionment about politics during 1884. In September the *Courier's* proprietor and the city's postmaster and Republican kingmaker, William S. Lingle, died of a heart attack unexpectedly. Not long before his demise, he had opposed what he called "the Gougars of the [Republican] party" who developed individual goals and one-issue campaigns at the expense of team play, compromise, and party loyalty.[5]

Another turn of events caused Helen to be disheartened. The Democratic victories in Indiana counties in 1882 had blocked the crucial second legislative approval of the prohibition and woman suffrage amendments in 1883 and delayed them indefinitely—until two more consecutive legislatures might some day revive, pass, and send them to referendum. Moreover, during 1884, in addition to her disgust with Republican critics such as Lingle, Helen's disenchantment with the Republican party surely must have begun to take shape.

President Chester A. Arthur wanted to run for the presidency he had assumed after James Garfield was assassinated in 1881, but his supporters had lost faith because of his reform activities. Instead, the leader of the "Half-Breed" wing of the party, Congressman-editor James G. Blaine of Maine, who believed only in moderate reforms, was nominated. But Blaine had a "pro-business" image that caused a new fracture in the Grand Old Party. A splinter faction, called the "Mugwumps," bolted and voted for the Democratic presidential candidate, the former governor of New York, Grover Cleveland. It was a campaign precisely of the sort Helen Gougar detested—a personal campaign of names, with principles left far behind in the order of business. Cleveland won with 219 electoral votes to Blaine's 182. It was the first Democratic presidential victory since the Civil War.

The combination of things gone wrong, commencing with the vicious Tippecanoe County campaign of 1882, took its toll on Helen Gougar's physical as well as mental state. She began to age noticeably and to put on weight, and by the end of 1884, her once-blonde hair was snow white. Then, too, she had passed her forty-first birthday and could hardly present herself any longer as a "rising young voice" in public affairs.

Helen apparently decided late in 1884 to shake herself free from the daily, weekly, and monthly responsibility of running *Our Herald*. Much of the fun and, perhaps, much of the profit had been removed from it. Advertisers may have resented Helen's personal conduct or the bad taste left by the slander trial testimony. Or they may simply have shifted their ideals, as people in general were shifting, away from such militant temperance and suffrage approaches. In any event, Helen marked the arrival of 1885 by selling *Our Herald*'s assets, perhaps little more than subscriber lists, to Elizabeth Boynton Harbert, who eventually merged them with Chicago's *Inter-Ocean*.

During the rest of 1885, Helen began a very slow climb back into activism. She returned to the Lafayette newspapers' attention spectacularly after a fight with John S. Williams, proprietor of Lafayette's spicy, venturesome *Sunday Times* and a Democratic political bureaucrat (he was then third auditor of the U.S. Treasury).

A gossipy item in the "Man about Town" column in the June 7 *Sunday Times* told of the president of the county fair association attending a WCTU meeting at a "very questionable place" the previous Friday. "If he thinks he is aiding the success of the fair by any such action," the column said, "he betrays a wonderful lack of discretion. The WCTU is all right in its proper sphere." The "questionable place" happened to be the Gougars' home. Helen let it be known she would pay one hundred dollars to any man who would publicly whip Williams. Helen felt it was a libelous article, and several friends, including some lawyers, agreed. But John Gougar disagreed. As Helen told the *Lafayette Daily Courier* on June 8: "My husband, dear, good man that he is, advised me to do nothing about it, and as you may imagine, this made me very angry and I decided to take the law into my own hands."

Rather than sue, Helen simply accosted Williams just outside the downtown Lafayette hotel where he roomed. She rapped him on the shoulder once with a small parasol and called him a few choice names in front of dumbstruck sidewalk spectators. Williams bopped Helen on the head with his cane, protested "I didn't write it! I didn't write it!" and hurried into the hotel lobby. The following Sunday, June 14, 1885, Williams explained and retracted:

> To satisfy some over-fastidious people it may perhaps be proper to remark that in using the words "questionable place" it was only intended to say that the residence of the person whose efforts along with other members of the WCTU, the wrecking of the Tippecanoe County Fair was mainly due, was not the proper place for the president of that society to hold a fair meeting. That was all that was intended to be said, and no inference of any improper character was meant or was to be inferred.

The *Chicago Inter-Ocean* picked up the whole story, ran it in mid-June, and also printed a letter from a woman in Lafayette:

> It is a pity the citizens of Lafayette cannot find someone to find fault with and give Mrs. Gougar a rest. I admire her for her gallant defense of herself. I suppose the gentlemen of the city are immaculate, not one of them ever having an immoral thought. This is the reason they are so opposed to one delicate woman, whom scandalmongers choose as a fit subject for their attacks, because she has what many of them have not—brains.

In late September and early October, Helen accepted several lecture invitations in Kansas where, unlike Indiana, woman suffrage in city elections still had a chance. Kansas women had voted on school issues since 1861. The trip expanded into an

Our Herald.

FREEDOM AND LAW KNOW NO SEX.

VOL. 6.   LAFAYETTE, INDIANA, SEPTEMBER, 1884.   No. 26

GROVER CLEVELAND AND HIS VICTIM.

Helen Gougar owned and edited Our
Herald *from 1881 through 1885.
During that time, she used the
publication to present her views and to
deliver verbal blows to opponents.*

OUR HERALD.

FREEDOM AND LAW KNOW NO SEX.

VOL. 6.　　　LAFAYETTE, INDIANA, SATURDAY. NOVEMBER 1, 1884.　　　No. 38

Modern Politician: To which shall I turn for success?

exhausting thirty-five appearances before she returned October 22, giving her little time to get ready for an October 26 trip to Philadelphia as one of five Indiana delegates to the National WCTU Convention.

In mid-November, Helen delivered two lectures on woman suffrage and one on temperance in Peoria, Illinois. She was home in time to celebrate the annual "John's birthday and our anniversary" at home on December 10 and plan a Friday night, December 18, Parlor Club program for their own parlor. There Helen read a new essay on Alexander Hamilton.

At the beginning of 1886, Helen Gougar apparently was restless to get back into lecturing in a bigger way but found the temperance and woman suffrage subjects, temporarily at least, to be simply worn out. She may indeed have discussed the situation with John, whose great leisuretime pleasure was travel. John may have suggested that Helen take a trip to Europe or the American West. Helen, may also have recalled how years ago she had arranged the visiting travelogue programs for the YMCA with a lady from Asia and a man from Egypt and how the audiences loved the programs. So it might have come about that in early May Helen left for a three-month trip to the British Isles to visit England, Scotland, Wales, and Ireland. It was an exciting enough experience for her on the face of it. Yet it also was restful and gave her hours of peace and solitude to think and write and observe and memorize lines for future speeches. The experience gave her not only new subject matter for lectures but also more worldly political experience with which to pen deeper articles of international worth.

The July 22, 1886, issue of *Inter-Ocean*, for example, contained one of many letters from Helen about the home-rule fight in England and conditions in Ireland. About the same time, John received a letter from Helen, postmarked London, in which she said that she was spending a week with a friend and that her trip so far had been "very pleasant." Helen returned to Lafayette by train on August 20, and five days later was re-elected president of the Tippecanoe County WCTU.

On August 30, the *Lafayette Morning Journal* published a long interview with Helen about her experiences abroad. She told of steamship life, travel costs, tipping customs, meals in England, and other details. But she concentrated, as she later would in lectures, on social conditions, religion, poverty, eviction laws, home rule, and economics in Ireland.

Helen gave a WCTU annual reunion program talk in Lafayette the afternoon of September 26, saying that the association was flourishing. Her formal speech criticized both a recent speech by Senator Benjamin Harrison of Indiana and the "whisky planks" of the Republican and Democratic parties. She also disclosed that the prohibitionist element in Tippecanoe County planned to call a convention soon and to put a county ticket in the election field before November.

Then on Wednesday night, October 6, in Cleveland, Ohio, Helen broke in her new travel lecture, "Ireland: Yesterday, To-day and Tomorrow." She apparently was now using a professional lecture booking agency in Chicago to arrange the itinerary, fees, and travel arrangements and to free her of myriad details. For the Parlor Club on October 15, Helen discussed "Foreign Immigration." She maintained that, since the influx of ignorance was greater than the moral forces at work to educate and Americanize, there should be restrictions on immigration. She suggested a poll tax of $100 upon every adult male who came from a foreign land to settle in America over the next twenty-five years, after which she thought "it might be safe to again let down the bars."[6] The October 21 *Lafayette Morning Journal* reported that Helen had been booked to give the Ireland lecture on October 27 in Goshen under sponsorship of the Knights of Labor. That organization was then avidly recruiting women wage earners as members. Next Helen would take the show on to Englewood, Rockford, and Sandwich, Illinois, in the Chicago area.

On Thursday night, November 11, Helen Gougar's lecture on Ireland was booked for Lafayette's opera house, with music by a "great child singer" named Gracie Jones, the "Welsh Nightingale," who specialized in Scottish, Irish, and Welsh dialect songs. The lecture was sponsored by the Knights of Pythias to benefit the widow and children of a Lafayette Irishman who had been a telegraph operator for the Louisville, New Albany, and Chicago Railroad. In the lecture, Helen reviewed the issues between England and Ireland, commending the works of priests and nuns among the Irish poor and denouncing the Orangemen as "landed or monied gentry, intensely loyal to the landlord," who take advantage of religious hatreds in order to direct public attention away from the real issues between landlord and tenant, home rule and foreign rule. The *Lafayette Morning Journal* heaped praise upon Helen, saying her manner of delivery had few equals on the platform:

> She speaks entirely without notes, is graceful, aggressive in her opinions, and incisive in language. She understands her subject thoroughly before handling it in public, and commands the closest attention of her hearers.

Mrs. Gougar has always had a complimentary hearing among those of our community who agree and labor with her in her special reforms of prohibition and woman suffrage. But she has reason to feel especially flattered at the reception rendered her on her new departure on behalf of Ireland.

The front-page headline over the *Journal*'s story held nothing back: MAGNIFICENT SPEECH BY OUR DISTINGUISHED CITIZEN MRS. HELEN M. GOUGAR.[7] For Helen, the bitter memories of 1882–83 must now have seemed more than overcome. The response to her lecture that night in the opera house must have brought a flood of very private tears of relief, joy, and vindication for this "unsexed, diabolical bulldozer" the *Chicago Herald* thought it saw in 1883. But, there was little time for self-congratulation. There were places to go, lectures to give, people to meet, experiences to digest, wrongs to right, and money to make.

Helen left Saturday, November 20, 1886, for a series of thirty bookings in Kansas. The *Lafayette Morning Journal* indicated she would be home through Christmas but then would return to Kansas and a few cities in Iowa to do thirty or forty more lectures on Ireland and woman suffrage.

Her lectures, the *Lafayette Morning Journal* said on December 30, had brought her a "series of ovations," and she was getting twice as many invitations to speak as she could accept.

CHAPTER 12

Talking for Fun and Profit

The year 1887 appeared to be a happy new year indeed for John and Helen Gougar. Certainly it must have been the most remunerative of their lives. In January John was appointed executor of the will of a wealthy farm widow who had died in March 1886. Meanwhile Helen was drawing big crowds and raking in lecture money in Iowa. Some newspapers commented, and the *Lafayette Morning Journal* proudly reprinted, that Helen was "the best lady platform speaker in all the land."

She returned on February 2 from a series of sixty-four lectures in five weeks in the Midwest. The *Journal* reported she would leave February 20 for a southern tour that would include Florida; then she and John would spend some of their newly earned money on a four-month trip to Europe in the summer.

Certainly part of Helen's January stumping in Kansas had to do with suffrage. An equal suffrage bill written and pushed by Helen had failed by a small margin in 1885. Now she was campaigning for it again. In late January, the Kansas Senate passed it, and success was predicted easily in the House. Of her work that winter, the *Wichita Eagle* noted: "Mrs. G. is, in many particulars, the most eloquent woman in America resembling in many respects Mrs. Elizabeth Cady Stanton, who is now too old to actively work on the platform."[1]

On her way back from the tour of southern states, Helen visited the Indiana Senate on March 2, pushing for equal suffrage legislation again and saying she would soon be going back out to Kansas where Leavenworth and Atchison had enacted "local option" woman suffrage and were preparing for city elections in April. The *Lafayette Morning Journal* said on March 12 as Helen left for Kansas that she was now getting requests from as far away as Rhode Island to assist in an equal suffrage amendment and from Michigan, which had a prohibition amendment pending. The April elections in Leavenworth and Atchison were especially noteworthy, not only because women would vote for the first time but also because the cities had openly defied prohibition laws. Helen boldly claimed that the votes of women would change that state of affairs. In Leavenworth Helen Gougar helped to register and coach more than a thousand women on voting. Their effect was negligible on municipal affairs, as things turned out. But woman suffrage, at the very least, had gained, and Helen Gougar returned to Indiana a heroine.

On April 21, Helen left for four lectures in Illinois and Iowa, and on April 25, 1887, the *Indianapolis Journal* published her letter about municipal woman suffrage in Kansas. In it she assailed the organized liquor lobby and said women would need more time to be felt in politics.

The *Morning Journal* in Lafayette noted that on May 25 the Gougars would sail for Europe from New York City aboard the steamer *City of Rome*. Until then, Helen was her usual busy self. In early May, she presided over the state woman suffrage convention in Indianapolis, where the *News* reported she was "grayer looking."[2] Helen had hoped to retire as the association's state president in order to replace Mary Livermore, now sixty-seven, in the stable of speakers in a lecture bureau. But the membership passed a resolution urging her to "remain a worker for the interest of humanity and woman's elevation." The convention re-elected her as president, and she consented to remain in suffrage work for at least another year. Although active for some years in the American Woman Suffrage Association, with which the Indiana society was affiliated, Helen now joined May Wright Sewall, Ida Husted Harper, and others in organizing a rival state auxiliary of the National Woman Suffrage Association at Indianapolis. Helen was president of the new group which in 1889 would absorb the older state unit, touching off infighting that would simmer for years to come.

One reason for the internal strife was the question of

whether the woman suffrage movement should link itself with any particular political party or remain neutral; or if it were to be partisan, which party would benefit. The rise in power of a prohibition political party in Kansas had prompted the WCTU's Frances Willard to ask Susan B. Anthony to "please send me the form of resolution which would be the least that would satisfy you as a plank in the [Prohibition] platform."[3] Miss Anthony answered, in part:

> Not until a third party gets into power or is likely to do so, which promises a larger percent of representatives on the floor of Congress and in the several state legislatures who will speak and vote for woman enfranchisement than does the Republican shall I work for it.
>
> You see, there as yet is not a single Prohibitionist in Congress, while there are at least 20 Republicans on the floor of the U.S. Senate, besides fully one-half the members of the House, who are in favor of woman suffrage.
>
> For the women of Kansas, or Iowa, to work for any third party would be ungrateful and suicidal.[4]

In mid-May, Miss Anthony went to the state suffrage convention at Indianapolis where the new auxiliary for her National association was formed. She was the guest of May Wright Sewall and was honored at a Bates House reception. From there she went on to meetings in Evansville, Richmond, and Lafayette and then to an Ohio convention in Cleveland.[5] On May 17, the touring Miss Anthony was a guest at the Gougar home; and that evening, she and Helen spoke at a WCTU benefit in Lafayette's Christian Church. In time, though, their camaraderie would end over third-party politics.

On May 20, Helen and John began the long trip to Europe, but with a pleasant sidetrip to Boston. There in the Vendome House, New England women honored Helen on May 23 at a banquet saluting her suffrage work in Kansas. The invitation had come from Mary Livermore, who five years earlier, during the slander trial, had told the *Lafayette Daily Courier* she regarded Helen as "coarse." The famous Julia Ward Howe presided at the banquet.[6] The banquet seems to have been one of many conciliatory events that led to the 1890 reunion of the rival National and American Woman Suffrage associations, separated since 1869.

Little is recorded of the Gougars' trip to Europe. They had planned to visit there about four months but stayed five because John became ill in England. They saw Great Britain, Holland, Belgium, France, Italy, Switzerland, Austria, and Germany.

On August 8, 1887, the *Lafayette Morning Journal* printed a letter written by Helen while in Venice and Milan to her sister Addie Sherry:

> The marble palaces now inhabited by the very dregs of poverty show the wealth of the past and the poverty of the present.
>
> Nobody in Italy stays under a roof who can possibly help it. Last night was a religious feast night, a feast of ancient times to give thanks for the lifting of the plague. It is now divested of every religious aspect and is a general riot. I think every native howled at the top of his voice all night. They stay up and at sunrise go down into the surf and all plunge into the water at once. We could not sleep for their howling and wished they had gone in last night and stayed forever. No one should visit Venice unless he wants the poetry of the place taken out of him.
>
> We have been to Naples and seen Vesuvius; walked through the ruins of Pompeii, but did not attempt the ascent of the mountain on account of the great heat. I was quite sick at Rome, and we were all glad to turn our faces into the Alps and Switzerland again.
>
> It is wonderful what a change the present liberal government is making in the country and the rapidity with which the people are throwing off priestcraft. But the Italians are not yet to be admired; they cheat, lie and do every other mean thing; and they do it all with so much grace that it makes an American feel impolite for even knowing that he has been stolen out of his eyes by them.[7]

John and Helen returned to Lafayette by train on October 7. Within a month, Helen was back at work. On November 4, she presided over a state Woman Suffrage Association meeting in Evansville and spoke in a packed Presbyterian church on "An Unrestricted Ballot." She also let it be known that, beginning November 20, she would perform platform work under the auspices of the Chicago branch of the Redpath Lyceum Bureau.

Susan B. Anthony and followers were busy during much of 1887, campaigning all over the nation not only for state woman suffrage amendments and laws but also for a sixteenth amendment to the U.S. Constitution. Miss Anthony traveled in state after state and spent November attending two-day conventions in each of Indiana's congressional districts: Evansville, Vincennes, Bloomington, Kokomo, Logansport, Wabash, Lafayette, South Bend, Fort Wayne, Muncie, Anderson, Madison, and New Albany. The biggest was at Terre Haute.[8] Ida Husted Harper, the state suffrage movement's secretary, arranged the meetings. In the series of Indiana meetings, Miss Anthony, Zerelda Wallace, May Wright Sewall, and Helen Gougar were the headline speakers who "aroused great enthusiasm and made many converts."[9]

Helen Gougar discussed "An Unrestricted Ballot" November 17 in the G.A.R. Hall in Logansport, then began a series of midwestern appearances that had her traveling in and out of Lafayette regularly through the end of what had been another memorable—and profitable—year.

CHAPTER 13

Third Party Politics

*I*f 1887 was a year of profit for Helen Gougar, then 1888 was a year of disillusionment and political action. In it she severed some old connections. She broke permanently with the Republican party and temporarily with the Democratic party and became a Prohibition party activist, defying Susan B. Anthony's advice against third-party work. To some extent, Helen also broke with the church and the mainstream women's movement as vehicles for a better America. Her Prohibition leanings also would, in time, estrange her from the likes of Frances Willard, even from Indianapolis's May Wright Sewall.

Her Redpath lectures had her crisscrossing the Midwest through January and February. She cut away from those assignments Saturday, March 10, to attend the convention of the International Council of Women in Washington, D.C. But on March 17, John Gougar's seventy-three-year-old mother died unexpectedly in the Gougars' Lafayette home. When word reached Helen in Washington, she cancelled all convention commitments and hurried home to help with the funeral and postfuneral amenities on March 19.

An item in the *Lafayette Morning Journal* on April 5 said Helen would speak on temperance April 8 at Delphi, maintaining that it was the site of her "first public address" on May 27, 1878. Since then, the *Journal* said, apparently using a figure estimated by Helen herself, she had given over three thousand lectures in nearly every American state, in Canada, and in England.

In mid-April, Helen stayed in Indianapolis a few days to preside over meetings of the Equal Suffrage Association's executive committee. On April 22, she left Indiana to lecture on suffrage in Illinois and disclosed that the Third Annual Indiana Woman's Suffrage Convention would be in Indianapolis on May 15, 1888.

Helen returned from the Illinois trip on May 10 and then opened the May 15 convention with a long address in which she said the fighters for woman suffrage could show great progress in the past forty years and had "much to be congratulated for . . . Thanks to progress that has been made, we [women] can now hold property, enter partnerships, sue and be sued." She stated a number of property laws still ought to be changed, especially laws relating to marriage partnerships. They must be absolutely equal, she claimed. "Time," she said, "will make things right. Colleges and schools now are open to women everywhere and the process of years will work out everything to the benefit of women." She advocated allowing women to practice law, medicine, or any of the professions that they saw fit to enter and said she believed that women needed the ballot to restore healthful industrial conditions in America. In Indiana, she warned, the policy of woman suffragists would be to petition the 1889 legislature for municipal suffrage, the same first step accepted in Kansas. "The work is organized in all congressional districts in Indiana," she said, "and the sentiment growing. Ministers, as a rule, are for it, and a good man can now ask God to bless the cause without choking!" She urged women at the convention to go home and to work to see that Democrat suffragists, Republican suffragists, and Prohibition suffragists were sent to the 1889 legislature so that something could be done when they had a majority.[1]

It is significant that in that speech Helen Gougar rated the Prohibition party with the other two, for she was on the verge of joining it. Helen lectured in Frankfort on May 21 and in Wheatland, Illinois, on May 22. On May 28, she and John entertained the interesting Rev. Isaac K. Funk, editor of a rising prohibition paper called the *Voice.* An Ohio-born Lutheran minister, he was intrigued by such things as prohibition, psychical research, and simplified spellings. In 1877 he and a partner formed a book business which became the noted Funk and Wagnalls Company. Funk would edit *Literary Digest* in 1890 and *Standard Dictionary of the English Language* during 1890–93. Funk gave a talk that night in the Lafayette Christian Church, and on May 30–31, he, and perhaps the Gougars, went to Indianapolis to the Prohibition party's national convention.

Helen spent much of June lecturing in Michigan and Illinois on assorted subjects and, upon her return July 2, learned that sister Edna Jackson had been hired as a reporter for the *Times-Star* in Cincinnati. On July 4, Helen delivered the oration of the day to a southern Indiana audience in Martinsville, celebrated her forty-fifth birthday lecturing on the road, and closed the tour in Decatur, Illinois, on July 29.

Then, in early August, she steeled her nerves for two confrontations. On August 4, she took a seat in the all-male Tippecanoe County Republican Convention, having been granted a chance to speak. There, on behalf of the Indiana WCTU, she requested adoption of a platform plank in which the GOP would agree to select candidates who would support prohibition. It was an unpleasant moment, punctuated with haughty hecklers' cries and a stony silence when Helen had finished and taken her seat. The convention went on about its business as though she had never spoken.[2]

On August 7, Helen doggedly left for Indianapolis to present arguments for woman suffrage to the Resolutions Committee of the Indiana Republican Central Committee. There Helen made it clear that she was the only prominent speaker and worker from the WCTU who had stuck to the Republican party in 1884 but that she was now a third-party Prohibitionist. The Republican national platform adopted in June had completely "read her out" of the party, she said. "To the women of the country I say that to the Republicans we owe no further allegiance any more than we do to the Democrats. The Chicago platform on which Benjamin Harrison stands and the principles which he supports are an insult to the intelligent and moral elements of society."[3] What chance did Harrison, Indiana's "favorite son," have to win? "Harrison is certain to be defeated," Helen Gougar said. "And I do not think it possible for him to carry Indiana." She said Prohibitionists would not support Harrison, and she found fault with the recently enacted Mills tariff bill, declaring it to be high on manufactured articles. "This has been my view since my visit to Europe two years ago," she said. She obtained a fifteen-minute hearing before the resolutions committee and gave a stirring appeal for adoption of an equal suffrage plank in the state Republican platform, but it was a waste of her time.

On August 10, Helen was seen poring over law books in the Tippecanoe County auditor's office and explained she was researching the constitutionality of "local option" prohibition for Indiana. The issue was mildly debated in the 1884 state election, but Helen was not convinced about the data, she said. A good crowd braved rain and lightning the afternoon of August 12 to hear Helen Gougar speak on prohibition in a rural church near Lafayette. She said Democrats were for free whisky and Republicans for local option; but since local option was unconstitutional, the only hope was to identify with the Prohibition party. She also sold a few subscriptions to Reverend Funk's prohibition paper, the *Voice*.[4] That 1888 church speech was a milestone in Helen Gougar's career, for in it she began engaging in partisan, third-party political debate. Until then, the comparatively cleaner and clearer issues of Christian morality, temperance, suffrage, and equal rights had been her fuel.

Helen gave a Sunday lecture in a tiny Illinois community on August 19, and on the twenty-fourth, she welcomed seventy-three-year-old Elizabeth Cady Stanton and her daughter as houseguests. On August 25, through the pages of the *Lafayette Morning Journal*, Helen announced plans for a nine-day national Prohibition camp meeting to start Sunday, September 15, in Lafayette. Speakers would include former Governor St. John of Kansas. Organizers planned a discussion day, a woman suffrage day, a WCTU day, a young men's day, an emancipation day for blacks, and more. Speeches, political workshops, musical entertainment, and special excursion-rate tickets on Lafayette's railroads and the electric streetcars kept the crowd busy and amused.

On August 29, Helen went by train with Mrs. Stanton to Logansport, where Helen spoke for two hours to a county fair "Prohibition Day" audience of one thousand, assailing Republicans and Democrats alike. The *Logansport Journal* saw the talk as "the tirade of a gifted public scold and reckless partisan."[6] On the thirtieth, Helen and John welcomed 150 guests to their home for a "parlor address" by the venerable, snowy-haired Mrs. Stanton, who spoke half an hour on equal rights for women.

On September 13, 1888, Helen and former Governor St. John spoke at a Prohibition meeting in Chicago, then journeyed to Lafayette to open the nine-day camp meeting on the fifteenth. Tents, platforms, chairs, and bunting, created a festive air. WCTU ladies wore white ribbons. The encampment drew encouraging audiences of both the faithful and the curious. On the final Saturday, residents filled a Tippecanoe County Prohibition ticket for the November balloting, with candidates for circuit court judge, sheriff, treasurer, commissioner, and state representative, and elected several women to the party's central committee.

Helen, though a guiding spirit, did not attend all the sessions, for on September 21, she began work on a bold new assignment in Richmond. The Republicans had begun sending two famous women orators—Ellen Foster, a Massachusetts attorney Helen had met in the 1884 suffrage meeting in Washington, and Philadelphian Anna Dickinson, the forty-two-year-old actress and labor and suffrage lecturer Helen had once praised in a "Bric-a-Brac" column years before—into the field to stump for the Grand Old Party. The Prohibitionists delegated Helen Gougar to challenge either or both by booking her for lectures that followed theirs. Helen gave the Richmond talk on the twenty-first as a rebuttal to one Anna Dickinson had given a day or two before; and, as Anna toured Indiana, Helen followed, calling her arguments about tariff and other issues "fallacious and ridiculous." "To the gentleman who said I could not answer her without making a Democratic speech," Helen said in Indianapolis on September 26, "I say he is ignorant of our Prohibition gospel. I am often accused of working in the Democratic interests, but such is not the case, though I believe they are the nearest right on many things."[7]

On September 29, the *Lafayette Morning Journal* reported Helen had been offered fifty dollars per night for thirty-one straight nights in New York state to speak on Prohibition and reply to Ellen Foster's speeches, but Helen was quoted as saying she would give New York just five dates, reserving the rest for "looking after political fences in Indiana." On October 2, 1888, a new Fisk Club promoting temperance and Prohibition politics was formed in Lafayette, and Helen agreed to be its speaker on October 5 in the WCTU Hall. An item in the October 8 *Lafayette Morning Journal* said Helen was about to speak in Hamilton and Henry counties and in South Bend to reply to Anna Dickinson and had addressed "immense audiences" in Valparaiso and Wabash. With a secretary's help, Helen deployed a dozen other Prohibition speakers around the state.

Helen Gougar spoke at a statewide Prohibition party rally in Indianapolis on October 31 and prepared remarks for two days of party work in Tippecanoe County prior to the November 6 election. She spoke to an audience in Lafayette's opera house on November 3, blasting Anna Dickinson, Republicans, and Democrats. "The only thoroughly good-natured people in the campaign," she told the *Morning Journal* on November 2, "are the Prohibitionists and it is the only party that is growing. Everywhere the Republicans have shown a ku klux spirit that would disgrace Mississippi. Why, they seem to think that no one has a right to an opinion who will not follow under the whip of the GOP, which means 'Gone Out Permanently!'"[8]

Clinton B. Fisk of New Jersey, a Civil War general and founder in 1867 of Fisk University for negroes, and Dr. John A. Brooks of Missouri were the Prohibition candidates for president and vice president. The Republicans were running Benjamin Harrison of Indiana for president, and the Democrats, Grover Cleveland. Helen Gougar finished campaigning in Fort Wayne the day before the election and awaited the returns. For her, they were devastating. In Tippecanoe County, Harrison received 5,072 votes, Cleveland 4,280. The Prohibition ticket attracted just 120 votes county-wide.

CHAPTER 14

Preaching Prohibition

*H*elen Gougar, who for years had based lectures and writings on documented facts, in 1888 saw facts which made her a fool in the merciless world of political rhetoric. Her predictions and her assessments of a growing Prohibition party were made to look both naive and ridiculous. Yet, true to the nature of the political creature she was becoming, she told the *Lafayette Morning Journal* on November 10 that she "greatly rejoiced" over the increased Prohibition vote in Indiana and other states since 1884. But again, it seemed, she had been the target of crude postelection celebrations. The November 13 *Lafayette Morning Journal* contained her bitter letter describing it:

> The following spectacle was presented last night by the Republicans in procession: Five wagons filled with men halted immediately in front of my house. They threw red calcium lights and in the full glare hoisted beer and whisky bottles, drinking or pretending to drink therefrom.
> Another wagon was filled with men, dressed like women; upon this they had a figure dressed to impersonate myself, while the mob hurrahed for "Helen Gougar."
> A Methodist preacher and a Sabbath School superintendent rode in the carriage with one of the most notorious saloonkeepers in the city. The city was a mass of drunken men and boys. Seated back of the log cabin, on a whisky barrel, was the beer-shaped clown.

I feel honored that my work for Prohibition has been of enough value to cause the enemy of decency and sobriety to make these unseemly displays; but my heart sinks within me when I think of the good men in this city whose votes were given to a party that is in the hands of such depraved men as were guilty of this display.

The churches and schools cannot overcome the debauchery of the young through last night's demonstration in months of labor.

Let our ministers of the gospel and all decent people take the lesson of this display and dare to speak for a better order of things. The saloons were veritable hells of pandemonia. How about the hundreds of homes to which these men returned last night?

Yours for Prohibition to the end of the war.[1]

Helen left Lafayette November 14 for a lecture in Freeport, Illinois, then went to Chicago on the eighteenth. On November 24, 1888, a new Indiana Prohibition League formed at Indianapolis with Helen as its treasurer. The war would indeed go on.

Then, on December 12, the *Lafayette Morning Journal* reported that Helen had agreed to return to the newspaper business, in a sense, as an "associate editor" of the *Lever*, a Chicago publication which called itself "the largest and most influential Prohibition Party paper in the West." The *Lever* described Helen as "one of the most sprightly writers on the continent" and said she would "undoubtedly add much interest to our columns. She will represent the paper at conventions . . . and in every way help to push the interests of the paper."[2]

Helen was invisible from the public prints during the first half of 1889 without a definitive explanation. It may be that she was lecturing far away and on noncontroversial topics. Or her new responsibilities with the *Lever* may have bound her to the writing table. Another possibility is that she and John embarked on a long trip through the South during the winter months, including a visit to Cuba. The wire services on January 21, 1889, told of the gathering of leading advocates of woman suffrage from all major states in Washington, D.C., for the Twenty-first Convention of the National Woman Suffrage Association. Helen probably was there, but her name was missing from the list of newsworthy luminaries. On Sunday night, July 21, she certainly was visible again in Lafayette, speaking on prohibition and temperance to a night gathering in a Methodist church on "Victories Won for Prohibition in Pennsylvania, Rhode Island and Massachusetts." The ninety-minute talk was enthusiastically received by a big crowd. Helen assailed Republicans, Democrats, and newspapers "bought by brewers' boodle" to gain editorials favoring high license and opposing prohibition.[3]

Helen drew big crowds with prohibition speeches in southern Indiana, then swung into Illinois in early August for a series that ended August 7 in Decatur. She then left on August 9, complaining of hoarseness, for two weeks of speeches in upstate New York. That jaunt ended August 26, but, after a brief rest, Helen was off for ten more engagements in Cortland, Syracuse, and eastern New York, apparently campaigning for Prohibition candidates in state election contests.

On September 12, Helen, former Governor St. John, and others were speakers at a Prohibition party rally in Frankfort. "I have great reason to be happy," Helen told the crowd. "I have just come from New York where we have made a fight, and I know the cause is right and we will win in time. But the cause of Prohibition must have a John Brown." She said people were getting tired of old political parties and predicted the Prohibition party would hold the balance of power by 1892.[4]

On October 10–11, she attended the state Woman Suffrage Association convention in Rushville and about a week later gave the dedicatory address at a cornerstone ceremony for a school being built in Fremont, Nebraska. It was an occasion that Helen simply "could not miss," as she explained in her speech, reported in the *Fremont Tribune*. "It gives me great joy," she said, "to know that a vast brewery whose only mission was to destroy and degrade manhood and pollute the souls of humanity, has been chosen as the site for a glorious institution of learning. Upon the ruins of that brewery, you exalt yourselves in rearing this magnificent building."[5] The *Tribune* described Helen:

> Mrs. Gougar is a powerful woman. She spoke for two hours at the rate of about 150 words per minute, exhibiting no symptoms of weariness. Her familiarity with the king's English and the control of the same is marvelous. Her voice is strong and pleasant to the ear. Her mine of knowledge is inexhaustible and there is not a phase of the political, social or religious questions of today in our land, or any other land, that she is not entirely familiar with, and could intelligently discuss with the ablest men of the age.[6]

The second week in November, Helen spoke to prohibition workers in a Methodist church in Chicago. She explained away recent Democratic victories in Iowa and claimed anarchism in Chicago was easily traceable to rum and beer. The *Chicago Herald* noted: "Mrs. Gougar is a handsome old lady, with snowy white hair and wears golden 'specs.' She spoke in a voice which was somewhat influenced by a cold."[7]

On December 1, 1889, in the jam-packed Lafayette opera house, Helen delivered a one and three-quarters hours' speech on temperance versus prohibition, the evils of high license, and political developments across the land. County prohibition organizations, who arranged the program, invited preachers, saloonkeepers, workmen, and men of all political notions. A six-year-old girl from Danville, Illinois, sang "The Drunkard's Lone Child," and after an opening prayer, Helen took over.

The licensed liquor traffic, she said, depends upon debased manhood, wronged womanhood, and defrauded childhood. "It holds a mortgage over every cradle, a deed written in heart's blood over every human life," she said. "Shall mothers know this and be silent? Shall fathers understand this and be indifferent?" Helen described the principle of high-license as nothing more than

> an adroit method of making poor men support the free schools, build sidewalks and light streets. It shifts the burden of taxation from the shoulders of bankers, real estate and able men upon the consumers who are largely the day laborers. Nebraska is the oldest and highest high-license experiment and after nine years the liquor league men say it is the best kind of a law for their business, that it has not decreased the amount of grog consumed, that there are 3,740 saloons, 50 breweries and three distilleries, and that the state is literally the slop bucket for her Prohibition neighbors which surround her on three sides. The Democratic and Republican parties, the Liquor League, and the Roman Catholic church all declare for this same high-license law.

Helen complimented the Catholic church for its work among the poor and sinful but disapproved of its high-license position and of what she felt was an attempt to secure political control in America. "This act alone," she said, "will compel the entire Protestant church to array itself on the side of Prohibition to prevent the temporal power of papacy in this country." She belittled a recent Lafayette City Council decision to raise liquor license fees, saying the action "will not cause one less drunkard, and be no control of the saloons in the city, but will drag that much more money away from half-fed children and poor homes." She put the blame for unjust laws upon the voters and urged them to send men to the legislature pledged to prohibitory legislation. "To declare that 'prohibition cannot prohibit,'" she said, "is to yield to anarchism instead of asserting republicanism."[8]

On December 10, 1889, Helen and John observed their twenty-sixth wedding anniversary and John's fifty-third birthday. Helen, the "handsome old lady with snowy hair" described in the *Chicago Herald*, was now forty-six.

VI

NOT-ALWAYS-GAY NINETIES

Lead on, O king eternal, till sin's
  Fierce war shall cease,
And holiness shall whisper
  The sweet amen of peace.
For not with swords' loud clashing,
  Nor roll of stirring drums,
But deeds of love and mercy
  The heav'nly kingdom comes.

From "Lead On, O King Eternal," Ernest W. Shurtleff,
1888, and Henry Smart, 1836

CHAPTER 15

Backing Losers and Losing Backers

The decade that later would be glamorized as the Gay Nineties was filled with change, dissatisfaction, and pressure for reform. Benjamin Harrison had been a successful Indiana lawyer and U.S. senator and was the grandson of former President William Henry Harrison. As a president, Benjamin Harrison saw his duty as carrying out the wishes of the Congress which, in turn, responded to the sentiments of the people. During his administration, therefore, Harrison reversed or repealed many of the precedents Grover Cleveland had set while in office. Under Harrison's leadership, politicians did little about the spoils system and the increased pension rolls, and they adopted the highest protective tariffs in U.S. history.

The 1890 Congress passed two laws for farmers, laborers, miners, small businessmen, and the general public. The lawmakers intended the Sherman Silver Purchase Act to help western mining interests and increase the amount of money in circulation in order to aid farmers, wage earners, and small business. Congress adopted the Sherman Antitrust Act to stop monopolies and other abuses of free enterprise that were rising with the growth of industry.

But it did not quite work out that way. Wage earners formed the American Federation of Labor, and most left the Republican ranks. Many farmers—disillusioned, like Helen Gougar, with the two major parties—joined with labor to seek control of government and to enact reforms.

Industrialization caused much of the bumpiness of the U.S. economy by creating new jobs for some while throwing others out of work. As a result, poverty and insecurity increased among many workers. The Prohibition party, in the 1884 and 1888 elections, reflected some of the uneasiness. Then the unrest rallied behind a different third party in 1891. The Populist party was organized by farmers, but it soon lured wage earners and many other voters as well.

Meanwhile, for Helen Gougar, the "gay nineties" began with controversy that reached all the way to the White House. In 1890 President Harrison would name Lafayette's new postmaster, either a Methodist minister or a saloonkeeper. Republican powers in Tippecanoe County backed the latter, but Harrison, wise to Indiana politics, told Hoosier visitors: "If I were to appoint him, unless she could be silenced in some way, there is a little woman in Lafayette who would turn that appointment into a club and use it with terrible force over the head of the Republican Party."[1]

The candidate himself went to see Helen Gougar, according to her detailed account printed in the *Lafayette Morning Journal* on January 3, 1890, to ask for her written endorsement. But Helen refused, pointing out she could never support a saloon man. She could not support the minister either, she said, for he had been one of the jeering crowd that demonstrated in front of her home after the November 1888 election. On January 8, Harrison named the minister, Wilson B. Smith. Helen was not in the least bothered by the Republican infighting for she was now a thorough Prohibitionist.

On February 8, 1890, the Tippecanoe County Prohibitionists convened in the WCTU Hall. Helen and four men were chosen as delegates to the state convention to be held February 21 in Indianapolis. About six hundred delegates and two thousand visitors attended. The *Lafayette Morning Journal* published Helen's account on February 22. The convention nominated candidates for secretary of state, auditor, treasurer, attorney general, superintendent of public instruction, supreme court judge, and clerk. Party members nominated the Reverend Brazillai M. Blount, board president of Butler University in Indianapolis, for secretary of state.

The convention also adopted a sixteen-point platform which called for legal prohibition rather than any form of licensing of intoxicating beverages; improved pensions for Union Army soldiers; settlement of international disputes by arbitration; prohibition of price-fixing by business trusts or combinations of capital; distribution of public school money on a basis of enrollment; and reduction of county officials' salaries, adjusted in times of high prices. The platform also favored awarding public printing work to the lowest responsible bidder; hailed the organization of wage-workers and farmers, and the "intelligent and just demands" they made for abolition of class and monopoly legislation; and condemned "the corruption of the dominant political parties."[2]

"Here," Helen Gougar wrote in the *Lafayette Morning Journal*, "is a platform that demands the support of every man who would see the saloon, with its great waste, outlawed; of every man who would see his farm mortgaged to eastern monopolists; of every wage earner whose small tenement, carpetless and bare rooms bespeak the ravages of high tariff and a saloon tariff, one or both."[3]

Next, Helen left for a series of lectures in New York, New Jersey, and Illinois, which would occupy her almost nightly until April 4.

A tip-off about the strength of the Prohibition party, at least in Tippecanoe County, came on the Sunday afternoon of April 19, 1890. An opera house audience of about two hundred attended a Prohibition program featuring former Governor St. John and Helen Gougar. Toward the end of her talk, Helen admitted feeling a sense of shame because of the small crowd. "Someone estimated to me that Sunday afternoon meetings were not well attended," she said, "so I sent a notice to be read from each pulpit. It was well-advertised, but where are the preachers and the Christian people?" She then proclaimed that, with one or two exceptions, the churches in Lafayette were "deader than any other churches between the two oceans. Why must the ministry secure evangelists? Because they are not brave in crying out against the evils of the day!"[4]

On Saturday evening, May 3, 1890, Tippecanoe County Prohibition party members met in the WCTU Hall to begin discussing a ticket for the November county and state elections. Helen Gougar spoke about the political situation. She also was about to take on a big load of platform lecture work. The *Lafayette Morning Journal* on May 9 said she had turned down an invitation to address alumni of Pritchett Institute in Glasgow,

Missouri, on June 3 because she was booked almost continuously from May 16 to November. Her itinerary, the *Morning Journal* said, would include Nebraska, South Dakota, North Dakota, Minnesota, Virginia, and Maryland. Most of the talks, presumably, had to do with prohibition. On June 28, the *Morning Journal* reported that Helen was home for a few days after giving thirty-three lectures in the West. Her schedule called for a return west to Fairfield, Nebraska, for Independence Day and later for a speech in Omaha before an estimated eleven thousand union members.

In early September of 1890, the *Lincoln Call* told how Helen had impressed an audience of 500 "of the best citizens, professionals and businessmen in the city" in a two-hour speech in Wymore, Nebraska. It was the "standard" prohibition speech, pleading for the American home against the saloon. The audience "listened and shivered and thrilled and applauded the terrific blows against the liquor traffic, accompanied with the iron logic and the burning invectives of this peerless platform speaker," the Nebraska paper said, adding that public sentiment for a Nebraska prohibition amendment was "growing rapidly."[5]

On September 25, 1890, Tippecanoe County's Prohibitionists met in the Christian Church lecture room to choose their ticket. John Gougar accepted nomination for judge of the county superior court, and party members chose candidates for state senator and representative, county auditor, treasurer, sheriff, clerk, recorder, coroner, and commissioner as well. The Prohibitionist candidate for Congress, Milton Hansen, was a guest speaker, and optimism ran high. However, the November 4 election returns deflated the Prohibitionists. In Tippecanoe County, where more than 7,800 persons voted, the most a Prohibition man could get was the 167 Reverend Blount captured for secretary of state. The top county candidate nabbed 120. Returns show, too, that John Gougar's name never made the ballot. Nationally, the Prohibitionists did little better.

In mid-November the *Lafayette Morning Journal* reported the Gougars expected to leave February 24, 1891, on an excursion train trip to Mexico. Helen, the paper said, had arranged for a Pullman car full of personal friends to go on the month-long trip, conducted by a professional travel agent.

During the first weeks of the new year, Helen lectured continuously in Wisconsin and Iowa, returning January 25 to catch her breath before leaving again for dates in Ohio and New York for two weeks starting January 27. On February 10, 1891,

Since its completion in 1885, the Tippecanoe County Courthouse has dominated Lafayette's central square. Helen and John Gougar probably were part of scenes such as the 1890 one captured here.

Helen left Lafayette for a reception in her honor in Chicago's Sherman House as well as to address the Illinois legislature on municipal suffrage for women. Chicago's *Evening Journal* reported that she said: "Give me woman suffrage in Chicago and I'll rid your city of the slum rule and then come up from Indiana and run for mayor."[6]

Helen appealed for municipal suffrage for women to the Illinois House of Representatives on February 12 and to the Senate the next morning. She was invited to return and speak to a joint session on prison reform and convict labor in April, after the trip to Mexico. On February 19, she spoke to the Indiana House and Senate at separate 2 P.M. and 7 P.M. sessions, urging legislation that would give women municipal suffrage and prohibit the sale and use of intoxicating beverages.[7]

Helen and John left Lafayette about February 22 for the tour of Mexico, with a February 23 side trip to Jefferson City, Missouri, where Helen spoke to the Missouri legislature. The train carload of excursionists then left Saint Louis for Mexico on the twenty-fourth. Again the *Lafayette Morning Journal* printed a letter from the traveling Helen Gougar to her sister Addie Sherry:

> It is not necessary for one to cross the ocean to see an ancient civilization, or, more properly speaking, an ancient barbarianism.
>
> In all Europe there is nothing more medieval than the sights which have met us since we left the Rio Grande. The long stretch of desert land, the miserable huts made of adobe, or of sticks and brick, the half-clad natives, sometimes covered with rags, always with a sarape, a bright red blanket or varicolored long shawl swung carelessly and gracefully over the shoulders, and the ever-patient donkey are the most prominent objects that make us realize that we have left our civilization behind and are in a strange country.

Helen went on to tell of beauty and squalor in Zacatecas, and of the people, the land, the cities, the homes and buildings. She complained of pickpockets in a cathedral and referred to Sunday bullfights and horseracing as "depraved entertainments."[8]

The Gougars returned home on March 27 by train. The *Lafayette Morning Journal* sent a reporter to visit the Gougars and inquire about more details of the trip. Helen, as one might imagine, did the talking. John was laid up with a sprained ankle suffered when he stepped off a train in El Paso enroute home.

According to the *Journal*, the Gougars brought home not only stories but also a collection of souvenirs:

> At Orizaba, Mrs. Gougar purchased a Mexican clarin, a drab bird resembling a mockingbird in size. It is a cross between the bobolink and robin and, when he sings, is an entire orchestra.
>
> Some new Mexican coins, fresh from the mint, are another curiosity. The finish is quite rough and the workmanship is comparatively primitive. A sarape, the popular wrap of the country for both sexes, and a pair of Mexican sandals, child's size, made of plaited grass, are other curios.
>
> The most valuable items in the collection are the specimens of onyx. The famous onyx quarries are at Esperanza and the workshops at Puebla. The onyx is transparent and contains all the colors of the rainbow.
>
> Mrs. Gougar also purchased a covering for a center table, a number of ornaments made to represent books, and several inkstands.
>
> At Guadalajara the party came in touch with an Indian of Puebla descent called the Rogers of Mexico. He and his son model from Mexican mud the most artistic images and busts imaginable. Their work is done outdoors and in an offhand manner. For some of the busts $100 is considered a fair price. The figures secured by Mrs. Gougar represent a peddlar and various phases of merchant life. The representations range from the lowest grade of salesman and saleswomen to the highest. In all cases the facial expressions are marked and the work is marvelous. All of the figures are made of mud and are sun-dried.
>
> Another feature of the collection is the feather work of Indian women. This work is done on cards and the figures represent persons. Different hued feathers are used to indicate the gaudy dress materials, the face and the foot coverings.
>
> A handsomely carved cane of coffee wood, grown at Cordova, the great coffee center of Mexico, was among the other articles of the collection.[9]

Helen resumed lecture work in April of 1891 but was called home for a few days in mid-May while John was ill. On May 17, she and John welcomed as houseguests former Governor St. John from Kansas, the WCTU's Zerelda Wallace from Indianapolis, and Miss Abbie Thomas, whom the *Lafayette Journal* described as "the whistling soloist from Elkhart." They all left for Cincinnati on May 18 when Helen, as president of the Indiana Woman Suffrage Association, spoke at the National Conference of Industrial and Alliance Workers.

The Cincinnati convention on May 20, with both farmers and wage earners in the audience, was one of many sessions around the country which led to the eventual development of the Populist political party which at this point was still nameless and groping. Helen's chief function was to urge adoption of a prohibition plank, but she probably defeated her own cause with an afternoon speech that denounced the banquet scheduled for conventioneers that night as "an instrument of the brewers."[10]

She returned to Lafayette but left again on June 7 for a series of talks in Ohio and Illinois. The *Journal* in Lafayette said she had declined over five hundred speaking invitations during the summer but still had only one "leisure day" in the next three months.

On July 4, 1891, Helen gave the oration of the day at Pittsfield, Illinois, where she had been credited with helping carry local option prohibition legislation in 1889. She returned to Lafayette on July 12 but by the fourteenth was in New York state for lectures and chautauqua talks in places ranging from Staten Island to Glens Falls and for a national temperance convention on July 16 in Saratoga.

Back in Illinois in early August 1891, Helen told the *Chicago Record*:

> There is $1 billion spent in this country each year by the people for liquor, while at the same time the running expenses of the government are $360 million.
>
> While I believe in absolute prohibition, yet I believe that the government is committing robbery by putting an internal revenue tax on the liquor business. It is robbing the people, for the consumer in the long run pays it, the same as the consumer pays the added price for an article under high tariff.
>
> Besides, the government by taking the money raised by internal revenue tax becomes a party to the crime of profiting by a business which it says is an evil. If selling whisky is an evil, stamp it out. If it is to be recognized as a traffic the same as selling dry goods, or groceries, let the saloons run without license.[11]

Helen Gougar spoke in the Grand Pacific Hotel in Chicago on August 6, 1891 and at nearby Crystal Lake, Illinois, on the seventh; in addition she was preparing next to stump for the Prohibition party in Ohio and make free-trade speeches against the McKinley Bill in various states until the fall state elections. Between April 1 and the Chicago visit in August, she told the

Record she had lectured seven days a week with only eight days off and had also finished "a large amount of writing for papers and magazines."

At the Good Templars convention at Crystal Lake, a prohibition orator from Missouri delighted the audience with a Helen Gougar story: in order to get statistical data for her speeches and articles, she had written the U.S. State Department, headed by Secretary James G. Blaine in the Harrison administration. Specifically, she wanted data showing the increase in the sale of beer and malt to Latin countries and South America by U.S. dealers. The object was to show how U.S. consuls in those countries, under Blaine's reciprocity system, were agents to boom the goods of the large brewing firms. The State Department's assistant secretary, a man named Wharton, wrote Helen regretting that such information was not given out to private individuals. She waited a few days then sent another letter giving the fictitious name of "Jacob Detscherner," supposed to be a big brewer, asking for the statistics of his own trade. A prompt reply contained the desired statistics.[12]

After eastern lectures against the McKinley tariff ended in November, Helen hurried off to Chicago for a speech to 400 Sherman House diners at the National Prohibition Party Central Committee banquet. Her subject was "What Shall We Do with Our Convicts?"

> This nation is living under the most fearful reign of crime ever recorded on the pages of history. Men murder each other apparently without motive; husbands shoot down their wives and murder their children; men commit suicide; our cities are burdened with the criminal classes.
>
> We see one state, Tennessee, in open anarchy, the authorities helpless in the hands of free labor outraged by competition with convict labor. It is best to reason from effect to cause. The daily papers record the reason for the present reign of crime. It is the legalized saloon.
>
> Elect the Prohibition Party to power, stop the manufacturing of criminals and we shall have answered the serious question: "What Shall We Do with Our Convicts?"[13]

On March 4, 1892, the *Lafayette Weekly Journal* reported that both John and Helen Gougar had left for Hot Springs, Arkansas, followed by a "lengthy stay" in Florida. By mid-April, though, Helen was definitely back as a platform orator and agitator on a Sunday evening in a Baptist church in New York:

I have more respect for a man who gets blind drunk 365 days of the year and then votes for the brewer and the barkeeper than I have for the deacon who prays all the year and on election day votes to support the saloon in opposition to the way he had been praying.

If it is necessary [for ministers to go undercover to trap sin and expose corruption] I'd like to see every minister in the city of New York playing "hop toad" constantly. And they might do much more good than by devoting so much time to preaching about Hezekiah, Uriah and all the other iahs.[14]

In all, Helen delivered forty-seven lectures in New York State for the Prohibition party by early June. On May 24, 1892, in the Lafayette Opera House, Tippecanoe County's Prohibitionists, with Helen Gougar as their chairman, chose state convention delegates and a county ticket.

On May 31, the party's state convention in Indianapolis nominated John Gougar for judge of the Third District Indiana Appellate Court. (He later withdrew.) It chose Helen as a delegate to the party's national convention to be held June 29–30 in Cincinnati. She left for New York immediately after the state convention, though, to work as Indiana's representative on the party's national executive committee. The national convention nominated General John Bidwell of California for president and F. B. Cranfill of Texas for vice president.

From July until the November election in 1892, Helen Gougar worked on the party executive committee, wrote pieces for the *Voice* and the *Lever*, and lectured in the Midwest, Pennsylvania, New York, and Connecticut, venturing east as far as Massachusetts. Her fifteen-day tour through that state ended with an October 18 address at Harvard College—and later, in a lawsuit.

Throughout this campaign, Helen's fervor for prohibition exceeded her zeal for woman suffrage, perhaps with good reason. In 1890 after twenty-one years of rivalry and through a negotiating committee on which Helen served, the aggressive National Woman Suffrage Association, led by Susan B. Anthony and Elizabeth Cady Stanton, merged with the more conservative American Woman Suffrage Association, launched by Lucy Stone, her husband Henry Blackwell, Mary Livermore, and Julia Ward Howe. Helen, always a friend of both camps, perhaps felt her presence was not so keenly needed now that the associations were pulling together. But as history would show, neither prohibition nor woman suffrage progressed appreciably in 1892; and the Populists stole the "third party" attention from the Prohibitionists. President Benjamin Harrison, running for re-election on the Republican ticket, was defeated by Democrat Grover Cleveland in a landslide. The Populists, a coalition of farmers and laborers, did poll one million votes; won twenty-two electoral votes for their presidential candidate, James B. Weaver, an Iowa lawyer and congressman; and gained seats in Congress and several legislatures. No third party ever had shown such strength. The "Prohibs" were a distant fourth.

Two weeks after the election, Helen left Lafayette again for New York for the national Prohibition party's executive committee meetings. She had served on the convention platform committee and on the national committee itself. The postelection organization was now badly split over what to do next. Helen, answering a questionnaire for the *Voice* before the next presidential election, expressed these opinions:

> I suggest a series of reform conferences under the auspices of the national executive committee in 10 different sections of the country, ending in Chicago with a grand joint conference. I urged this at the last meeting of the committee but they decided to hold conferences of Prohibitionists alone, under the direction of our chairman.
>
> Such conferences arouse no public interest and are time and money thrown away. There is a very general desire all over the land, on the part of reformers, for a coalition at the ballot box. If the Prohibitionists do not take the lead in this, some other party will, and Prohibition will be ignored.
>
> In every community smaller conferences should be held. Women must be organized in leagues auxiliary to the Prohibition Party, to do distinctive party work by way of extending the circulation of the party press, arranging meetings, distributing literature and raising funds. National headquarters must be removed from Podunk to some one of the larger cities where press facilities are at hand, and the prime wires should be used more than they are.
>
> The platform should be as broad as it is now, subject to such revision as the enlightened sentiment may demand.[15]

The *Voice*, published from New York, said sentiment through the party executive committee was evenly divided between taking steps toward a coalition of various reform forces and accepting single-issue prohibition as a platform. It must have been a gloomy and discouraging conclave. Yet on December 16, 1892, in a long letter to the *Lafayette Morning Journal*, Helen Gougar displayed her usual fight. She blamed both Populist and Prohibition election failures on unjust election laws enacted by Republican legislatures in several states. She also declared a press conspiracy to disguise or suppress true third-party programs and progress.

From all the hard work, defeat, and bitterness of 1892, though, Helen ended the year with a new career in the making. Her sister Edna Jackson Houk from Cincinnati came for a pre-Christmas visit with Helen. The *Lafayette Weekly Journal* explained:

> The two ladies are putting the finishing touches on a book which is entitled "How Can Women Make Money?" The Cincinnati press speaks in high praise of the advance sheets. Mrs. Houk, who has long been recognized as a writer of great force and wit, does the main part of the book while Mrs. Gougar, who is not only a writer but a practical businesswoman, who has been actively identified with the "women's movement" during the past 20 years, contributes the introduction and associates her name with the work.[16]

CHAPTER 16

Writing, Speaking, and Suing

*A*t the end of 1892, Helen Gougar must have ranked as a leading moneymaker among American women. At that time, she was giving over three hundred lectures per year at $50 to $100 a turn. She probably also drew dividends from stocks in banks and from business and land ventures invested for her by John. Now the book, reportedly entitled *Women Wealth Winners*, might itself provide income. Also, Helen was contributing a prodigious volume of material to national publications such as the *Voice* and the *Lever*, possibly gratis but more likely for pay. Some examples:

• On February 4, 1892, her article "Funeral Today" appeared in the *Lever*. It described a drunkard's funeral and the effect of liquor on surviving women and family, and called for new voters to vote the Prohibition ticket, saying "the saloon cannot be legalized and the home protected under the same fiat."

• In the same issue of the *Lever*, Helen's letter to the editor discussed "Union but No Compromise." In it, she criticized the national WCTU's Frances Willard for endorsing "municipal suffrage only" in a Sherman House speech in Chicago. Elaborating, Helen wrote:

> Let Miss Willard contend for the full measure of rights with the minority rather than sacrifice one jot of principle for the sake of a temporary majority. Only by such a course will she maintain respect for her political sagacity and secure a following.
>
> Let her remember that all permanent and worthy reforms are built upon righteousness and exact justice, never upon compromise.

• On March 24, 1892, Helen's letter in the *Lever* told of a rift at an industrial conference in Saint Louis. There the committee on suffrage issued a majority report favoring municipal suffrage "with educational qualifications" while Helen and former Governor St. John in a minority report demanded "suffrage on equal terms regardless of sex."

• The November 3, 1882, number of the *Lever* printed Helen's article "For Whom Shall I Vote, and Why?"

• The December 15, 1892, issue of the same periodical carried her "Why They Rejoice." In it she criticized her old benefactor, Chicago's *Inter-Ocean*, which had said the Prohibition party had nothing to celebrate. To this Helen replied that it had elected a principle and was a party that was not corrupt.

• In early 1893, her article "Christ and the Liquor Seller" appeared in New York's the *Arena*, a journal of religious reform. It was a reply to an article by a physician, Henry A. Hartt. Among her points: "The laws of Christ are all prohibition laws. With as good reason should He repeal the Ten Commandments, and declare them impracticable because they are disobeyed by a large part of the human family, as for men to declare prohibition to be impracticable because in some instances it is violated."[1]

Helen entered 1893 carrying her customary heavy load of speaking engagements. The first was before the Indianapolis Prohibition Club on Monday, January 2. The March 4 issue of the *Arena* carried her article on "Alcohol in the Bible." During March, April, and into May 1893, Helen lectured in Indiana, Iowa, and Illinois.

In late May Helen weathered a significant week-long interlude in Chicago. She discussed "Universal Suffrage" in All Souls Church, then took in the world's fair known as the Columbian Exposition, which marked the 400th anniversary of Columbus's voyage of discovery to the New World. A historic part of the exposition was a one-week Woman's Congress, the largest, most visible and prestigious of all the many women's rallies and conventions to date.

The growth of the National Council of Women and, later, an International Council of Women—with Indiana's May Wright Sewall a leading force—had given the women's movement additional numbers and more organizational savvy, and had attracted women of means like Mrs. Potter Palmer, a leader of Chicago's social elite. Here at the Woman's Congress, all the famous names in the long struggle for equal rights for women were booked for talks and panel discussions. Susan B. Anthony, seventy-three years old, was everywhere. But for Helen Gougar, the long-awaited Woman's Congress proved to be a bitter and ugly chapter, one which for all practical purposes severed her relationships with the movement's most noted leaders.

May Wright Sewall had strongly opposed Helen Gougar's drift into third-party politics—a view also held by Miss Anthony and most others in the mainstream leadership. A feud had simmered since 1889 between Mrs. Sewall and Helen Gougar because Mrs. Sewall had tried to unseat Helen as president of the Indiana Equal Suffrage Association because of her Prohibition leanings and had failed.

Now Mrs. Sewall schemed to have Helen's name omitted as a panelist on "Civil Government and Woman Suffrage" at the congress. But the moderator of the panel naively welcomed Helen's remarks, which drew strong applause. Hearing of this, Mrs. Sewall upbraided the moderator, saying "the official board of lady managers have made an order that the voice of Helen M. Gougar must not be heard within this Woman's Congress!"[2] The two women coldly left the congress to go their separate ways on lecture tours. Helen headed west before returning June 1, 1893, to Lafayette from Kansas City, Kansas, and from Des Moines, where she had attended the Iowa Prohibition Convention. She next organized a state collegiate oratorical contest.

On June 3, Lafayette's Prohibition Club sponsored opera house temperance meetings and the oratorical contest. Helen gave a talk on the legalities of prohibition and presided over the awarding of prizes to the young speakers. Early the next week, she was off again to Iowa for talks in Mason City on June 7–8. She also accepted an Independence Day oration invitation from Decatur.

Back in 1892, Hillsdale College had recognized Helen Gougar's reform work and had accorded her an honorary Master of Arts degree. Later that year, Hillsdale College representatives named her a member of the school's alumni association. From this body, she was one of twenty-five women named to the college's first woman's commission, created by the board of trustees in 1892, and was elected its first president.

At the request of the trustees, two from the woman's commission were then named to the board of trustees itself. Helen was one of the two and served on the board from 1893–96. On June 23, 1893, she officially joined the Hillsdale board. A week later, she attended a national Prohibition oratorical contest in Harvey, Illinois.

The July 6 issue of the *Lever*, meanwhile, contained Helen's opposition to a proposal to nationalize the liquor industry. "If we can demand government control," she wrote, "we can demand prohibition." The same issue said Helen's Fourth of July oration at Decatur on equal suffrage was "an epoch-making speech, the kind from which men and women date conversion to a new life."

Now turning fifty, Helen headed east again for a series of talks in Pennsylvania and New York, then returned for the World Congress on Civil Government in Chicago where, on August 9, she spoke for "Universal Suffrage." She next left Chicago for Silver Lake, New York, and a series of talks that would keep her in the East until August 18. She and John left Lafayette again August 22, 1893, for a few leisurely days at the Columbian Exposition.

In September, Helen also completed plans to file a libel suit. Through an attorney in the East, the suit was filed about September 15 against Republican Congressman Elijah Morse of Massachusetts and against the *Attleboro Sun* (Massachusetts) newspaper. Helen asked $25,000 damages from both because the *Sun* had printed Morse's letter accusing Helen and other prohibitionists of being "soldiers of fortune" who sold their services to the Democratic party while campaigning in Massachusetts. A rare document that tells of the suit is a letter, dated September 15, from the congressman's defense counsel to Lafayette's postmaster, Wilson B. Smith, whose 1890 appointment by President Harrison had drawn Helen Gougar's opposition. The letter says in part:

> The defense may wish to prove the publication by the plaintiff of a certain scandalous paper entitled "The Black Record of Benjamin Harrison," with which, possibly, you may be familiar.

> Although the face of the paper shows that she was its author, it is doubtful whether we may not be driven to proof of its actual publication or distribution by her.
>
> I accordingly take the liberty of asking you whether you can give any information which may help us in this direction; as, who printed the paper, who posted the copies at the post office in Lafayette, etc. Anything you can give us, we shall be very thankful for.[3]

The postmaster's response is not to be found.

During early September 1893, Helen returned to the land of earlier triumphs, Kansas, for about twenty speeches in a campaign backing a referendum giving full woman suffrage. Because she had participated in the successful Kansas effort to give women municipal suffrage in 1887, she might have expected this to be a pleasant trip. But this time she tasted the bitterness of deal-making. Laura M. Johns, president of the Kansas Equal Suffrage Association, also was president of the state Woman's Republican Club. Mrs. Johns had agreed with the Republican party that neither prohibition nor woman suffrage would be mentioned in Kansas that fall. But Helen Gougar had every intention of campaigning for both causes in her speeches. Mrs. Johns vowed she would "not permit" Helen to campaign anywhere in Kansas and tried to cancel Helen's talks. But Helen responded from Kansas City, "This association cannot muzzle or gag me. I have been at work in the interest of suffrage too long to allow some unknown suffragist to switch me off the track. I propose to say what I please about prohibition in every speech I make."[4]

On September 16, Helen left the Kansas travail behind and embarked on a three-week lecture tour through New York, Maryland, and West Virginia. She returned to Lafayette on October 11, telling friends about the thrill of having watched the America's Cup yacht race between the *Vigilant* and the *Valkyrie* on October 7.[5]

Then on October 13, Helen traveled to Chicago where the Single Tax Club honored her at a reception in Orpheus Hall. Her address was entitled "Which Promises the Greater Benefit to Wage Earners, the Single Tax or the Prohibition of the Liquor Traffic?" It was an unusual invitation, and Helen responded with an unusual speech. The *Lever* of October 26 printed excerpts:

> I thank the members of this club for the compliment implied by this kindly reception, the more because you

know that I am not an advocate of the single tax, although we are together in desiring the same results, that is the reclamation of the land from all speculation and non-use, that the people, to whom God gave the land as He has fresh air, sunshine and all the natural resources for their sustenance, may have the benefits in their pursuits of life, liberty and happiness.

Horace Greeley said: "The man who has no right to live everywhere has no right to live at all."

In these hard times, as I read of weary men seeking work, hopelessly tramping day in and day out, finally sinking down to mother earth to rest their tired bones and the policeman's order to "move on" deprives him of even this little boon; when I see our granaries bursting with the bounties of the land and yet so great hunger in all our large cities that charity bread is thrown out like bones to the dogs, I know there is something wrong in society; for the Almighty has never made such a mistake as to put one mouth more on earth than the earth's bounty can fill.

Our present widespread poverty need not be. It is caused by unjust and unwise legislation. I would allow no man to hold one foot of real estate more than he made legitimate use of, and I would tax all land held for speculation so high that no man could afford to hold it for such purposes. This would relieve the congested centers in our large cities and extend their borders. It would take people out of crowded apartments where it is difficult to rear modest girls and virtuous boys and put these people under their own vine and fig trees. I would give them room.

On all these things we are agreed, but the single tax on land would make things worse instead of better because of its manifest injustice. I believe the banker, bondholder, merchant or mechanic who owns property, not land, should be taxed. I do not look upon this tax as a "fine upon industry" but as a fee for the protection vouchsafed them by good government.

But as important as is this reform, it is of small value compared with the prohibition of the waste of the liquor traffic. If the $40 million spent last year in Chicago for liquor, largely by the working classes, had been saved or spent in the legitimate channels of trade and commerce, there would be no men on the lakefront crying, "give us bread or give us work," and if the $1,253,000,000 spent in the nation was so diverted, real estate would be owned more largely than now by the masses and the land question would be half solved thereby.

In thanking the club for the invitation, she concluded: "I believe the single-taxers are the most consistent, persistent and courteous reformers in the country. You have me to convert to single tax; I have you to convert to prohibition, and both are willing to hear, read and conclude in the interest of the greatest good to the greatest number."[6]

In October 1893, the *Arena* contained Helen's 4,000-word article entitled "Is Liquor Selling a Sin?" She pointed out:

> God's word says, "Thou shalt not kill." Liquor nerves the hand of the murderer.
> God's word says, "Thou shalt not steal." Liquor palsies the honor and makes the thief.
> God's word says, "Thou shalt not commit adultery." Liquor is the parent of the social evil.
> God's word says, "Thou shalt not bear false witness." Liquor thwarts justice with perjury.
> The Bible is filled with admonitions against drink; therefore the man who deals in that which brings such a train of evils in its wake fails to conform to and transgresses the law of God, and wilfully commits sin.
> No, the Prohibitionists have received no special new dispensation . . . they find the old one sufficient for their demands.

On October 12, 1893, the Indiana WCTU named Helen Gougar to head its new committee on the relationship of temperance to labor.

The several state elections in November resulted in no progress for woman suffrage, but on November 23, there was victory of a different sort for Helen in Boston. There the U.S. Circuit Court returned a libel verdict in her favor and awarded her $1,000 damages against the *Attleboro Sun* for publishing Congressman Morse's letter. It gave her hope for victory in the $25,000 suit against Morse himself.

On December 6, Helen left Lafayette for several days in Chicago. On Saturday night, the ninth, she gave the opening address at a public meeting called to explore ways to combat wife and child abuse by drunken men. On Sunday, she spoke on "Give Us Work or Give Us Bread; the Way Out for the Unemployed" at a mass meeting called in the interest of those who were out of work. With that she returned to Lafayette and to John for their thirtieth wedding anniversary and John's fifty-seventh birthday party and for a restful holiday season. It was literally a calm before the storm, though, for 1894 would prove to be one of the stormiest in years.

CHAPTER 17

Fighting the Tariff and the Courthouse Club

*I*n late January 1894, in a long letter to the *Lafayette Morning Journal*, Helen Gougar flashed her knowledge of economics by tearing into the McKinley tariff in terms hometown folks could understand:

> One evening last week I was the guest of Joseph Baer in the village of Transitville. Mr. Baer found it necessary to reach beyond the limits of his own town in order to derive the income necessary to enlarge the comforts and educational advantages of his children. He decided to ship a carload of winter apples from the orchards of Michigan fruit growers to sell to those who must eat in Lafayette.
>
> He came to our town, visited the wholesale dealers in fruit and found such apples as he proposed to handle selling for $4.25 and $4.75 per barrel. He could make a handsome profit by selling these apples to the wholesalers at $2.75 per barrel. These dealers offered but $1.75. He refused this paltry sum and proceeded to open a temporary store and sell his apples directly to the consumer for $2.75, thus saving $2 per barrel and enabling many to eat apples who could not do so if compelled to pay the exorbitant price exacted by certain dealers in fruit who have grown rich and

are growing richer by the large profits they are making on these necessities of life which they handle.

Now these dealers had the effrontery to petition our city council to give them a monopoly, or trust, not only on apples but on all other provisions by exacting a prohibitive tariff, called "license," on Mr. Baer and all farmers or gardeners who are willing to take a reasonable profit on their produce and live and let live.

Suppose the city council granted the prayer of the wholesale dealers and local retail grocers and placed this tariff on apples and other provisions, who would have suffered and who would have received benefits?

First—Men living on small wages would have been compelled, with their brood of children, to go hungry for apples; only those of ample means can afford to eat apples at $4.25 per barrel.

Second—Those who bought these apples would have been robbed out of $2 per barrel more than is necessary to warrant a living profit to resident wholesale dealers.

Mr. Baer would have been deprived of the privilege of using his energy in the market, his income would have been cut off, he would have sighed for something to do that would have enabled him to support and educate his bright children and consequent poverty must have been his lot all on account of this "protective" tariff on apples.

The Michigan fruit grower sees his beautiful apples, with ruddy cheeks, blacken and rot on the home market, and nine times out of ten will declare that overproduction is the cause, for there being no demand for his apples. On account of this, next year the Michigan farmer refuses to hire his half dozen aides in pruning his orchard, while packing and shipping clerks count their fingers as they tramp the roads seeking employment.

The links of this chain are the wage-earner out of employment, the apple-hungry man, the impoverished fruit grower, welded hopelessly to poverty by the would-be protective tariff law of the city council which "protects" only the monopolist wholesaler, who is becoming independently rich by this system; and if the city council had granted this petition pending, he would have the 20,000 consumers of Lafayette by the throat and be able to demand his "pound of flesh" from all who eat—and men must eat.

Was there ever a more patent attempt to legislate in the interest of monopoly and trusts which make the few rich and the many poor? The McKinley tariff has its perfect illustration in its results upon producer, consumer and monopolist in this proposed apple transaction. Surely no one with a thimbleful of common sense will declare that the consumer does not pay the cost of the $4.75 apples. The same principle applies to the woollen coat or carpet, the steel and iron rail or farming implement and everything upon which a so-called protective tariff is placed.

The result of this system of continual robbery of the masses has been the steady decrease in the savings of the people until inability to buy has reduced consumption to such a limited amount that factories have closed and millions of wage earners are fed at free soup houses.

If the present Democratic Congress had the nerve, it would strike out the last vestige of the McKinley tariff and tax the people on what they possess instead of upon what they consume, sufficient in amount only to support the government, economically administered, and not one dollar more.

This would put the whole country under the law of demand and supply with no privileged class, and the Almighty alone—whose justice and wisdom can be trusted to administer with equality population and production, opportunity and results—would be the arbitrator of man's condition.[1]

On February 18, Helen attended a woman suffrage convention in New York, then left Lafayette on February 21 for a week of lecturing in Kansas. In her absence, on February 24, the Tippecanoe County Prohibition party elected delegates to district and state conventions. Helen attended a state Prohibition convention in Indianapolis March 15 and left for Danville, Illinois, for speeches on April 10–11. Then during two weeks in April, Helen and Mary E. Lease of Kansas toured Indiana cities for a series of unusual lectures on "Money, Monopoly and the Masses." Helen spoke on prohibition and Mrs. Lease on populism. Mrs. Lease told audiences of her party's ideas about reclaiming thousands of square miles of land virtually given to railroads and corporations, federal control of the railroad and telegraph, remonetization of silver, and abolition of the national banks. She predicted the day when "man will be held equally responsible with woman from a moral standpoint." The *Lafayette Morning Journal* editorialized that "it was an enjoyable and interesting privilege to hear these two famous, brainy women."[2]

On May 1, the Tippecanoe County Prohibitionists chose candidates for nine county and three state legislative offices and promised to later choose men to run for prosecutor and two judgeships.

On Sunday, May 6, 1894, Helen Gougar spoke on municipal government at a Chicago meeting called by the Populist party. She said there was "something radically wrong in the government of American cities" because so many were "under the reign of anarchy. It is almost impossible to enforce the laws. A remedy for the slums and crowded tenements, from which come vice and crime, is legislation which will take the people out of tenements and remove the land both in city and country from the hands of corporations and speculators. There should be no actual ownership in land beyond what is actually occupied. The American saloon must be destroyed, or it will destroy the republic."[3]

The *Chicago Record*, meanwhile, interviewed Helen about the recent campaign with Mrs. Lease in which "centralized reform" was evolving. "Several months ago," Helen responded, "I conceived the idea that if all the reform forces in the political field were welded into one great party, everything would fall before it and some of the modern Utopian dreams could be realized." She said she met Mrs. Lease in Kansas, told her about her ideas of centralized reform, and "before we had talked an hour, a plan of procedure had been mapped out." They closed their Indiana speeches with a joint call for development of a Union Reform party, she said. "The country is ripe for a new organization which will represent the interests of the people and not simply work for its own aggrandizement."[4]

On May 19, 1894, John and Helen Gougar hosted a Prohibition party meeting in their home to map "centralized reform" campaign strategy. The reformers planned that two meetings would be held in each of an estimated one hundred fifty schoolhouses outside Lafayette and in surrounding townships. They put together a list of speakers which included Helen Gougar, former Governor St. John of Kansas, and a Huntington judge named Henry B. Sayler.

Helen spoke in Indianapolis on May 24 at a Populist party convention, then prepared for a trip east to lecture. During May, two significant articles of hers also created controversy and comment. In the May issue of the *Arena*, she published a 3,000-word piece called "A Prohibitionist Points the Way Out." Basically she called for:

- Education of the rising generation as to
  the physical effects of alcohol and narcotics
- Punishment for intoxication
- Legal prohibition of the indiscriminate
  sale of alcoholic beverages

- Incarceration in the penitentiary of
  those who violate the law
- Enfranchisement of women
- Election of the Prohibition party to power
  in all branches of the government.

At the same time, in an article in the *Voice* summarizing the fight for woman suffrage, Helen released long pent-up disgust and assailed seventy-four-year-old Susan B. Anthony for being a "moral coward" and a "failure as an organizer" who was against any Prohibitionist taking part in the suffrage crusade.[5]

On June 9, 1894, the *Lafayette Morning Journal* reported that Helen was home from New York City where she had attended the International Prohibition Convention and delivered two addresses. Helen was quoted as saying 10,000 persons had attended.

Helen left Lafayette on June 10 for Michigan to sit with the Hillsdale College board and woman's commission and then embarked for Kansas and Colorado to speak daily until July 18. The *Voice* reported that Helen visited Greeley, Colorado, on June 23 and weathered a "vicious attack" in the town's pro-Republican newspaper, the *Sun*. Helen fired back, with documented facts, forcing publication of a retraction June 27. The *Voice* also reported from Boston that a September 11 trial date had been set in the oft-delayed libel suit Helen had brought against Congressman Morse in 1893.

On July 12, the *Lafayette Morning Journal* teased its readers at Helen's expense with a chilling headline; MRS. GOUGAR IN JAIL. But the item told how, on July 2 in Denver, Helen had met with a longtime Lafayette temperance and Parlor Club friend, now matron of the county jail in charge of women prisoners. Helen spent the night in jail and told the *Denver News*:

> I want to see jail life as it is, not as visitors see it, and I accepted the invitation of my old friend with a great deal of pleasure.
>
> Our jails are filled with the offscouring of saloons. An arrest for drunkenness makes a man callous and hardened. He loses respect for himself and in time becomes embittered against the world. He menaces society and for the protection of the latter jails are provided. How much better it would be if the monster drink could be throttled before the demon it nourishes enters men's souls and blights men's homes and fills our jails, asylums and graveyards.

Helen returned to Lafayette from thirty-five lectures in the West on July 23, saying the mountain sojourn had been "more like a summer outing than hard work." She said she found that the repeal of the Sherman Silver Purchase Act by the Cleveland administration in 1893 had people "intensely wrought up" in Colorado. The measure had "prostrated all kinds of business, and if the state could secede, it would do it. It would be worth the life of any speaker to attempt to advocate the single gold standard before any audience in the state." She predicted the Populists would carry the next election and Prohibitionists would poll a large vote, owing to the suffrage of women. "It is probable," she said, "the Populists and Prohibitionists will unite, and if they do they will sweep the state."[7]

On July 28, Helen Gougar, former Governor St. John, and Judge Sayler began their series of Indiana rallies on behalf of prohibition, the Populist party, and woman suffrage. Beyond that, Helen rapidly filled her schedule book with speaking engagements in Illinois, Ohio, and New York; then she would return to Colorado for three weeks in October.

The first day of the series, nearly five thousand persons came to Oxford to hear the "fusion" of Populist, woman suffrage, and Prohibitionist thought. Gradually the phrase "fusion meeting" became part of the lexicon. A thunderstorm interrupted the rally after Helen's talk on woman suffrage. But the throng repaired to the town's opera house to hear Judge Sayler's talk on the economy and the Populist party's plan for free coinage of silver, as well as Governor St. John's talk on "The Waste of the Liquor Traffic."

But the *Lafayette Morning Journal* editorialized that recent elections in Tennessee and Alabama demonstrated that the decay of the Populist movement in the South already had begun. "The southern people are above all things conservative," the *Journal* opined. "They have, it is true, flirted with the Populists, but they are rapidly recovering from this political inebriety, and are getting back into the party of sound principle in government. The recent elections show that Populism has failed in the states where circumstances should have made it strongest. That party may not break up forthwith, but there is every evidence that it has reached the limit of its influence and that its future will be one of steady decline."[8]

Helen Gougar could not be convinced of that, after seeing 4,000 people crowd the town of Clarks Hill. In her portion of that "fusion rally," she compared the Republican and Democratic parties. She talked of the nation's steady decline in wages and farm produce and the rise in taxes and debt despite promises that repeal of the Sherman Act would make good times. She quoted from an 1876 report of the silver commission to show what demonetization of silver would do, and had done, then said that only by remonetization of silver and prohibition of the waste of the liquor traffic could America hope for better times.[9]

On September 2, 1894, at Staten Island, New York, Helen extended the fusion speech approach with a talk on "The Shotgun or Justice: Which Shall the Laboring Classes Have in the Settlement of Strikes and in the Battles between Labor and Capital?" A few days later, she spoke on "Why the Saloon?" in Westerly, Rhode Island, where the *Daily Sun* reported:

> Mrs. Gougar is a lady of commanding appearance and a marked personality. She is a believer in woman suffrage, Prohibition (large P), free silver and foreign immigration; is inclined toward free trade; and, apparently for all evils both in the moral and financial world her panacea would be the prohibition of the manufacture, sale and importation of liquor.[10]

Helen then went to Boston for the trial against Congressman Morse. It lasted three days, and on September 14, the libel suit for $25,000 in damages ended. The jury deliberated ninety minutes and found in favor of Morse. Helen's attorney applied on September 22 for a new trial.

But now Helen Gougar was telling political associates both nationally and at home of her plan for a different sort of lawsuit, and the *Lafayette Morning Journal* was the first to report it: she would challenge Indiana's election laws by attempting to vote in the November balloting, then file a friendly suit based on the anticipated refusal because of her sex. The try came on November 6, and the *Lafayette Morning Journal* described it:

> By previous arrangement with the election board every courtesy was extended and she was permitted to enter the booth, ask for a state, county and township ballot, and was refused each and all on the simple ground of her sex.
> She then demanded the privilege to make an affidavit of her citizenship which was also denied her on the same ground. She was accompanied by her husband and next best friend, legal voters, witnesses to her demand.
> This is the test vote for a case to be carried to the Supreme Court of the state under the instructions of the Indiana Suffrage Association, of which Mrs. Gougar has just been re-elected president for the 18th year.

A recent decision of the Supreme Court on the right of women to practice law in Indiana had inspired this action. Indiana has a constitutional provision that a voter, with certain qualifications, may practice law, and the court holds that this does not bar a non-voter, therefore women may be admitted to the bar in this state.

The qualifications for suffrage in the state say that a male may vote, but does not say a female shall not; therefore, if the recent decision is good law, women may vote as well as practice law.

Mrs. Gougar has been studying the development of constitutional rights and law for over two years that she may watch and direct every step of the proceedings of this suit. She has the assistance of some of the ablest constitutional jurists of the state and widespread interest has been awakened even beyond the borders of Indiana.

A recent decision of the Supreme Court of the United States makes for the side of woman suffrage. Judge Everett of the Tippecanoe Superior Court will hear the case about the middle of December and the case will go up from whichever side is defeated in his court. S. M. Sayler of Huntington appears for the suffragists and A. A. Rice, of Lafayette, for the election board. Both are ardent friends of woman suffrage.

Many test votes have been tried, but no other on the lines of law that will be presented in this. Mrs. Gougar is better posted in constitutional law than many men at the bar and her management of the case will be thorough and searching. In a sketch of her life published in "Woman of the Century," this statement occurs: "She has a keen insight into character, and in selecting those to serve her in the promotion of reforms she seldom makes a mistake." She has shown this trait in her preparation for this case. The women of Indiana are giving her loyal support.

The case will be watched with unbounded interest. This is a novel and most effective manner of agitating woman suffrage. Indiana promises to be the storm center for woman suffrage the coming year.[11]

The 1894 election otherwise was "business as usual" in Tippecanoe County. Republicans won almost every race, Democrats ran a strong second, but the Populist and Prohibition tickets were buried. The strongest Prohibition candidate received just 184 votes.

On December 17, Helen's suit, asking $10,000 in damages, was filed against the election board in superior court. Judge Frank B. Everett said he would hear arguments January 10, 1895.

The Christmas holiday season was intensely busy for both Helen and John. They had to make several arrangements for the holidays and for a voyage to the Mediterranean. The Gougars set sail February 6, 1895, from New York and planned to leave Lafayette in late January for business and pleasure in Washington, D.C., before the voyage. But there was more immediate, and serious, business. Helen was busy writing her brief and rehearsing to argue her suit before Judge Everett.

January 10 was the history-making morning when Helen was sworn in as the first female member of the Tippecanoe County bar; then she delivered her carefully documented, four-hour argument. The *Lafayette Morning Journal* told of the drama of the courtroom and of the many women seated in the audience, giving "the fragrant odor of flowers" to the high-ceilinged room. On the table, behind which Helen stood to speak, sat a basket of yellow roses, an emblem of the woman suffrage movement, given by ladies in support of Helen. A basket of carnations and smilax brightened another table. The flowers were a gift from working women of Lafayette who attached a card telling Helen: "We need the ballot for industrial protection." Alexander A. Rice, Helen's legal foe of the day, but truly an old friend from Parlor Club and temperance lecture days, voiced the motion for her admittance to the bar.

Her argument lasted until 3 P.M. Her Huntington friend and lawyer, Samuel Sayler, and his brother, Milton, added arguments for another hour before Judge Everett ordered a recess. The next day, Rice defended the election board after the Sayler brothers' father, Judge Henry B. Sayler, summarized for Helen. Printed copies of her argument were made available, as she and Samuel Sayler had prepared the brief in advance for the Indiana Supreme Court. The sixty-page document, printed in pamphlet form in the *Lafayette Morning Journal* job shop, was on sale by local and state suffragists and in a Lafayette bookstore owned, ironically, by one of the election board defendants.[12]

The document was entitled "The Constitutional Rights of the Women of Indiana." Helen devoted sections to the significance of the issue; the history of woman suffrage in the world and nation; abuses in various states under existing laws; definitions of suffrage and citizenship; a brief history of human liberty over the world; selections from the U.S. Declaration of Independence, the Articles of Confederation, and the U.S. Constitution; a discussion of the nature of state governments; the Bill of Rights; the construction of law; the two opposing views about interpreting the law; and numerous suffrage case

*Alexander A. Rice (top left),
John S. Williams (top right),
Benjamin Harrison (bottom left),
and F. E. D. McGinley (bottom*
right)—*two were attorneys, two
were mayors, one was a U.S.
president, and all felt the impact of
Helen Gougar's strength.*

histories. An appendix contained this summary of suffrage laws in every U.S. state:

> In all the states except Colorado and Wyoming the right to vote at general elections is restricted (by custom only, we believe) to males of 21 years of age and upwards. In 19 states, male foreigners who have merely declared their intention to become citizens; in 16 states insane males; in 33 states male paupers; in 39 states male illiterates; and in five states male criminals may vote.
>
> In none of these states can intelligent, law-abiding, native-born women vote, except in general elections in Colorado and Wyoming, city elections in Kansas, and in school elections in 24 states.[13]

"The decision of this court," Helen told Judge Everett, "will affect the liberty of one-half the citizens of every state in the Union, except Massachusetts." There, she pointed out, women were specifically prohibited from voting by law. In the rest, the law simply said males shall vote but did not say females shall not. She characterized the suit as a "trial for human liberty vs. human bondage. Without suffrage no citizen is free, and with one-half the citizens of a state disfranchised there is no free state or consistent republican form of government." She pointed to the folly of apportioning members of the U.S. House on the basis of free inhabitants which included all women and then prohibiting the female half from voting. She noted that the word *male* does not occur in either the Declaration of Independence or the Constitution of the United States and said, "I am told that the state, not the national constitution, delegates suffrage, and to the state must the women look for relief."

Later in her argument, she opined: "There is absolutely no protection to life, liberty and happiness but the bludgeon, the bullet or the ballot. Civilization has outlawed the first two and has adopted the God-intended weapon of defense, the ballot or the will of the mind. Indeed, is the ballot the right preservative of all rights." She concluded: "On behalf of the women citizens of Indiana, it is my prayer that this court may arise to the dignity of this great occasion and with unbiased judgment give the decree that shall make me and my sex free."[14]

Judge Everett recessed the January 11 session at noon, then began deliberations, conferences, and research that would last until April.

CHAPTER 18

Crusade: From Holy Land to Bryan

*H*elen and John Gougar left Lafayette for Chicago to shop and attend a banquet the night of January 17, 1895, in the Sherman House. Helen served as both the main speaker and guest of honor at an after-program reception sponsored by the now-unified National American Woman Suffrage Association. It was, in fact, a celebration of her test case; Samuel Sayler and such equal suffrage association leaders as the Reverend Olympia Brown from Wisconsin stood in the receiving line with the Gougars.[1]

On January 28, Helen, John, and Helen's sister Addie Sherry left Lafayette for Washington for the annual National American Woman Suffrage Association Convention. Next, they joined friends aboard the Red Star Line steamer *Friesland* in New York and departed for the Mediterranean on February 6 in an adventure that would last until May.

The steamer touched Bermuda, then crossed the Atlantic to Gibraltar. The Gougars reached Alexandria, Egypt, on February 26 after seeing Gibraltar and edges of Spain and Algeria. They toured Malaga, Grenada, and noticed terrain similar to mountainous California. They steamed across the Bay of Tunis

155

to the site of ancient Carthage. The *Friesland* ran aground while leaving Port Said on March 6, damaging its steering gear and occasioning worldwide wire service alarms. The Gougars were safely sightseeing in Jerusalem at the time. At the end of March, they visited Rome, and John Gougar took a turn at travel writing for the *Lafayette Morning Journal*. In his letter, he told of steamship and railroad trips to Malta, Cairo, the lower Nile, and the pyramids, where he said "the horde of beggars and guides who are like packs of wolves in their demands are human pests who destroy much of the pleasure of sightseeing in the Orient." The tour, from John's account, also included Joppa, the valley of Sharon and Ajalan, the mountains of Judea, and Jerusalem. He wrote:

> I can assure you if a person wishes to have a favorable impression of Jerusalem and a belief in things and places here held sacred by so many of the Christian faith, it would be the better part of wisdom not to see it; but I am glad that I have been there, as I know the many false ideas and impressions people get from the descriptive writings of sentimental tourists to the Holy Land.[2]

The tourists pressed on to Beirut, Cyprus, Smyrna, and Athens; they stood at the Acropolis, saw the ruins of the Parthenon, the prison of Socrates, and the domain of Demosthenes. From Greece they crossed the Aegean Sea and the Sea of Marmora, sailed up the Bosphorous to Constantinople and on to Naples, then traveled across Europe via Pisa, Nice, and Paris to London and Southampton. On April 20, the party left Southampton for home. On the same day, 5,000 miles away in Lafayette, Superior Court Judge Everett ruled in a fourteen-page decision that he could find no Indiana law giving women suffrage. The essence of his decision was:

> It cannot be denied that for some cause our Constitution has, since its adoption, been understood by most persons to limit suffrage to certain males. The general understanding of any law has always been some guide as to its real and intentional meaning.
>
> That the framers of our Constitution intended to limit suffrage to certain male citizens over 21 years of age is a proposition so plain to me that I cannot disregard it.[3]

Within a few days after the Gougars returned to Lafayette from Europe, Helen faced new challenges. She and John visited Henry Sayler in Huntington to review Judge Everett's decision and plan the appeal to the Indiana Supreme Court. In the meantime, Helen decided to return to the platform to advocate remonetization of silver, a philosophy called "bimetallism."

Under the Sherman Silver Purchase Act, the U.S. Treasury had begun to buy large quantities of silver in 1890. Mine owners had had a sure market, but the price kept falling. The Populist platform of 1892 demanded more—free and unlimited coinage of silver. By 1893, though, the Treasury had become nervous about bimetallism, wherein both gold and silver furnished the security for the nation's currency. The value of silver had fallen until its content in a dollar was worth only sixty cents. More Americans began to grow uneasy. Many began to cash their silver bank notes for gold coins. By early 1893, the nation's gold reserves had plummeted to $100 million; by midsummer, the value of silver in a dollar had fallen to forty-nine cents, threatening runaway inflation. Congress repealed the Sherman Act over the protests of silver miners, farmers, and other "cheap money" people. Repeal stopped the flow of silver into the Treasury, but Americans continued to redeem millions of silver bank notes in gold.

By 1895 gold reserves had dropped to $41 million. At this point, President Cleveland accepted an offer from a group headed by banker and financier John Pierpont Morgan to lend gold to the government and receive government bonds as security. This restored confidence in government and ended the gold run but riled people who felt bimetallism was a smarter policy.

Her bimetallism talks did not mean that Helen Gougar had abandoned her other causes. On May 27 in an open meeting sponsored by Good Templars in Lafayette, she called for formation of a citizens league to oppose the state legislature's newest attempt to regulate liquor through an eight-section measure known as the Nicholson Law. It regulated business hours, sale to minors, licensing and license fees, and many other concepts used to this day. Helen Gougar opposed it because it provided only regulation instead of outright prohibition.

The *Lafayette Morning Journal* on July 2, 1895, published the substance of Helen's view on bimetallism:

> I am neither a gold bug, a silver bug nor a straddle bug, but here is my scheme. If there is anything wrong in it, I wish the bankers and financiers of this city or roundabout would show me the errors of my plan.
> 1. Demonetize gold; by that we mean abandon its coinage and cease its use as a circulating medium.

2. Complete the demonetization of silver, and let its coinage, except for sums less than one dollar, be abandoned.

3. Destroy the gold certificates and the silver certificates as fast as redeemed, and issue no more of either.

4. Make all remaining forms of legal tender exchangeable in either gold or silver bullion at the option of the U.S. treasurer. Such exchange to be at the rate of 25.8 grains of gold, or an amount of silver equal in market value to that amount of gold, for every dollar of legal tender.

5. Let the treasury purchase all gold and silver offered, issuing therefor treasury notes to the extent of one dollar for every 25.8 grains of gold, or for an amount of silver equal in market value thereto.

6. Empower the secretary of the treasury to issue additional treasury notes on the bullion purchased until the amount of outstanding legal tenders shall equal in face value three times the market value of the gold and silver in the treasury, such treasury notes to be legal tender for the payment of all debts, and to be issued directly by the treasury in payment of government expenses.

In July Helen reviewed Samuel Sayler's research and draft of the election law decision appeal to the state supreme court. She then finished plans for a series of suffrage conventions. These one-day events commenced in Delphi in the middle of July and included visits to several other northwestern Indiana counties and towns. Helen spent August, September, and early October lecturing, writing, and working on the appeal brief. The September 19 issue of the *Voice* contained her views on why young girls wanted factory work instead of domestic work. The reasons, she reckoned, were more freedom and better social and living conditions.

On October 3, Helen, John, and the three Saylers from Huntington filed the appeal in the state supreme court. A few days later, Democrats won the Indianapolis election, pitching out a Republican administration. In the October 10 *Lafayette Morning Journal*, Helen commented that the Liquor League was responsible. The long letter was significant in her political life, too, for it reflected the beginning of her disillusionment with all political parties. By late October, she again concentrated on serious courtroom preparations—for the retrial of her libel suit against Congressman Elijah Morse. Helen left Lafayette on November 4 for Boston. The court heard testimony on November 6, 7, and 8. Again the jury ruled for Morse. Helen reviewed it all in the December 12, 1895, issue of the *Voice* and concluded: "The verdict was that an alleged retraction by Mr. Morse was a bar to any action in court. The retraction did in nowise touch the libelous charge in my declaration, and was incompetent as evidence."

The retrial also produced an ironic twist in that Boston's seventy-five-year-old suffrage leader Mary Livermore, who had been an off-and-on supporter of Helen's for twenty-five years, testified for Morse that Helen was "severe in speech, addicted to personalities and unsafe" on the platform. Yet in cross-examination, Mrs. Livermore conceded she had invited Helen to the 1892 reception in Boston after the woman suffrage victories in Kansas—then complimented her. In any event, Helen abandoned the libel suit and returned to Lafayette to open an eight-day "reform conference" on November 17.

This conference utilized the "fusion meeting" format, with guest speakers and musical groups from as far away as Chicago and New York. Helen gave the keynote speech. The parade of orators covered temperance, prohibition, liquor licensing, "The Sabbath School and the Saloon," "Our Money Problem," "Bimetallism," "Woman in Literature," "Woman's Work," "Wealth and Waste," "Organized Labor," and "Is It Just and Expedient That Women Vote?" Helen reincarnated her old illustrated lecture on "The Physical Effects of Alcohol" and closed the conference saying "our object has been to educate. We may write success as the result of this experiment."[4]

On November 27, she left for Illinois with former Governor St. John for a four-day "reform conference" in Rochester. Her last appearances in 1895 were speeches in Chicago on December 10 and in Lafayette on December 22.

Helen Gougar's early 1896 activities included a talk in Cincinnati on January 25. On February 11, she left Lafayette for a speech in Racine, Wisconsin, and a debate two days later in Milwaukee. The debate with a Populist party leader was over the premise: "Prohibition is Wrong, Impracticable, Leads to Hypocrisy and Unjustly Infringes on the Rights of the Individual." The debate was but a hint, however, of the deeply divisive political year Helen would experience.

On February 19, she and John hosted a Prohibition party meeting. Helen and eight men were chosen delegates to the state convention to be held February 26–27. The delegates were instructed to back the gubernatorial ambitions of Helen's attorney friend Henry B. Sayler. A county nominating convention was set for June 10. A tiff was brewing within the party itself, however; and Tippecanoe County party members, adopting a resolution approved by their brethren in Marion County, agreed to "discountenance all organizations and movements in the name of temperance reform that have for their prime object the holding of present voters in old parties and the leading of prospective voters into those parties instead of the Prohibition Party."[5]

While Helen prepared for the state convention, she and John made plans for nearly seven weeks in California, where Helen had twenty-three lectures booked after March 1. The state Prohibition convention at Indianapolis nominated Rev. E. C. Shouse of Terre Haute for governor. The platform demanded outright prohibition of liquor, equal suffrage, bimetallism, and other planks to which Helen Gougar subscribed.[6] The Gougars returned from California on April 21.

On Sunday night, May 10, Helen mounted the pulpit of a Lafayette Methodist church to speak on "Crime and the Liquor Traffic." After lectures in Wisconsin, she headed to Pittsburgh for the Prohibition National Convention. There, splits occurred over both money and suffrage issues. The result was a "national" faction that emphasized prohibition and the gold standard, while Helen and others led a new "national reform" wing, demanding that free silver and women suffrage be in the platform. Back in Indiana, the Prohibition state committee met to decide what to do.

The "national reform" faction hurriedly organized itself, naming L. B. Logan of Ohio as its chairman and selecting his home town, Alliance, as party headquarters. Helen went on the executive committee, along with a woman from Ohio and men from New York, Michigan, Kansas, and Kentucky. The thirteen-point platform included unalterable opposition to liquor, free coinage of both silver and gold, and equal suffrage.

Efforts to mend the rift took place in early June; but by June 20, Helen was in Chicago to help form a National Prohibition party out of the old "national reform" wing. By June 24, it was accomplished, and members called for a meeting in Indianapolis to set up a National Prohibition party state campaign. Helen was nominated to run for secretary of state. Eight days later, she addressed a National Prohibition party meeting in Lansing, Michigan. Her abrupt change of political colors typified sweeping changes and surprises in all American politics in 1896. By the time of the summer presidential nominations, both major parties were also split between "sound money" and "cheap money" advocates.

The Republicans chose as their presidential candidate William McKinley, a lawyer and congressman from Ohio. McKinley waffled on the money issue but eventually sided with the people who favored gold.

The Democratic convention opened with the same split. The silver wing prevailed, and a new battle erupted over naming a candidate. Rejecting Grover Cleveland, the "silver" Democrats picked William Jennings Bryan of Nebraska, a thirty-six-year-old, two-term congressman, who declared:

> Having behind us the producing masses of this nation and the world, supported by the commercial interests, the laboring interests, and the toilers everywhere, we will answer their demand for a gold standard by saying to them; You shall not press down upon the brow of labor this crown of thorns, you shall not crucify mankind upon a cross of gold!

With his stunning "Cross of Gold Speech," Bryan began the crusade to seize power from big business. But the naming of Bryan and adoption of the Democratic platform left the Populists and people like Helen Gougar and her new National Prohibitionists in an awkward position: the Democrats had stolen their thunder. When they met in convention in the summer of 1896, the Populists decided to support Bryan but to preserve some identity by naming Thomas E. Watson, a forty-year-old Georgian lawyer and congressman for vice president.

During August 1896, Helen Gougar seemed to spin in several political directions. On August 1, the *Lafayette Morning Journal* told of her speaking in Potomac, Illinois, and of having organized a Bimetallic Union that would back Bryan. But on August 6, the *Journal* printed the official call for a county meeting of the National Prohibitionists with Helen listed as secretary. That convention on August 11 chose W. D. Wattles of Reynolds to run for Congress and heard talks by several candidates, including Helen Gougar who pledged: "If I am elected, I will see that the corporations in the state pay their just proportion of the taxes."[7] That evening Helen spoke more than two hours on bimetallism. A series of speeches followed on the money question at such towns as Chalmers on August 14 and Mulberry on September 8, as well as several places in Ohio.

Helen returned to Lafayette on September 26, predicting for the *Journal* that Bryan and the "free silver" issue would carry Ohio in November. Meanwhile, near Scottsburg, a township club composed of lady Democrats for Bryan invited Helen to speak in mid-October. So it was a strange campaign. Helen had

begun the year a Prohibitionist. She became a National Prohibitionist, then a "free silver" advocate, then a pro-Bryan
speaker, and finally, a guest of the Democrats.

She ended the campaign on November 2 back in Lafayette's opera house. The *Journal* said that hundreds were turned
away from her "non-partisan" meeting for the laboring man
and that her speech dwelled on bimetallism and the protective
tariff question. Helen appealed to voters to ignore party lines
and "vote intelligently upon an issue that, if adopted, will crush
the power of trusts and syndicates and restore prosperity to the
country."[8]

McKinley received about seven million votes, with six and
one-half million for Bryan, but won the electoral vote more
easily, 271 to 176. Defeat in the 1896 election and the arrival of
better times for farmers ended the power of the Populist party,
while the badly split Prohibitionists showed election turnout
losses nationally.

Political defeat was nothing new for Helen Gougar; yet this
one had a certain bitter finality about it. She was becoming such
a consistent loser, and she had burned so many political bridges
that she was barely welcome in any party except her own small
National Prohibition group in Indiana. She was weary, too, of
platform speaking and battles in court, of combat with candidates and congressmen. Helen had led the state National Prohibition ticket by 105 votes, but it proved nothing: out of some
630,000 votes cast for secretary of state, she received a mere
2,372, finishing fourth in a field of five. In Tippecanoe County
where 10,700 people voted, she received twenty-five votes.

In 1896 Helen was fifty-three years old and tired. She celebrated John's sixtieth birthday and their thirty-third anniversary
at home. Between them, John and Helen had banked thousands
of dollars. They felt they needed to reward each other for that,
at least, so they began plans to build a new home and to spend a
month in the Bahamas in the spring.

On January 7, 1897, Helen announced via the *Lafayette
Morning Journal* her withdrawal from the National Prohibition
party and her intention to support Bryan in 1900. "I hold principle paramount to party," she explained. "I care more for my
country than I do for the name of any party, and I care more for
the triumph of principle than I do for the person of any candidate." Helen said she now embraced Bryan's ideas about
restoration of silver and about a series of other reforms to be
decided by the adoption of the initiative and referendum. "I
believe this is the perfection of popular government," she told

the *Morning Journal*, "and will enable people to bring about reform they [can] enforce when it once becomes law." She vowed that, between then and 1900, she would introduce bills for initiative and referendum in several legislatures and would herself be "stronger for being free" from any party alliance.[9]

On January 7, 1897, in Canton, Ohio, Helen was one of many speakers at a testimonial for Bryan, who handed her a personal, autographed note: "I beg to express my appreciation for your efforts in behalf of bimetallism. I learned through the press and otherwise of your devotion to the cause, and deem it right that you should know that I feel very grateful."[10]

On the same day that Helen was enshrining Bryan in Canton, the Indiana Supreme Court justices in Indianapolis announced they would hear arguments on February 19 in the appeal of her suit against the Tippecanoe County election board. The hearing was businesslike and uneventful. The *Indianapolis News* remarked that "more women than often grace the courtroom" were in the audience. Helen, the *News* said, was the third woman ever to present an oral argument in the high court. The others were not named.

Alexander A. Rice presented the election board's side of the case only briefly, then "resigned the remainder of his time to his opponent," the *News* said. Helen Gougar argued sixty-three points relating to constitutional law to convince the five male judges that women have an equal right with men to vote in general elections.[11] The hearing was held more than twenty-seven months after the 1894 election which launched the suit, but the justices needed just five days to say no to Helen's pleadings. In substance, the tribunal decided that under Indiana's 1851 Constitution women could not vote and that this did not conflict with the U.S. Constitution.

CHAPTER 19

Castle Cottage and Cuba

*A*s soon as the severe winter weather started to mellow, construction of the Gougars' home began. The *Lafayette Morning Journal* reported that the building would somewhat resemble a pink brick and limestone castle built over a full cellar. On March 15, as workmen began digging for the cellar and installing water and gas pipes, John and Helen left for a three-week trip to the Bahamas and Cuba. On April 8, 1897, the *Morning Journal* printed a 3,000-word letter from Helen, dispatched on March 29 from Nassau. In it Helen described the climate, the sights, the people, their dress and customs. But she touched deeper themes as well:

> I have found in my travels that the extent of the boundaries of a country indicate the average comprehensiveness of the inhabitants thereof. Boundaries and climate have much more to do with the mental grasp of a people than is usually supposed.
>
> Add to the sleepy movements of the tropics the sluggish blood of the English colonists and time suffers a relapse in the motions of men. They will never die with nervous prostration unless they wear themselves out putting things off until some other time. It is a capital place to rest from the hustle of northern business life.
>
> These islands teach us of the United States a valuable lesson. They depend upon us entirely for bread, meat and

nearly all their imports as we are their nearest market. The imports from the U.S. in 1895 amounted to $680,700; imports from all other countries $225,200. Total exports from this colony into the U.S., $182,790.

Last year we exported to this colony nearly one million dollars' worth of our farm and factory productions. There is the greatest excitement here now over the proposition of the Dingley tariff to put the duty, which will be prohibitive, on pineapples and oranges. If this law goes into effect it will prostrate these struggling colonies until they can open a market with Canada. When they do this we lose these islands as a market, and forever divert this growing trade to other countries. Was there ever greater financial idiocy? I blushed for my country as I listened to this discussion, and realized that the great United States should propose a plan so contemptible as these fruit tariffs, and one so well calculated to reduce the prosperity of our own agriculturists.

Here again we see the hand of corporate power and class legislation. The pineapple lands are limited in extent at best in our country, but the East Coast Florida Railway Company and Mr. Flagler, the corporate octopus of Florida, own these lands. Prohibit the importation of pineapples and it will increase the value of Mr. Flagler's lands and make thousands of dollars on every farm sold and cultivated for this corporation. Thus for the sake of enriching this single man and a few fruit growers, we divert our trade from these colonies just to that extent impoverishing our corn and wheat raisers, besides closing several canning factories in Baltimore that depend upon the Bahamas for their fruit.

To such results does our vicious "protective" tariff legislation drive us commercially. Give us absolute free trade with these colonies. Let our people have all the pineapples they can get, under the law of supply and demand, and in turn let us feed and clothe these people from our broad acres and bountiful harvests.[1]

The Gougars returned on April 13 but continued to rest and view the progress on the new home. Helen's load of political speeches lightened dramatically. For one reason, there was no election campaign. For another, Helen's record of supporting defeated causes may now have reduced her drawing power as a speaker and logician after so many futile years. But tensions in Cuba and elsewhere which would lead to the Spanish-American War were rising, and Helen saw in it a good subject for travel lectures. She had arranged for a photographer to shoot scores of pictures that could be made into slides to illustrate the talks.

In 1897 Helen mixed the speeches she did make with involvement in some new social work projects outlined in her letter to the *Lafayette Morning Journal* on July 21:

> For the past year a small company of young women have been trying to sustain a Rescue Mission for the reformation, shelter and protection of unfortunate, misguided girls of our city. That there is necessity for this work of woman for woman is evident when I state that I am officially informed that there are 31 houses of prostitution with their base followers and procurers, male and female, doing their deadly work in this city, beside 15 houses of assignation.
>
> These facts are certainly appalling. Some of the incidents pertaining to the work of rescue and the necessity for this mission would doubtless startle you could you learn of them from the noble band of girls who are trying to promote their much-needed work.
>
> Permit me to state one of the cases. A mother, poor, ignorant and degraded, for seven years a resident of this city plying her deadly business, had led her two daughters, aged 15 and 17, into her own life of shame. By her attempt to sell her remaining girl but 12 years old she was discovered and the child's rescue begun.
>
> This is but one of the many cases that have come under the care of the Rescue Mission. It is the earnest desire of the police that this mission be sustained. I cannot believe that the women of Lafayette with all their wealth and womanliness will refuse to give ample support to this work. Let it not be said that women will not extend help and aid to woman.
>
> The fact that this is a university city and so many young men come within our gates to be tempted by these denkeepers should add renewed efforts to support the Rescue Mission.[2]

Helen left on July 29 for a Chicago speech, returning August 2; and between August 11 and 17, she gave three chautauqua speeches in Salem, Nebraska. These seemed to mark her debut with stereopticon slide-illustrated travel lectures. She chose as her subjects "Cuba," "The Turk at Home," and a religious, inspirational lecture she had been giving for some time called "The Power of Habit."

Upon her return, Helen, as president of the Indiana Woman Suffrage Association, organized an excursion train trip for Indiana and Illinois association members. The group left Chicago on September 1 for an exposition in Nashville, Tennessee, and joined suffrage activists in a series of programs.

Toward the end of September, Helen traveled to Springfield, Ohio, to speak at a ten-day "silver camp meeting." She was in Chicago on October 15, then hurried off to Ohio for political talks that supported "free silver" candidates in several local, county, and state campaigns.

In mid-November, Helen returned to Lafayette, this time engineering a move to replace the abandoned rescue mission with a WCTU-backed Young Women's Christian Home. She called leading women, the chief of police, and others to her lavish new home, called "Castle Cottage," to establish a nine-woman board of directors and a twenty-five-man advisory board, select a matron and housekeeper, plan a budget, begin a drive to raise $3,000, and select a home.

Her interest in a home for wayward young women seemed to coincide with completion of Castle Cottage. The Gougars' three-story house had steep roofs, exquisite stonework, and a southeast corner tower that gave it a castle-like demeanor. The December 11, 1897, issue of an illustrated weekly Indianapolis magazine called *Indiana Woman* profiled Lafayette. The weekly featured photographs of John and Helen and Castle Cottage, depicting it as one of the city's most prominent and interesting buildings.

On December 15, 1897, organization of the new Young Women's Christian Home continued. At a meeting in the elegant parlor of Castle Cottage, Helen directed elections and helped put more committees into operation.

As 1898 arrived, Helen Gougar tore into another year hard at work. She accepted numerous bookings for her Cuba lecture, illustrated with nearly one hundred slides. On January 5, she left for twelve days of lecturing in Ohio. Then, in February she delivered two benefits for Lafayette organizations. On Sunday night, February 7, at the Salvation Army barracks, the subject was temperance. On February 21, she did "Cuba and the Cubans" in the First Baptist Church to benefit the Young Women's Christian Home fund. Tickets sold well, as the newspapers carried accounts of the growing prospect of war with Spain daily.

Both Puerto Rico and Cuba remained part of Spain's shrinking empire; and for nearly thirty years, both had been scenes of rebellion. Now, in the 1890s, most Cubans worked at starvation wages for wealthy landowners. Spanish misrule plus economic problems brought more bloodshed. American tariffs made life worse. Spanish-American relations fell apart, and newspaper exposés of conditions in Cuba inflamed public opinion. By 1898 growing numbers of Americans felt the United States had a moral responsibility to restore order in Cuba. On February 9, some papers quoted a Spanish minister to the United States as having insulted President McKinley. On February 15, the American battleship *Maine*, sent to Cuba in January to protect American lives and property, was sunk in Havana harbor, killing more than one hundred fifty. "Remember the *Maine*!" became the warcry while McKinley tried talking to prevent war.

Amid this background of growing fear, concern, outrage, and patriotism, the *Lafayette Morning Journal* printed a generously long account of Helen Gougar's lecture. She spent thirty minutes alone on Cuban history, showing a map projected on a stretched white canvas screen. Helen lauded the bravery of the Cuban natives and condemned the brutality of the Spanish, the occupying Spanish Army, and American inaction:

> Cuba will free herself from Spain before this war ends or the island will be decimated and the Cuban race entirely destroyed. God grant that the United States that was helped in just such an hour of extremity by France, else we would not be a nation, as Cuba is in today, shall speak the word, granting belligerent rights, before brave people are exterminated by barbaric methods, the most inhuman in the annals of war.
>
> That we have allowed this brutal war to go on within five hours of our own doors will ever remain a stain upon the name of America. President Cleveland said in his conciliatory message to Congress upon this subject: "The United States has a character to maintain."
>
> We have not only a character to maintain, but we must ever defend our cowardice and our lack of humanity for not having long ago spoken the word that would have made Cuba one more republic, prosperous and at peace with the world.

Helen said she opposed the annexing of Cuba by the United States because she wanted "no more Spanish, Creole, ignorance or foreign blood made a part of the voting, political influence in the United States until the intelligent American woman has direct political power through the ballot. We have enough territory now upon which to test the refinement of a free government without annexing Cuba, Hawaii, or any other outlying territory."[3]

Completed in 1897, the Gougars' Castle Cottage was Helen's home for only ten years. John lived there until his death in 1925. Today *Castle Cottage serves as a mortuary. (Top, an 1897 drawing; bottom, a 1900 photograph)*

She gave the "Cuba and the Cubans" lecture again on February 22 for residents of the Indiana Soldiers Home, which had opened north of Lafayette in 1895 for Civil War veterans; on February 24 in Watseka, Illinois; and on February 25 in Crawfordsville.

VII

CHANGING SCENES

A mighty fortress is our God,
A bulwark never failing;
Our helper He amid the flood
Of mortal ills prevailing.

From "A Mighty Fortress Is Our God,"
Martin Luther, 1529

CHAPTER 20

Riling Republicans; Writing a Book

Though most women still lacked the vote, some took part in other reforms aimed at influencing government in the 1890s. The National Consumers League, in which a social reformist from Chicago and New York, Florence Kelley, was a leader, uncovered stores and companies that paid women less than men for equal work. The league urged consumer boycotts to protest unhealthy working conditions and child labor. Through its many campaigns in churches, schools, and public meetings, the WCTU doggedly stressed the physical, psychological, and social dangers of drink and showed the effects on the well-being of families. Perhaps as a result of Helen Gougar's years of prodding, Frances Willard, leader of the WCTU from the beginning, now began to persuade its members to support woman suffrage as a means to attain prohibition. Many other women took part in the more militant Anti-Saloon League, which supported candidates who pledged opposition to the liquor interests and opposed those who did not.

Helen certainly had strong sympathy for all three of these movements; and in February 1898, when Frances Willard died

173

at age fifty-eight, Helen felt a strong sense of personal as well as national loss. On Sunday, February 27, several WCTU branches in Lafayette met for a memorial service. In "Miss Willard as a Politician," one of five testimonials, Helen said:

> Miss Willard taught the 19th-century woman to discover herself. She taught women to organize and to lead meetings. Her refining and spiritualizing influence was felt in whatever work she was engaged in. Not at first a suffragist, her efforts were directed chiefly toward the betterment of drunkards. She was a growing woman, one who has left the impress of her character on American politics as a Christian socialist. Her wonderful tact and ability in dealing with turbulent women in large conventions, and her high accomplishments as a parliamentarian deserve recognition as well. She is honored the world over because she stood unflinchingly for principle.[1]

On March 1, Helen greeted members of the Young Women's Christian Home board in Castle Cottage, and they decided to move ahead to secure property and set up a home. On March 16, again at Castle Cottage, the Young Women's Christian Home became a reality. The trustees and advisory board members agreed to rent a home for $150 per year. They named Helen treasurer and dedicated the home to "all women who are homeless or unemployed, or those stranded in the city without money or friends. In addition, young women who wish to rest and are without homes, by the payment of a proper sum, will be received if the capacity of the home shall be sufficient, preference always being given to those most in need," the by-laws said.[2] A matron was chosen and an advisory board formed, consisting of one woman from each of fifteen Lafayette and West Lafayette churches. The home opened on March 16, 1898. Open house and a business meeting were held in the clean, neatly furnished home on April 1; but on April 7, an outbreak of scarlatina forced it to be quarantined for seven weeks.

On April 13, Helen delivered an address for Thomas Jefferson's birthday in Salem, Ohio; and the next day in Alliance, Ohio, she discussed bimetallism and money policy. On May 2, coincident with Commodore George Dewey's naval victory over Spanish forces in Manila Harbor in the Philippines two weeks after Congress rather blandly declared war in Cuba, Helen left Lafayette for another week of lectures about Cuba. The itinerary included Lebanon, Peru, and Converse, as well as Kankakee, Illinois. On May 8, Helen spoke in Lafayette's

WCTU Hall, newly renamed Willard Hall, on an old subject: "Indiana Convicts—What Shall We Do with Them?" Her solution had not changed over the years: stop the liquor traffic, eliminate saloons and the criminal atmosphere she claimed they create, and prevent the broken homes that spawn criminals.

Judging from her speeches both before and after the 1896 presidential campaign, Helen supported William Jennings Bryan. Her sentiments became obvious the weekend of May 26–28, 1898, when the Indiana Democratic Editorial Association members and spouses held their convention in Lafayette. Helen and John hosted a reception for the visiting ladies in Castle Cottage; and on Friday night, May 27, at a pro-Democratic Jackson Club rally, Helen delivered her popular travelogue about Cuba. The following Sunday night, Helen spoke on "The Little Things in Life That Make Christian Character" to members of the Epworth League, a Methodist youth organization founded in 1889 to promote fellowship, worship, Christian service, and study of the Scriptures.

In mid-June 1898, Helen finished a typewritten manuscript, "Wall Street's Bold Threat," apparently designed to be submitted to the *Arena* and also to be adapted for use in speeches. She concluded the piece by saying:

> The Republican Party stands for the power of Wall Street. From the redeemer of the people, it thus brazenly announces its determination to become the oppressor of the people by a platform that is in harmony with the desires of Henry Clews [a New York banker, financial reporter, and mouthpiece for Wall Street] and his associates.[3]

Independence Day 1898 fell on Monday. Helen spoke that afternoon at a temperance rally in Lafayette's Columbian Park. On Sunday night, July 10, she spoke at a mass meeting in Lafayette's Trinity Methodist Church to inform the public about the Young Women's Christian Home and widen support for it. Helen expressed her joy at seeing women so active in social work, citing the creation of the children's home, a free kindergarten in operation several years, and this home for young women.

While Helen's activities engaged the interest of a segment of Lafayette's population that July, the appearance in town of three men driving a dusty "horseless carriage" caused a buzz among the general population. Built in Kokomo and called the Haynes-Apperson, the vehicle was one of the first American motor cars.

Helen spent the rest of the midsummer of 1898 completing the manuscript for a short book, giving chautauqua lectures in Illinois, planning a lecture tour "throughout Canada" in a plebiscite campaign for prohibition, and preparing for several talks to be given in Indiana about 1898 campaign issues.

She expressed her views about election issues in a letter published in the *Lafayette Morning Journal* on September 22. Her long and viciously anti-Republican tirade included among its targets J. Frank Hanly, a Lafayette attorney. Hanly, then thirty-five, had served one term in Congress before being redistricted into political oblivion. He had moved to Lafayette from Warren County in 1896 and was making an ambitious comeback into Republican political circles. Helen ended her letter:

> It is no wonder that the Republican Party wants to transfer their campaign issues to the Sandwich Islands, Philippines, Cuba, yes, good Lord anywhere to get rid of facts and figures at home. It is their only hope.
>
> If they are out after truth let them have all they want of it. The opposition will have nothing to lose by it.
>
> A Republican majority in Congress this winter means a continuance of the policy of financial ruin that besets the country now, and has since 1873.
>
> A Republican Congress means unnecessary taxation to maintain an Army of occupation in remote islands.
>
> A Republican Congress means whitewash of the official criminals of the war.
>
> A Republican Congress means the endorsement of political corruption in every department of government.
>
> A Republican Congress means more trusts, more tramps and vagabonds, more mortgages and a harder struggle for existence than at any other time. Let the people be undeceived as to the real purpose of campaign speakers who indulge in bombast about "expansion" and neglect the weightier matters of political justice.[4]

In November 1898, oblivious to rhetoricians such as Helen Gougar, voters gave the Republican candidates easy election victories in Indiana.

Helen was too happy to brood. Her book *Matthew Peters: A Foreign Immigrant*, which she had completed during the summer, appeared in bookstores in time for Christmas sales. Bound in cinnamon brown, the volume measured five inches in width, six and one-half inches in length, and half an inch in thickness. The protagonist, who lived from 1846 to 1898, emigrated from western Germany and was orphaned in New Orleans. Helen intertwined with Peter's life material about the underground railroad, the Civil War, temperance, suffrage, charity work, and America as a land of opportunity.

Matthew Peters's wife was Clara Lyon Peters, vice president for a time of the Woman's Press Association in Illinois, a philanthropist, and worker for women's emancipation. Helen probably came to know Clara Peters and the story of her husband's life through her many visits, speeches, and meetings in Illinois.

Helen opened her book with the dedication: "To the memory of my sainted father, whose dying message to me was: 'Daughter, be kind to everybody.'" She ended her book with a plea for "worthy" foreign immigration allowances in the United States: "Every man is my brother, and every land my country."[5]

In 1898, the same year as Helen's book appeared, a literary benchmark for the women's movement was released: the first two volumes of *Life and Work of Susan B. Anthony*, written by Ida Husted Harper and published by the Bowen-Merrill Company of Indianapolis.

Ida Husted Harper, who was born near Brookville, became a well-known writer and lecturer during her lifetime. She attended high school in Muncie, studied at Indiana and Stanford universities two years each, and eventually became a high school principal at Peru. After spending several years in literary work in Terre Haute, she moved to New York to live and work.[6] The author spent ten years under Miss Anthony's roof sorting through copies of speeches, letters, diaries, and personal reminiscences, as part of the research for the work. In 1881 Ida Husted Harper with Miss Anthony had written *History of Woman Suffrage to Close of Nineteenth Century*.

The two volumes (a third would follow in 1908) contained 1,100 pages, with forty-two references to Indiana's May Wright Sewall, fourteen to Harper herself, twelve to Zerelda Wallace, but only five to do-it-my-way Helen Gougar, whose third-party leanings, pithy criticisms, ventures for personal wealth, and frequent vacations from the cause evidently weakened her esteem in the movement's hierarchy.

On November 17, 1898, Helen left for Joplin, Missouri, to spend a week visiting her sister Edna Houk and her husband (who had moved there from Cincinnati) and sisters Etta Cosgrove and Mary Robinson. The *Lafayette Morning Journal* in a social item revealed that the sisters all had interests in a booming industry in the Joplin area—zinc and lead mining—and were "realizing handsome returns."

Helen's chief social involvement early in 1899 was a signed report in the *Lafayette Morning Journal* of January 9, in which she appealed for funds for the Young Women's Christian Home. She disclosed that the board had proposed to finance the home on a budget of $1,000 cash, plus property donations. The cash was to be raised by enlisting 500 women to give one dollar per year and 100 to give five dollars per year. "When this is done," Helen wrote, "there will be no tickets to concerts, dinners or other calls made for the institution." But the pledges were not coming in. So Helen appealed for $500 within a week, adding: "Please do not tell me that the work has your 'cordial sympathy' without supplementing the wish with practical sympathy of your fives and ones."[7]

CHAPTER 21

Viewing Money, Labor, and Nationalization

*P*ublic interest in the nation's "money question" and economics in general brought Helen Gougar back in early 1899 to familiar territory after many years: the YMCA lecture programs. A lecture course was established under the auspices of the Lafayette YMCA and the University Association of Chicago, which had offered extension work for three years. Helen, local pastors, Purdue University professors, and other townspeople with expertise gave the lectures. Helen's, on the topic of "Municipal Ownership of Public Service Systems," was booked for April 17, 1899. Within a month, the Economic League had 128 members in Lafayette and held its sessions in the high school. In her lecture, Helen advocated government ownership and control of railways and other means of public transportation and communication, including the telephone and telegraph. She reasoned:

> While the prosperity of a country depends largely upon its productiveness, the importance of proper facilities for the expeditious transportation and ready exchange of its various products can scarcely be overrated. The free circulation of commercial commodities is as essential to the

welfare of the people as is the unimpaired circulation of the blood of the human organism.

The interest taken by man in the improvement of roads over which he must travel is one of the chief indications of civilization, and it might even be said that the condition of the roads of a country shows the degree of enlightenment which the people have reached.

The evolution of road-building is most interesting but in these later days when we take note of the conduct of the railroad system, we might add, the control which the people exercise over their means of public transportation and communication show equally their degree of enlightenment.

It is not so much how to build roads but how to manage the roads already constructed that most concerns the welfare of the people of the most civilized countries. We will leave the history of road-building to the curious and deal with the latest developed highway, the railroad.

These arteries of the commercial life of the nation are mainly owned and controlled by a very few men, about 70 in all. The small stockholders have nothing to say, but resign the control to these self-constituted managers who hold a majority of the stock.

It is said that through this concentration of railroad power, five men can stop every wheel in the United States at will. Kings, under "divine right, " and whose yoke it is our proud boast we have thrown off, never possessed such supreme power.[1]

On April 25, 1899, Helen spoke at a WCTU institute in Indianapolis on 'Echoes from the Legislature on the Enfranchisement of Indiana Women," appealing for support of a woman's reformatory in Indiana. In May and June, she spoke in Cincinnati and then in Mattoon, Illinois. Twice she visited Joplin with John and sister Addie Sherry to look into mining business matters. In early June, she wrote the *Lafayette Morning Journal* a long letter about how American labor was being degraded by immigrants. She based the argument on press dispatches from Victoria, British Columbia, saying that nearly seven thousand laborers would soon leave Yokohama under contract to work on Hawaiian plantations, the result of permission given by the U.S. government for the importation of Japanese both to assist in cultivating of land and to attempt to offset a large Chinese population already at work. Helen said:

> So far as labor is concerned a cheap Jap is as great a menace to free labor as is a Chinese coolie and this excuse

for overriding the law of the land against foreign contract labor will avail nothing with the people who recognize the high-handed outrage committed by this present administration.

These plantations belong to the sugar trust. The remnant of liberty left labor by the trusts will be most effectually destroyed by this foreign importation.

She closed by urging vigilance until "McKinley is retired to private life or a Congress fresh from the people can rebuke and hinder him in his destructive policy."[2]

In mid-July, Helen spent a week in Joplin on mining business, then traveled to Nebraska for several chautauqua talks on U.S. imperialism. On Labor Day, she spoke at a program at the new Tecumseh Trail Park a few miles up the Wabash River from Lafayette. She gave a general talk, blending her philosophies about politics, labor, money policy, and imperialism. She had been speaking out much of the year against "imperialism in the interest of patriotism and Americanism," saying that "it is a fact that women regardless of party proclivities are opposed to the course of the McKinley Administration in the Philippines." She made some other points as well:

> [The Philippines fight was] an unwise, uncalled-for, unnecessary, un-American and unconstitutional war. It was neither the people nor Congress that declared it, but William McKinley, and this without authority in law or principle.
>
> We paid Spain $20 million filched from the pockets of our overburdened taxpayers for goods she had no right to, and that she has been unable to deliver. In the words of the immortal Bryan, "We paid $20 million for an option to do what Spain has not been able to do in over 300 years."
>
> This government is in the wrong and the people should demand that the troops be withdrawn from the Philippines at once and leave the islands to govern themselves.
>
> We have the timely warning of Washington, Jefferson and other honored statesmen against such a policy, besides we have the lesson of history in the colonial policies of other nations that have been weakened and finally overthrown.
>
> England's weakness is today in her colonial policy; she is obliged to keep a standing army in India of 100,000 men and she dares not put a gun in the hands of a single native, so royally and justly is she hated.
>
> These [Philippine] islands can not be of enough bene-

fit to us in the way of trade to offset our expense to secure and hold them.[3]

On October 5, the *Lafayette Morning Journal* said Helen would be leaving for a series of ten speeches in Nebraska, beginning in Lincoln, where she was the guest of honor at a five-course dinner in the home of Mrs. William Jennings Bryan. It was strictly a ladies' affair, with the entire party attending Helen's 8 P.M. address.

She finished the year—and the nineteenth century—with a lecture in Crawfordsville. The date was December 21 and the theme a well-rehearsed one: "The Criminal Record of the Licensed Liquor Traffic."

VIII

THE TURN OF THE CENTURY

This is my father's world,
  And to my list'ning ears,
All nature sings and round me rings
  The music of the spheres.
This is my father's world,
  I rest me in the thought
Of rocks and trees, of skies and seas,
  His hand the wonders wrought.

From "This Is My Father's World," Maltbie D. Babcock,
1901, and Franklin L. Sheppard, 1915

CHAPTER 22

Training the Modern Girl; Turning Democrat

Now in the twentieth century, America continued to grow. Cities had museums, libraries, freight yards, warehouses, stockyards, railroad depots, slums, electric lights, telephones, a few motor cars, littered alleys, and people who ranged from rich to poor.

The wealth was in a few hands. Some of the very rich gave money for churches and colleges, art galleries, libraries, or opera houses. Lower on the economic pecking order were professional people, small business proprietors, clerks, and skilled workers. They had raised their standard of living and now enjoyed gas heat, modern plumbing, and household appliances. They bought magazines and books and sent their children not only through high school but also to college. In religious and social welfare work, many women were winning international reputations. Mary Baker Eddy had founded the spiritual and metaphysical system known as Christian Science. The Church of Christ Science was chartered in 1879. A number of Catholic women had started religious orders; an example was Mother Frances Xavier Cabrini, who established the Missionary Sisters of the Sacred Heart in 1880, orphanages, and schools. Born in

Italy and naturalized in 1909, she was the first U.S. citizen to become a saint in the Roman Catholic Church. Helen Gougar's long-time favorite, Clara Barton, famous for her Civil War work of soliciting and distributing supplies for the wounded, developed the American Red Cross in 1882.

The growth of coeducational universities and establishment of such women's colleges as Mount Holyoke, Wellesley, Vassar, and Smith meant more young women could obtain an education equal to that of men. By 1900, there were 1,000 women lawyers, 3,000 women ministers, and 7,500 women doctors in the United States. Women now had careers in business, in offices, and in industrial plants.

The growth of women's clubs—a movement Indiana's May Wright Sewall still helped lead—continued. By 1900 women's clubs were fighting corruption; improving health and recreational facilities; and battling on for temperance, prohibition, and woman suffrage. The liquor industry, which feared the female vote might outlaw alcohol, continued to block, frustrate, and openly fight the suffragists into the twentieth century. Although by 1900 only a few western states had given women the right to vote, in the next fifteen years, the number would grow. And in certain states that granted limited suffrage in 1900, women took part increasingly in school board and city elections.

The Illinois-born social worker, author, and peace advocate, Jane Addams, became famous for her work in Chicago's slums and for opening Hull House in 1889. There she pioneered day-care centers for children of working mothers and classes in child care.

To many Americans, McKinley's victory in 1896 had ended the "reform movement." Yet by 1900, a new reform impulse known as the Progressive movement was under way. It served as a successor to the Populist crusade but with different aims: (1) return control of government to the people, (2) stop abuses and injustices resulting from urban industrialization, and (3) draw up new rules for the conduct of business to restore equal opportunity. Helen Gougar could not agree with these goals alone, though, for they did not include prohibition or woman suffrage. Anyway, she was now, privately at least, a Bryan Democrat.

By 1900, too, Americans had made other political reforms. The secret, or Australian, ballot replaced the practice of voting on paper ballots in open view. The use of the initiative, referendum, and recall gained support, first from Populists, now from Progressives. The initiative enabled voters in a state to initiate or introduce legislation at any time. The referendum provided people with power to force questions to a popular vote by petition. The recall enabled voters to remove officials before a term expired. The Progressives also aimed to institute a direct primary election in place of the political party nominating convention.

While the arrival of the twentieth century in the fifty-seventh year of her life signaled a gradual slowing down, Helen Gougar remained interested in national, state, and local affairs and continued to write and lecture, only less frequently or passionately. She spent more time in Joplin dealing with mining concerns. She entertained guests in Castle Cottage. She attended local meetings and went to funerals of old friends. She and John traveled more.

In January 1900, Helen made one trip to Joplin, gave a Young Women's Christian Home progress report on the fourteenth, spoke at a Methodist and Baptist union service in West Lafayette on the twenty-first, and spoke in a local Methodist church on "Industrial Training for Women" on the twenty-ninth. She drew up a blueprint for the twentieth-century girl:

> Put her in the first years of her school life in the kindergarten, which should be made part of the free school system in every state in the union. Up to 12 years of age she should be taught the "three R's" and kindred rudimentary English branches. I would even require her to study hygiene with special reference to the care of the body and the home; she should devote part of her time in learning to do plain sewing and skillful darning, and no girl should be permitted to graduate from the free schools until she could cut and make a simple, plain, entire suit of her wearing apparel; she should also learn to prepare a wholesome meal and have thorough training in household management that her head might save the weariness of her heels.
>
> Every free school should be thoroughly equipped to give so much of industrial training as is necessary for everyday life. The common English branches, with industrial training, are all the instructions which the free schools have any right to impart. The dead languages and French, German, Spanish or Hottentot are out of place in the free schools. Drawing and music, however, should be taught in all the common schools for these train the head and hand and sweeten the daily toil of the school room. The state should also supply the institutions for the higher and special training.
>
> If a girl is found to possess a superior talent in any

direction such as music, authorship, art, architecture, medicine, law, politics, domestic science, platform or pulpit, then she should be thoroughly equipped in these lines that nature has evidently laid down for her and this should be done at the expense of the state.

I would make no difference in the training of a country girl or city girl, for in this democratic land of ours a country girl stands as good a chance to become the first lady of the land as a city bred miss.

If the state would train specialists under proper restraints and examinations, there would be more good housekeepers and fewer half-done musicians. The free schools are not educating too much, as many claim, but much of the education is misdirected. The state can more economically educate its children than it can support incapacity, indolence and crime which are the direct traits of not knowing how to do any work well.

A woman trained as indicated by my plan would be well-rounded and symmetrical in character. She would honor and grace any position in life to which she might be called.[1]

Later, the *Lafayette Evening Call* published the full text with some explanatory remarks which Helen had given in an interview: "Heretofore women have been taught that the chief aim in life should be to attend prayer meetings and learn how to die. I hold that if we live right, we will die right, and the chief lesson for every human being to learn is how to live."[2]

Later in February, Helen visited Joplin on mining business and was in Chicago on the thirteenth. On Sunday, March 11, 1900, she spoke at a WCTU seminar on practical Christian citizenship in Lafayette's Willard Hall. On March 13, she spoke on "Civil Government and Municipal Law" in Battle Ground at a WCTU "White Ribbon" temperance camp meeting. On May 11, Helen entertained seventy-five WCTU members in Castle Cottage and remarked about woman suffrage, referring to New Zealand as having one of the best and most progressive governments in the world. That nation, she said, had adopted the initiative and referendum in regard to all its legislation and had given women the privilege of voting.

In mid-May, the *Globe* in Joplin mentioned that Helen was preparing for the presidential election campaign:

> Mrs. Gougar will take an active part during the coming campaign, speaking for Mr. Bryan. She is already engaged for 15 days in June in South Dakota. She thinks that

Indiana can be safely counted in the Democratic ranks, as the result of the municipal elections show.

The assaults upon the constitution by Mr. McKinley, and the imperial militarism of the Republican Party are most unpopular in Indiana and elsewhere.[3]

Helen confirmed her decision to work for Bryan and the Democrats in 1900 within a week when, on May 21, she spoke at a Democratic rally in Knightstown. An Indianapolis paper later reported:

> Mrs. Gougar is with the Democrats heart and soul. She called at Democratic Headquarters today and a group listened with great attention while she discussed the issues. She wore a corsage bouquet of beautiful flowers.
>
> "It is high time for us to withdraw from Cuban soil, and cease stealing the natives blind," she said. "The sooner the Democrats get their speakers upon the stump the better it will be, for the people want to know about the sins of the administration and an explanation of affairs will make votes without number.
>
> "I delivered my first campaign speech in Knightstown last night. The subject was 'The Trusts and the People.'
>
> "I succeeded in making some of the Republican pothouse politicians mad, but that is a first-class indication. There are more Republicans about Knightstown than I ever saw, considering the population—so many that I didn't find out who the Democratic county chairman is. Four of those Republicans came to me voluntarily and told me the McKinley Administration is the rottenest they ever knew.
>
> "I am going to do a great deal of work in this campaign, among the women. I'm going to explain to them our treaties with the Sultan of Sulu and show to them how we have raised the flag of polygamy and slavery and put the master of the harem on our pension list. When I tell those things to women, they throw up their hands in astonishment and declare they never knew that before."[4]

On June 24, Helen left Lafayette for a long swing through South Dakota, Nebraska, Kansas, and Missouri, making chautauqua speeches and stopping in Kansas City to see her forty-year-old hero, William Jennings Bryan, renominated for president at the Democratic National Convention. She returned to Lafayette on July 14, spoke in Crawfordsville on the twenty-fourth, and made several talks in August.

On September 21, 1900, Helen began to engage in earnest presidential campaign stumping. At Bryan's specific request, she left for two weeks of talks in Wyoming, sponsored by the Democratic National Committee. During October, she set a strenuous pace, speaking in Nebraska, Ohio, and Indiana. During one brief rest stop in Lafayette, she agreed to chair a committee on county fair work at the annual meeting of the Tippecanoe County WCTU. In mid-October John Gougar spent a week on mining business in Joplin while Helen lectured again in Nebraska. She finished that tour in Auburn, Nebraska, on October 22, then hurried back to Greenfield to speak at a Democratic rally. With just forty-eight hours' rest in Castle Cottage, she then campaigned until election day in places ranging from Logansport to Canton, Cleveland, and Wooster, Ohio.

President McKinley, his running mate for vice president, Theodore Roosevelt of New York, and the other Republicans entered the 1900 campaign confident of winning. The Democrats with Bryan again tried to make free silver a major issue. But the nation in general, including most farmers, was enjoying prosperity. Tippecanoe County, its voters pumped up by an October 10 speech in downtown Lafayette by Teddy Roosevelt himself, overwhelmingly voted Republican in the November 6 balloting. McKinley defeated Bryan 6,317 to 4,673, and the GOP won virtually every Tippecanoe County contest. Ironically, one of Helen Gougar's "fellow Democrats" in 1900, who lost his race for township assessor, was Henry Mandler, the former police chief and barber who was the defendant in Helen's sensational 1882 slander suit.

CHAPTER 23

Women in Church: A Merciless Missive

*H*elen Gougar retreated quickly and quietly from the 1900 election back into Lafayette WCTU and Young Women's Christian Home affairs and into mining in Joplin. For their December wedding anniversary that year, she and John began planning a long voyage, across the Pacific Ocean this time, to New Zealand, Australia, the Sandwich Islands, Hawaii, and Tasmania. They left by train for the West Coast in mid-January 1901 to begin the trip "down under." It ended when they arrived in Lafayette by train June 12, 1901, having survived a Union Pacific derailment on June 7 near Laramie, Wyoming. They were riding in the last car of the train, the only one to remain on the tracks in the accident.[1] While Lafayette newspapers may have approached the world travelers for interviews, they published no stories about them. Nor were any letters published while they were gone. Perhaps Helen decided to assemble pictures and notes from this trip and from the earlier trips to the Mediterranean, England, and Ireland and put them all into a book.

For a while, the summer of 1901 promised to be a leisurely one for Helen. It was shattered in late July when she wrote a scathing, almost classic letter about women, religion, churches, and hypocrisy for the *Chicago Record-Herald* in response to an Illinois minister's printed sermon in which he said he expected to be lonesome in heaven because of the scarcity of men there. Helen's response read like this:

> I suppose as a woman I should defend Rev. W. B. Leach in his belief in an Adamless Eden and hold that my sex will most largely people heaven. But I cannot agree with him.
>
> To be sure, there are more women than men found in the churches, but this does not signify that these women are more pious and more given to religious work that counts than the men are who remain outside the pews.
>
> The majority of women found in the churches are there because they are empty-headed. They do not give a rap for true religion, and nine-tenths of them could not repeat a thought uttered by the pastor in the hour they have dozed away in the pews. They go to church for a mild and easy sort of entertainment, for they are not mentally strong enough to apply themselves to self-entertainment, and they go to church to see and be seen, and to prevent being bored to death by themselves.
>
> Not one woman in 100 can tell the first tenet of the church creed to which she has subscribed for years. Surely, if her religion were well founded she would know her creed. If she happens to know anything of it she learned it, like a parrot, in a Sunday School when a child, and she can give no intelligent elucidation of the same.
>
> About the most these church-going women know of the Bible is its shortest verse, "Jesus wept," and they can sometimes stagger through the Lord's Prayer and the Ten Commandments.
>
> Given 100 men and 400 women, all church-going, there is more genuine piety in the 100 men than there is in the 400 women. What proof have I of this? Ask for a donation for some worthy object. The women will be moved to tears in their momentary flush of pity, but ask them to give the price of a pair of kid gloves or the latest belt ribbon—ask them to make genuine sacrifice and they will not do it.
>
> The men who work 18 hours out of 24 to support their families, men who hustle until nervous prostration

overtakes them, will hand over the cash and relieve suffering, though they may not snivel about it. Show me a woman who professes "sanctification" and she will almost invariably try to pay off her poor laundress in old clothes or cold victuals though she knows her poor servant has a half-dozen mouths to fill and bodies to clothe out of her meager earnings.

If the depth of piety of the majority of church-going women needs to be fathomed, examine the contents of the missionary boxes ready to be shipped to the poor heathen. They will be found to contain the rubbish that could not be sent to the junkshop because of its worthlessness.

Women will not in any large numbers make sacrifices for their religion, so we justly conclude that it is not more than skin deep. To be sure, they manage church socials and missionary teas, but they do this for the mild sort of social excitement and entertainment afforded them. It is not from religious zeal. Note the small number of rich women who give to any religious or educational institutions or for the uplifting of their own sex, or make sacrifice for the common good of humanity; such women will beg of men to give, but carefully guard their own treasury.

Men may not so generally hear the word, but they are doers of the word, and are therefore more genuinely religious than women.

It makes me weary to think of going to an Adamless Eden, and then to find only Brother Leach there, with all the women making golden slippers for him alone (for women are not loyal enough to their own sex to make slippers for each other). It would be no summer day picnic, not even for a female angel.

If, as some of us believe, we are to enter heaven on the same mental and spiritual plane as we leave the earth, to evolve through all eternity toward and into the great Godhead, it stands to reason that the best, most desirable and most numerous companions will be the men who have, through the strength of will and intellect, been translated into the better sphere of an eternal existence.

No, Brother Leach will find numerous brethren in Eden, if he gets there, and he will have no "corner" on golden slippers and dear sisters.[2]

This remarkable letter reflected the bottled-up disillusionment and disappointment that followed Helen's years of work with and for women, churches, political parties, and charitable institutions. It seemed, in many ways, to openly insult much of what she had struggled for; perhaps part of it also reflected her disgust with yet another staggering political loss—Bryan's in 1900. The letter coincided with the beginning of the end of Helen Gougar as a sought-after leader and speaker. It carried a bitter tone of someone who did not care as much anymore about other people. Photographs of Helen from this period show physical change as well. Approaching age fifty-eight, she was growing heavy, round-shouldered, and somewhat mis-shapen. Her cheeks were puffy, and eyeglasses masked the blue eyes that once flashed and darted in front of countless spot-lights. Her snow-white hair was thin, wild, and windblown, while her jaw jutted in a menacing, unbudging, righteous way. The *Lafayette Morning Journal* reprinted Helen's letter to the *Chicago Record-Herald* on July 29, and on July 30, lit into her views with its own editorial, "She Is Wholly Wrong." This, too, marked the breaking up of a long relationship of respect and tolerance.

On September 6, 1901, a half-crazed assassin shot President McKinley, who died a few days later leaving the nation with progressive Theodore Roosevelt as the chief executive. Early the next month, Helen received another jolt: the closing of the Young Women's Christian Home. The board said it closed the home because of chronic money problems and the inability to find a suitable matron. By early November, with some help from Helen, the board opened a different home with ten rooms.

CHAPTER 24

World Tour; Time to Chat

*E*arly in 1902, John and Helen Gougar had nearly finished plans for yet another long trip abroad, this time a veritable world tour that would span ten months and provide Helen with additional material for a book.

On January 31 and February 1 and 2, according to a *Lafayette Morning Journal* item, Helen spoke to labor union audiences in Dixon and Rockford, Illinois. In early February, she scorched President Roosevelt's appointment of Iowa's Governor Leslie Mortier Shaw as secretary of the treasury. In a letter to the *Journal*, she nailed Shaw, a Denison, Iowa, lawyer, banker, and politician, for having pardoned 473 criminals. "It is no wonder," she concluded, "that anarchy and lawlessness run riot over the country when the governor of any state can make such a record as this."[1]

The remainder of that winter and into the spring and summer of 1902 may have been the period when Helen produced another book called *Strange Incidents in One Life*. Such a book is mentioned in her obituary a few years later, but no copies or library references can be traced today. Possibly it was an unpublished account of life on the lecture circuit as well as on world travels.

By spring, Helen had begun to be friendly with a protégé, Bertha Foresman, "society editor" of the *Call*, a struggling

195

Lafayette evening daily newspaper. All the Lafayette papers mentioned in late June that the Gougars would leave on their world tour on October 6, 1902, from Vancouver, British Columbia. On February 25, 1903, the *Lafayette Morning Journal* published Helen's long letter, dated January 3, from Java. Helen probably sent the letter first to her sister Addie Sherry, then a widow living on a farm southwest of Lafayette. In the letter, Helen described the volcanic, mountainous beauty of this island 800 miles south of the equator. She said both she and John were well, "though Mr. G. tires easily and we cannot travel as rapidly as if he (not I!) were younger." Helen indicated she was writing a series of dispatches about her trip for publication, perhaps for papers in New York or Chicago or for a magazine. Between October and January, she said the couple traveled to Japan, Hong Kong, China, and Singapore. She spoke of the intense equatorial heat, the lazy, slow-motion nature of the barefooted, sarong-clad Javan natives and said, "I have longed for an hour of our home, snapping cold weather for the past two months, for we have been in the hot countries."

Helen wrote that she and John had become used to ocean travel and neither suffered from seasickness any more. She said they were surprised to find electric lights, automobiles, typewriters, "and everything else about as we have it in our cities. The world seems small after all." Helen rated Java "a fine place for winter residence if a person cares to come so far, but California is more desirable a place than any we have seen yet. One wants to see [other] countries once, then stay within God's country, America, for permanent residence." In another part of the letter, Helen's views about race emerged rather bluntly: "I am convinced by what I have seen in the Orient that the Anglo-Saxon race is the one to finally dominate the world."[2]

Later, in a letter to an Indianapolis friend published in July 1903, Helen showed little respect or appreciation for Russia:

> Russia has a miserable government of absolutism. The masses are desperately poor, ignorant and hopeless. Aristocracy, backed by an immense standing army and police, public and spy, and a priestcraft that is the worst we have ever met within any country, tax and rob to the greatest extent possible.
>
> No one can visit Russia without having a contempt for its government and a deep pity for its subjects. The passport system and the complete espionage of individuals and the press censorship are more like the practices of the Dark Ages than of the 20th century spirit of progress.

We have enjoyed our trip, we have sat on throne chairs and stepped into the gilded chariots of empresses and queens; and withal, we will enjoy the solid comforts of home and the American way of living.[3]

The Gougars returned from the trip on July 12, 1903. The *Lafayette Evening Call* recapitulated:

They were gone nine months and 15 days and traveled many thousands of miles. The trip was made at leisure and all the points visited were carefully studied. Mr. and Mrs. Gougar came from New York, where they landed in the "Wilhelm de Grosse" after a trip of six and a half days from Bremen, Germany. The boat carried 750 immigrants and a vessel that landed the day before brought over 2,000. Mr. and Mrs. Gougar remained four days in New York.

Mrs. Gougar decided to combine business with pleasure and wrote many interesting newspaper letters while on the trip. She also occupied a portion of her spare time jotting down important and interesting facts observed by her in different lands visited.

These she will combine in a book form and as she has the work nearly finished her friends will soon have the pleasure of reading of the journey.

Mr. and Mrs. Gougar visited, among other places, China, Japan, the Philippines, Singapore, India, Java, Ceylon, Egypt, Hungary, Russia, Sweden, Norway, Denmark, Germany and also touched at Cherbourg, France, and Southampton, England.

Where it was necessary they employed a guide and an interpreter. Speaking of the trip, Mrs. Gougar said: "I was most favorably impressed with Egypt and Japan. They are to me the most beautiful and interesting countries. After all, we have decided that the world is not half so large as it seems."[4]

The Gougars spent the remainder of the summer at leisure. On September 12, 1903, Helen spoke in the Methodist Church in West Point on the world tour and her observations about foreign Christian missions. On September 30, a speaker at Purdue University paid homage to Helen, Frances Willard, and Anna Dickinson when he said they were the "three greatest lady orators in the United States." But except for a few talks on foreign missions and the progressive government of New Zealand, Helen devoted the rest of 1903 to the typewriter. Her consuming project was the travel book *Forty Thousand Miles of World Wandering*, in which she planned to reflect in detail on the people, politics, land, and customs of every foreign country she had visited. Helen also planned to furnish the book with black-and-white pictures she or hired photographers had taken, or which she had purchased abroad.

On November 30, 1903, Helen briefly returned to an old love—newspaper column writing. She wrote for the *Lafayette Evening Call* under the title "Weekly Chat with the Call Readers." Unfortunately, the *Call* was in wobbly financial circumstances and undergoing management changes. The "chats" turned out to be hardly weekly at all. The next one appeared December 1, just one day after the debut; another on December 7; the fourth appeared on December 10 in the newly combined *Home Journal and Weekly Call*; and the fifth on December 15 (repeated verbatim on December 16), after which the paper suspended the "chats" until February 24, 1904, and then dropped them. The "chat" columns were long, laborious, highly opinionated, and at times obnoxiously egotistical: "I went to church yesterday. All persons ought to go to church at least once every Sunday, no matter whether they get just such meat as they think they ought to have or not. They probably get better spiritual food than they would provide for themselves by communing with self at home."[5]

Somehow, Helen's column-writing had lost much of its pep. Perhaps she dashed the columns off while her mind was tired from other things, such as the travel book. And she had been a woman of leisure sufficiently long that her work sprang from memory and old impressions rather than the sharp edge of daily combat and discourse with people, crowds, and ideas. Her work also now indicated that she read less and was rewriting her own old themes: churches, pastors, government, men, women, the rearing of children, families, crime, charitable works; but the prose was tired. Some of her columns even lacked unity, skipping randomly from some obscure pastor's sermon on "Women" to the government of France. It was uninspired, hack journalism which bore little reflection of the mind and the talent behind it. On December 16, 1903, though, she did write two of her more significant "chat" passages:

> It is gratifying that many of the leading university faculties are repudiating football and will have no more of it in their institutions. Already we have "professors of football." Before long we may expect to see chronicled among the faculties of these institutions "professors of prize fighting" and "professors of bullfights." It is but a

few paces from the present conduct of the popular game to the matador and his ring.

An old farmer said to me the other day, "If my boy has to study athletics on the football team I will keep him home and let him study his athletics behind the plow and my old team of white horses."

Unless the conduct of this game is radically changed many a young man will be denied the privilege of a university training on account of the impression being made on the public mind by the wild craze for football.

A new name for divorce is "disespoused." It has come to such a pass that when one alludes to a widow the question is asked, "Is she a grass or a sod?" Every fifth case on the court calendar of Tippecanoe County is for divorce. Drunkenness of the husband is the cause of over ninetenths of all divorces. Stop the liquor traffic and the divorce mills will soon cease to grind.

CHAPTER 25

What the World Needs Now

*H*elen's December 7, 1903, "chat" column brought one stinging rebuke, published as a letter in the *Lafayette Evening Call* on January 15, 1904. In her column, Helen had upbraided young married couples who paid for household furnishings or other goods by installments. She contended that this was a "ruinous habit." She maintained that people should always live within their incomes and urged "total abstinence from debt." The reply, from a Waukegan, Illinois, woman named Winona Fitts, a local equal rights club leader, said in part:

> If these ideas of Mrs. Gougar's were to be carried into effect, civilization itself would be set back more than one cog in the wheel.
> Women, as a rule, despise and fear debts, and through this fear are kept back and occupy a negative position in the business world today. This fear of debt is of the feminine gender. Men of broad scope, successful men, assume debts as a matter of means and ways toward successful accomplishments. To run in debt and fail is no longer a "hanging matter."

The letter continued with an especially well-aimed shot: "William Jennings Bryan has sent word across the water that the solution to the Irish land problems is to 'sell the land to the tenants upon the installment of payment.' In conclusion, let me advise all salaried people to assume financial responsibilities in the shape of houses, lands, life insurance, or for the necessities and comforts of life."[1]

Helen Gougar herself seemed to be disenchanted with Bryan after his presidential election losses in 1896 and 1900 and by his solutions to Ireland's problems. By late February 1904, Helen expressed support for Congressman William Randolph Hearst the newspaper tycoon from New York. Both Democrats, who longed for a winner, and conservative Republicans, who did not like the colorful, crowd-pleasing, progressive Teddy Roosevelt, billed Hearst as a potential presidential candidate. On February 23, 1904, the *Lafayette Evening Call* printed Helen's assessment of Hearst, an acquaintance of several years. She said she liked him because he was "a strict moralist and holds women in high esteem . . . no vicious sentiments or vulgarity are permitted voice in his publications . . . he is a devoted advocate of the principle of 'equal rights for all, special privilege for none' . . . he is an aggressive foe of the new form of human slavery known as trusts . . . he is the friend of legitimate capital but the aggressive enemy of predatory monopoly. With such a man for a candidate on a wise and conservative platform, the Democratic Party will doubtless make a lively campaign."[2] On March 24, 1904, the Tippecanoe County Democratic Central Committee endorsed Hearst for president, possibly influenced by Helen's testimonial.

Helen spoke of the work of foreign Christian missions on May 4, 1904, at a West Lafayette Methodist church mission society meeting. She said that, before her world travels, she had been opposed or at least indifferent to missions, but now she felt that "the only bright spot in all the Orient is the work of the foreign missions."[3]

On July 5, 1904, John, Helen, and Addie Sherry left Lafayette by train for a ten-day visit to the Saint Louis World's Fair and the Democratic National Convention. To their disappointment, the convention bypassed Hearst in favor of Judge Alton B. Parker of New York as the candidate for president to oppose Teddy Roosevelt.

On Saturday, July 16, Helen left again for the Illinois chautauqua circuit for speeches about New Zealand. Then, on August 10 at Tecumseh Trail Park up the river from Lafayette, she engaged in a favorite, well-mined medium—the temperance rally. Her speech contained old arguments fitted up with new statistics and was entitled: "The Financial Side of the Saloon Question." Among her points:

> If the $1.7 billion spent in this country in the last year for liquor had been diverted into the legitimate avenues of trade in building and furnishing homes, churches, schools, etc., industrial and economic questions facing the nation would be largely settled.
>
> The saloon is the nursery of the poorhouse, the penitentiary and the insane asylum. Every dollar spent for liquor is a signpost directing the American people to destruction. The organized liquor forces of the country are the greatest trust in the land.

Helen even resurrected the old complaint about the beer stand which would be in business again in a few weeks at the Tippecanoe County Fair. She condemned those who would run it, permit it, and patronize it.[4]

Lafayette's and Indiana's interest in temperance was reviving for an unexpected reason. The ambitious attorney and former Congressman J. Frank Hanly, who had been practicing law in Lafayette for several years now, had in April 1904 gotten the nomination for governor from the Republicans. Hanly had advocated prohibition legislation, at least on a local option basis, in his early 1904 campaigning. Although Helen Gougar had been no great admirer of Hanly and was certainly not a Republican in 1904, she approved of prohibition.

On Sunday night, September 11, Helen repeated her address about foreign missions for the West Lafayette Methodist Church. Then on September 23, she mailed off the thick, typewritten manuscript of her book, *Forty Thousand Miles of World Wandering*, to the Monarch Book Company of Chicago. She gave her New Zealand talk to a Lafayette audience September 28 and on October 3 left for Chicago to discuss the book with Monarch editors. Helen made several more trips to Chicago on book business during that fall when, in days gone by, she would have been on the platform in the heat of a presidential campaign. For Helen's sake, maybe it was best that she left the 1904 campaign alone. Roosevelt was unstoppable. In November, he defeated Judge Parker by 336 electoral votes to 140.

On December 10, the Gougars entertained thirty friends at a dinner in Castle Cottage celebrating their forty-first anniversary and John's sixty-eighth birthday. The *Lafayette Evening Call* reported that Castle Cottage was decorated with red and white carnations and that a photographer took "flash light pictures."[5]

When 1905 arrived, Helen anticipated an exciting event—her book rolled off the press at Chicago in January. A thick, expensively bound book, it opened with a picture of Helen smiling broadly, a large rose at her bosom, and a facsimile autograph: "Cordially Yours, Helen M. Gougar." The dedication read: "To my husband, whose love of travel and desire to promote my pleasure and happiness have enabled me to visit many parts of the world and encircle the globe, this volume is affectionately inscribed." The 432-page book measured approximately seven by nine inches; was printed on thick, slick paper stock; had a dark brown cover; weighed three pounds and six ounces; and contained 270 pictures, three in color. For the title page, Helen borrowed a theme from Samuel Johnson:

> All travel has its advantages. If the traveler visits better countries, he may learn to improve his own; and if fortune carries him to worse, may learn to enjoy his own.
>
> The use of traveling is to regulate imagination by reality and instead of thinking how things may be, to see them as they are.[6]

In a brief preface, Helen explained her own aims and philosophies:

> I care less for ancient history and ruins in stone than I do for the sights, conditions and customs under which the human family is living at the present. I have aimed to give an accurate account of my daily experiences and the scenes I have witnessed.
>
> A tour of the world is so much time spent in going to school. The one great lesson I have learned is that the people of the earth are of one household, at the head of which is the great divine Master, and just to the extent His teachings are accepted are the children of men physically, mentally, morally and spiritually happy.
>
> When these facts are universally recognized, then will the immense treasure now expended in the armament of nations to promote the inhumanities of war be diverted into building homes of comfort, schools of learning and spiritual development, and the promotion of justice between man and man, and among all the nations of the earth.
>
> Electricity, commercialism and Christianity are making for the oneness of the whole world, in which glad time all will accept the great truth of the common brotherhood of man, and the Fatherhood of God.

She organized the book into thirty chapters, dwelling on such topics as Yokohama, Tokyo, the Japanese home, travel in

Japan, southern Japan, Hong Kong, China, the Philippines, Singapore, Java, Ceylon, India, Cairo, the Nile, Austria, Russia, Moscow, Stockholm, Denmark, the islands of the Pacific, New Zealand, Tasmania, and Australia. She wrote detailed and factual chapters, yet closed several with strong editorial opinions. Some examples:

> It is a good thing for the civilized world that the Chinese millions do not know their power. Before coming to this knowledge they must be humanized. (p. 89)

> At this moment Japan and Russia are engaged in the bloodiest war in all history. From the present outlook Japan will be victorious over Russia. (p. 347)

> The Christian missionary, whose work has been slow and most discouraging, sees his labors, like an accumulating snowball, grow larger and larger at every additional turn, until hope sees its reward in the next century in the redemption of India from the ignorance and idolatry of the past.
> India is an interesting study, and she should be visited by the traveler who wishes to know the nations of the earth, either as a passing picture or for a deeper study of the races and possibilities of the human family. (p. 221)

> The one bright, sweet hope and memory of a visit to the Orient is the work of Christian men and women sent from foreign shores to labor among the inhabitants thereof. (p. 283)

> My tour of the world has taught me that the treatment of woman is a perfect gauge to the degree of civilization attained by a nation. (p. 383)

> To be a good and happy traveler . . . a fine landscape must sometimes atone for an indifferent supper, and an interesting ruin or picture charm away the remembrance of a hard bed. The bee, though it finds every rose has a thorn, comes back loaded with honey from his rambles, and why should not other tourists do the same? (p. 432)

Forty Thousand Miles of World Wandering never became much of a seller by book industry standards. *Out to Old Aunt Mary's* and *A Defective Santa Claus* were two of the reasons. These two works in a long list of volumes by the beloved Indiana poet James Whitcomb Riley also appeared in the bookstores early in 1905 and overshadowed Helen's work.

On March 15, 1905, the *Lafayette Daily Courier* reported that John and Helen Gougar had left for a six-week vacation trip

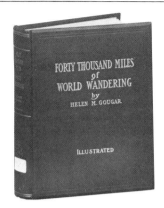

Published in 1905, Forty Thousand Miles of World Wandering *was Helen M. Gougar's last major work. Its frontispiece showed an aging yet elegant author.*

to California. They returned on May 12. Helen lectured on "The Condition of the Negro and What to Do with Him" on Sunday, May 28, 1905, at Lafayette's all-black African Methodist Episcopal Church. There is no record of her conclusions.

The same week, Helen's long-time friend and sometimes critic and adversary, Mary Livermore, died at the age of eighty-four in Melrose, Massachusetts. And on August 31, her old friend "Harry Burton" died in Argentine, Kansas. The former railroad fireman and temperance warrior, actually named Joseph T. Landrey, founded the *Argentine Republic* after selling his *Temperance Herald*, turning its editorship over to Helen in 1881.

On February 13, 1906, John and Helen left Lafayette for a trip to the West Indies on the steamer *Praetoria*. The ship departed New York on the seventeenth. The itinerary included Bermuda, Cuba, the Bahamas, and other Caribbean islands. While the Gougars were at sea, Susan B. Anthony died in Rochester, New York, at the age of eighty-six.

IX

LIKE

AN EVENING

GONE...

A thousand ages in thy sight
  Are like an evening gone,
Short as the watch that ends the night
  Before the rising sun.
Time, like an ever-rolling stream,
  Bears all its sons away;
They fly, forgotten, as a dream dies
  At the op'ning day.

From "Our God, Our Help in Ages Past," Isaac Watts,
1719, and William Croft, 1708

CHAPTER 26

End of a Rocky Road

Now, in 1906, John and Helen Gougar were semi-retired "old folks" in an energetic city that was plunging into the twentieth century with gusto. A corporation financed and built an interurban line from Lafayette to Indianapolis. Officials took steps to build a large YMCA and a gymnasium for rapidly growing Purdue University. Home Hospital, a product of Helen's early work with the Home for the Friendless, opened a two-story brick addition. The venerable opera house where Helen had spoken so many times closed through disuse; later a meatpacking magnate reopened it as a theater. Purdue University added schools and departments and developed an alumni association. John T. McCutcheon, a Tippecanoe County native and Purdue grad, made a name as a cartoonist in Chicago. His brother, George Barr McCutcheon, wrote novels such as *Graustark* and *Castle Craneycrow*. A nine-hole golf course opened in Columbian Park. New railroad depots were built. The operator of a famous horse farm east of Lafayette received the town's first radio message via Marconi wireless from a brother aboard a ship 1,500 miles away on the Atlantic Ocean. A rollerskate polo craze developed, and a Lafayette professional team, the Sycamores, played for four seasons. An Oldsmobile agency opened. J. Frank Hanly became governor. The motion picture came to town, first in the summer of 1905 at a firemen's benefit show, then by 1906 in a theater across the street from where a church had stood. Lafayette built a stockyard, remodeled the 1885 courthouse, raised $5,800 for victims of the San Francisco earthquake, welcomed 25,000 visitors to a GAR encampment, and heard Bryan, still the great orator, on November 15, 1906, at a YMCA benefit. (Bryan always paid his respects to his old friends at Castle Cottage.) Lafayette built homes and bridges and blacktopped streets, put up churches and opened a public swimming pool, cheered college and high school football, loved the new game of basketball, and backed a semipro baseball team in a ball park near the Wabash River.[1]

The Young Women's Christian Home report for 1906 listed Helen Gougar, near the end of the *Lafayette Daily Courier's* account, among the donors of food, bedding, clothing, and furniture. She made chautauqua speeches on temperance in upstate New York for two weeks in August 1906 and gave a talk in a private home on October 10 to a WCTU chapter.

Helen spoke on "Municipal Suffrage" for the WCTU in Willard Hall on November 9, 1906 and at the Soldiers Home November 11. For the December 10 wedding anniversary and seventieth birthday party for John, the Gougars invited 300 guests to Castle Cottage. The next day Helen hosted 100 young women for a program on woman's rights and woman suffrage. On January 31, 1907, Helen gave her New Zealand lecture as a benefit to a new English Lutheran church congregation which had taken over the WCTU's Willard Hall. During January and February, Helen and other women from around the state lobbied ardently for woman suffrage and prohibition legislation at the Indianapolis sessions of the 1907 legislature. Outright prohibition simply did not have enough support for a serious attempt, but the old approach of "high license" got a serious airing before it was defeated in committee. As usual, the prohibitionists were the targets of harsh criticism, and Helen Gougar heard much of it back home in Lafayette.

The 1907 woman suffrage effort came close to success, with the Indiana Senate evenly divided over the issue. Again the matter failed in the House, though, and the *Lafayette Daily Courier* continued to hammer woman suffrage into the ground. On February 20, 1907, the *Courier*—once a springboard for the rising young Helen Gougar but now under much more conservative management—editorialized:

> For the sake of the women and the homes of the state,
> it is to be hoped that there will be no foolish experiments

tried of giving women a voice in even local matters of
political nature.

The truth of the matter is that the women, the majority of them, do not want the right of suffrage. They
haven't time for such things. Probably one woman in 10
understands the political matters that affect the country.
She doesn't want to understand them. She has more elevating and congenial duties that keep her busy.

The proper rearing of her children is more to her than
the rise and fall of whole political parties. It is a safe venture to say that if the question of woman suffrage should
be presented to the women of Indiana themselves for
settlement they would reject it.

The claim is made that women in politics would ele-
vate and purify it. That is a most fallacious belief. The
politics of the world differs little in one place from another.
There is much that is bad in all politics and there is some
that is good. But women could not eradicate the bad. Instead of placing politics on a higher plane they would only
bedraggle themselves in the mire.

The women will thank the lawmakers if they are not
given any voice in the government of even the schools
except such voice as they exercise through their influences
over father, brother, husband and son.[2]

In early March 1907, John and Helen left Lafayette for a
six-week trip through the South, returning April 11. On May
3, Helen spoke on "The Home Situation for Children" at a
WCTU meeting in Castle Cottage. The *Arena*, the Boston-
based national magazine devoted to religious, political, and
cultural thought, published several of Helen's essays in 1906 on
such topics as "America in the Philippines" and "Shall Educated
Chinamen Be Welcomed to Our Shores?" The *Arena* printed a
most complimentary profile of Helen, too, in a piece about
"Noble Type of Twentieth-Century American Womanhood."
It described her as "strong, incisive, logical as a writer, possess-
ing the power of presenting her subject in an engaging manner
not infrequently enhanced with wit, humor and satire, while
sincerity, earnestness and clarity of thought are marked charac-
teristics of all her work." The article, by *Arena* editor Benjamin
Orange Flower, placed Helen's life and work in this perspec-
tive:

> The civilization of the 19th century in the New World
> was enriched by the influence of the most illustrious group
> of public-spirited women that up to that time had appeared
> in the life of any nation.

Indeed, they may be said to have been the advance guard that ushered in the larger and freer day for woman. The voices of most of this chosen band are silent now, but their splendid work and influence live and blossom in all that is best in our civic, social and domestic life, and their names will be revered more and more as the years vanish and the greatness of their work and the heroism of the stand they so courageously took in the face of a growing conservatism is more and more appreciated.

Dorothea Lynde Dix is only today beginning to be valued at anything like her worth. She wrought far more than any score of men in the 19th century to improve the condition of the insane in America and Europe. Lucretia Mott, Lydia Maria Child, Harriet Beecher Stowe, Julia Ward Howe and Mary A. Livermore are only particularly brilliant lights among the historic coterie of American women who dealt Herculean blows for the emancipation of the black man while ever working for the elevation of the moral ideals of the people.

Lucy Stone Blackwell, Elizabeth Cady Stanton, and Susan B. Anthony were noble representatives of the woman's suffrage movement in its early days, as they were also effective defenders of democratic ideals and the vital demands of an expanding civilization.

Later came a noteworthy group of younger workers who fought not the less ably or valiantly for humanity's weal and the moral progress of the people. Among these apostles of emancipated womanhood Frances E. Willard and Helen M. Gougar stand preeminent. Miss Willard has passed from view, but her great work for temperance, for social purity and for juster social conditions has left its imprint on the nation and will be felt for generations to come.

Mrs. Gougar alone of all this chosen band remains strong with the vitality of a fine intellect in its rich maturity.[3]

Helen summoned that strength, vitality, and intellect toward the end of May 1907 to write an article for the *Lafayette Leader* describing woman suffrage's progress abroad. She had planned to write an immense book about the full, worldwide history of woman suffrage. While Helen and John were also planning a long winter trip to South America in 1908, Helen tinkered with revisions and expansion of her old book *Matthew Peters*.

She wakened and arose in early sunlight just before 6 A.M.

on Thursday, June 6, 1907, but suddenly felt ill and dizzy. She sank to her knees and died even before the startled John or the housekeepers nearby could guide her back to bed or telephone a doctor. She had been treated for suspected heart trouble for about a year, it was disclosed later, but at the time the fatal attack was wholly unexpected.

CHAPTER 27

Old Times That Are Soon Forgotten

The *Lafayette Daily Courier's* front page contained four decks of headlines:

HELEN M. GOUGAR EXPIRES SUDDENLY

NOTED ADVOCATE OF WOMAN'S RIGHTS DROPS DEAD AT HER HOME IN THIS CITY

WAS APPARENTLY IN BEST OF HEALTH WHEN SHE RETIRED

HEART TROUBLE ENDS ACTIVE LIFE OF ONE OF THE LEADING WOMAN SUFFRAGISTS AND TEMPERANCE ORATORS IN THE COUNTRY— HISTORY OF HER CAREER

The obituary reported that Helen's sisters and brother were still living.[1] The next day, the *Lafayette Morning Journal* added these editorial opinions:

> Not always consistent, not always logical, and not always charitable in judgment, she was always earnest. It mattered not whether she was making speeches for the Republican or Democratic Party, she convinced the public that she was in dead earnest.

> A woman of less ability, power and earnestness could not have made the political changes she did without losing value as an adviser.
>
> Mrs. Gougar drew the audiences, and she never failed to entertain them. She was graduated into the political arena at a time when it was considered profitable to abuse one's opponents. In turn Mrs. Gougar arraigned the two old parties in scathing language that delighted sympathetic audiences.
>
> A woman of such force and earnestness would necessarily be bitter in her hatreds. Mrs. Gougar's temperament was that of the agitator; it was her mission to arouse and awaken.
>
> Mrs. Gougar was a remarkable woman. She thrived on antagonism, knew not the meaning of fear and had all the zeal of a martyr.[2]

On the afternoon of June 7, the members of the Lafayette WCTU voted to attend the funeral as a group. The Second Presbyterian Church pastor performed the rites the next day in Castle Cottage. Daniel Simms, a corporation lawyer, school board Democrat, and a Methodist, gave an address about Helen's life and work. There were six active and six honorary pallbearers. Telegrams, letters, and telephone calls with messages of condolence flowed in for days. For the funeral, Castle Cottage was packed with people and walled with baskets of flowers. Helen Gougar was buried beneath a gray marble headstone in a cemetery two miles northeast of Lafayette.

On Sunday, June 9, the *Lafayette Leader's* weekly edition summarized the events of the death and funeral and added editorially:

> No lawyer ever came into court with his facts better arranged than Mrs. Gougar when she went before the public. A woman with her talents and her fearlessness, with a less aggressive or combatative nature, might have made her influence and power felt over a much greater number of people; but her belief that she was right was so deeply fixed in her mind that she had little patience with those who could not see as she saw.
>
> She did not live to see the ideas she advocated framed into laws, but the seed she has sown will yet bear fruit.[3]

The *Leader* thus touched upon an interesting point. Within twelve years, the United States did put total prohibition into effect. The experiment ended with repeal in 1933. In 1920, thirteen years after her death, the nation did grant the power of the ballot to women. But experience has shown that it has made no difference either in the war against dirty politics, crime, or sin. For Helen Gougar, prohibition and woman suffrage might well have been limited victories indeed.

For John Gougar, life went on without her. He lived another eighteen years in Castle Cottage. He learned to play bridge and bought an automobile. John was a thin, wispy relic of a man, beloved as a downtown character, walking to his law office, puttering about with the books and papers, visiting the bank, telling stories of the olden days. "John was just a gem," an elderly Lafayette woman recalled in a remembrance in 1982, not long before her own death at age ninety-five. "I remember going to the Gougar house once when I was a girl of maybe fourteen. I remember John as being kind and friendly while Helen was . . . well . . . rather hard to get along with. She treated her hired help quite severely. She was not an entirely agreeable person. But she was smart and believed in doing things the right way.

"I remember going to a ladies' tea or some such function with my mother. It was the first time any of us had ever seen, or heard about, or tasted a casaba melon. I don't know where Helen got it. Probably had tasted one during her travels and had them sent. I don't know why I would remember that!"

In later years, this girl of fourteen would work at the bank where John was a director and frequent visitor. "He was always friendly and easygoing. He always wore a gray felt hat," she recalled. "And when people ever asked him about Helen, he always spoke of her, and her work, with the greatest pride. He really was a gem."

In 1925, John Gougar died suddenly at the age of eighty-eight in Castle Cottage, just as Helen had. His will, covering the $200,000 estate he and Helen had earned, was filed for probate in Tippecanoe Superior Court. He gave Castle Cottage to Addie Sherry. Today it is the Landis-Loy Mortuary, 914 Columbia Street, with a plaque telling of the building's history and interesting occupants located near the front steps.

Many of the nation's newspapers of 1907 carried wire service stories about Helen Gougar's death. The *Message*, official organ of the Indiana WCTU, eulogized her. As far away as Portland, Oregon, the *Woman's Tribune* published Helen's photograph and a long obituary on the front page of the June 29 issue. The funeral eulogy delivered by Daniel Simms and copied in the *Leader* concluded with these thoughts:

Her contribution to civilization, to the forward march of progress, has been of great and lasting and beneficial effect. Her name will live and go down in history indissolubly connected with those of Anthony and Willard.

She believed that in a long and tireless march of civilization, God's children all, without respect to sex, should take their place. She knew full well that the unit of civilization was the family—the home. She knew that ignorance is the bane of the race, and that intelligence, knowledge and wisdom is the morning light that leads to God.

The talents which God, in His wisdom, had entrusted to her have been returned, burnished, improved and multiplied many fold.

She was courageous, and ever ready for a battle—indeed, her soul thrived on conflict. She wrought along and upon lines that made for the betterment of mankind; and may we fight life's battles as fearlessly and courageously, and discharge life's duties as nobly and as truly as did she whose mortal remains we today consign to the tomb, and whose spirit has taken its flight and returned to the God who gave it.[4]

So the life and work of Helen Gougar ended in tears and sadness and pretty words. But history would write a sadder ending still. For Helen Gougar's name would not, as Daniel Simms so sweetly predicted, "go down in history indissolubly connected with those of Anthony and Willard." Instead she would be forgotten. Instead she would vanish from memory like the countless ranks and files of other soldiers in that mighty army who, in their own ways, in their own lands, in their own times, spent their lives marching where the saints have trod, urging a better life for us all.

NOTES

Editor's note: Frequently in the following, a note will show as its source a Lafayette newspaper while the text will attribute the same quotation to another newspaper in another city. According to the author, during the period in which Helen Gougar lived, one newspaper would regularly quote an article directly from another one and give credit to the original source.

I. FROM FARM TO FORUM

CHAPTER 1. **Childhood and Beyond**

1. "Gougar-Mandler," *Lafayette Daily Courier*, 8 Mar. 1883.

2. Lillian A. Comer, historian and archivist, Hillsdale College, Hillsdale, Mich., letter dated 29 Jan. 1975, to Mary E. Anthrop, Lafayette.

CHAPTER 2. **Sweet Land of Liberty**

Extensive use was made in the sweeping review of U.S. history before 1860 of the high school textbook *Rise of the American Nation* by Lewis Paul Todd and Merle Curti (New York: Harcourt Brace Jovanovich, 1977).

1. Blanche Foster Boruff, *Women of Indiana* (Indianapolis: Matthew Farson, 1941), 13.

2. Ibid., 31.

CHAPTER 3. **Lafayette: Young and Confused**

1. Descriptions of life in early Lafayette were selected from city directories, assorted newspaper articles, and from *Headline History of Lafayette*, a compilation by the author in 1977–79. This unpublished reference document was presented to the Tippecanoe County Historical Association and is housed in its Alameda McCollough Library, Tenth and South streets, Lafayette.

2. Cecil S. Webb, *Historical Growth of the Schools of Lafayette, Indiana* (Lafayette : Lafayette School Corporation, 1972), 5.

3. Ibid., 7.

4. Helen M. Gougar, *Matthew Peters: Foreign Immigrant* (Lafayette: Browne, Murphy & Co., 1898).

5. "Gougar-Mandler," *Lafayette Daily Courier*, 8 Mar. 1883.

CHAPTER 4. **Marriage and Mission**

1. Edward T. James, Janet Wilson, and Paul S. Boyer, *Notable American Women, 1607–1950*, (Cambridge: Belknap Press of Harvard University Press, 1971), 11: 69–71.
2. "Gougar-Mandler," *Lafayette Daily Courier*, 8 Mar. 1883.
3. Ibid.
4. "Gougar-Mandler," *Lafayette Daily Courier*, 27 Feb. 1883.
5. Eleanor Flexner, *Century of Struggle*, (Cambridge: Belknap Press of Harvard University Press, 1959), 151–52.
6. "The Woman Suffrage Convention," *Lafayette Daily Courier*, 10 Nov. 1869.

II. WAITING GAME

CHAPTER 5. **A Modest Beginning**

1. "Gougar-Mandler," *Lafayette Daily Courier*, 8 Mar. 1883.
2. "Woman Suffrage Convention," *Lafayette Daily Courier*, 25 Sept. 1869.
3. "Mrs. Livermore at the Lahr House," *Lafayette Daily Courier*, 5 Oct. 1869.
4. "Woman Suffrage Convention," *Lafayette Daily Courier*, 10 Nov. 1869.
5. Ida Husted Harper, *Life and Work of Susan B. Anthony* (Indianapolis: Bowen-Merrill Co., 1898), 1: 267.
6. "The Suffrage Convention," *Lafayette Daily Courier*, 12 Nov. 1869.
7. "The Home for the Friendless," *Lafayette Daily Courier*, 13 Nov. 1869.
8. "Y.M.C.A.," *Lafayette Daily Courier*, 19 Nov. 1870.
9. "The Lafayette Home," *Lafayette Daily Courier*, 1 Dec. 1869.
10. "Y.M.C.A.," *Lafayette Daily Courier*, 10 Dec. 1870.
11. Harper, 1: 380.
12. "Miss Anthony's Lecture," *Lafayette Daily Courier*, 8 Apr. 1871.
13. "Y.M.C.A. Literary Reunion," *Lafayette Daily Courier*, 16 Dec. 1871.

CHAPTER 6. **Patience Rewarded**

1. "Winter's Art Union," *Lafayette Daily Courier*, 30 Dec. 1872.
2. "Temperance Meeting Last Night," *Lafayette Morning Journal*, 24 July 1873.
3. "Southern Relief Committee," *Lafayette Morning Journal*, 21 Oct. 1873, and "The Relief Committee," *Lafayette Morning Journal*, 23 Oct. 1873.

4. Jacob Piatt Dunn, *Indiana and Indianans* (Chicago: American Historical Society, 1919), 4: 1057.

5. Ibid., 1059.

6. "Temperance Convention," *Lafayette Daily Courier*, 14 Feb. 1874.

7. "Mass Temperance Meeting," *Lafayette Daily Courier*, 3 Mar. 1874.

8. "Temperance," *Lafayette Daily Courier*, 13 Mar. 1874.

9. "Temperance," *Lafayette Daily Courier*, 27 Mar. 1874, and "Additional Local," *Lafayette Daily Courier*, 28 Mar. 1874.

10. Boruff, 94–96.

11. "Temperance," *Lafayette Daily Courier*, 17 Oct. 1874.

12. From *Headline History of Lafayette*, 1979.

13. Dunn, 4: 1060.

14. Boruff, 24, 26, 31, 42.

15. "Gougar-Mandler," *Lafayette Daily Courier*, 8 Mar. 1883.

16. "The Blue," *Lafayette Morning Journal*, 29 Apr. 1878.

III. RISE OF A FEMALE FANATIC

CHAPTER 7. **As a Writer: More than Bric-a-Brac**

1. "Bric-a-Brac," *Lafayette Daily Courier*, 2 Nov. 1878. All further references to this column appear in the text of chapter 7.

2. "Meeting of the Parlor Club," *Lafayette Sunday Times*, 18 May 1879.

CHAPTER 8. **As a Speaker: "Eloquent and Logical"**

1. From *Headline History of Lafayette*, 1979.

2. "Personal," *Lafayette Daily Courier*, 11 Oct. 1879.

3. "Our Gentlemen," *Lafayette Sunday Times*, 23 Nov. 1879.

4. "A Plea for Homeless Children," *Lafayette Daily Courier*, 27 Jan. 1880.

5. "Mrs. Gougar at Fowler," *Lafayette Sunday Times*, 15 Feb. 1880.

6. "Card from Mrs. Gougar," *Lafayette Sunday Times*, 21 Mar. 1880.

7. "Mrs. Gougar's Lecture," *Lafayette Sunday Times*, 18 Apr. 1880.

8. "The Libel Suit," *Lafayette Daily Courier*, 17 Apr. 1880.

9. "Bric-a-Brac," *Lafayette Daily Courier*, 8 May 1880.

10. Harper, 2:515–17.

11. "Bric-a-Brac," *Lafayette Daily Courier*, 29 May 1880.

12. "Feminine Franchise," *Lafayette Daily Courier*, 17 June 1880.

13. "Bric-a-Brac," *Lafayette Daily Courier*, 7 Aug. 1880.

14. Ibid., 28 Aug. 1880.

15. "Blue Ribbon Lecture Course," *Lafayette Daily Courier*, 18 Dec. 1880.

16. "Working for Women," *Lafayette Daily Courier*, 28 Jan. 1881.

IV. SPOILING FOR A FIGHT

CHAPTER 9. Our Herald; Political War and Personal Bloodshed

1. Janice Marie LaFlamme, *The Strategy of Feminine Protest* (master's thesis, Indiana University, 1968).

2. "Our Herald," *Lafayette Daily Courier*, 13 Aug. 1881.

3. "Mrs. Gougar at the Woman's Suffrage Meeting," *Lafayette Daily Courier*, 18 Oct. 1881.

4. "Personal," *Lafayette Daily Courier*, 25 Nov. 1881.

5. "Personal," *Lafayette Daily Courier*, 12 and 23 Dec. 1881.

6. "A Beardless Youth's Reply," *Lafayette Daily Courier*, 13 Jan. 1882.

7. "Mrs. Gougar for Congress," *Lafayette Weekly Courier*, 24 Jan. 1882.

8. Ibid.

9. Harper, 2: 541.

10. "Mrs. Gougar's Address at the New York Suffrage Convention," *Lafayette Daily Courier*, 10 Feb. 1882.

11. "The W.C.T.U.," *Lafayette Weekly Courier*, 11 Apr. 1882.

12. "Mrs. Gougar at Anderson," *Lafayette Weekly Courier*, 11 July 1882.

13. "Mrs. Gougar's Sarcasm," *Lafayette Daily Courier*, 15 Aug. 1882.

14. "The Course of the Lafayette Journal," *Lafayette Weekly Journal*, 1 Sept. 1882.

15. "Mrs. Gougar's Joke," *Lafayette Daily Courier*, 29 Aug. 1882.

16. "Personal," *Lafayette Daily Courier*, 7 Sept. 1882.

17. "A Popular Game," *Lafayette Daily Courier*, 9 Sept. 1882.

18. "Who Is the Herald Company, Any How?" *Lafayette Weekly Journal*, 29 Sept. 1882.

19. Ibid.

20. "Women in the Campaign," *Our Herald*, 25 Nov. 1882.

21. Ibid.

22. "Republican County Ticket," *Lafayette Daily Courier*, 2 Sept. 1882.

CHAPTER 10. The Gougar-Mandler Trial

In describing the Gougar-Mandler slander trial, extensive use was also made of an untitled, undated, unpublished summary researched, footnoted, and written by Mary Anthrop, a history teacher at Central Catholic High School, Lafayette. Miss Anthrop's study and analysis covering eighteen typed pages is housed in the Alameda McCollough Library, operated by the Tippecanoe County Historical Association at Tenth and South streets in Lafayette.

1. "Gougar-Mandler," *Lafayette Daily Courier*, 19 Feb. 1883.
2. "Hissing in a Court Room," *Indianapolis Journal*, 6 Mar. 1883.
3. "Gougar-Mandler," *Lafayette Daily Courier*, 30 Mar. 1883.
4. "Gougar vs. Mandler," *Lafayette Daily Courier*, 24 Jan. 1883.
5. "Woman Suffrage Not on Trial," *Lafayette Daily Courier*, 24 Feb. 1883.
6. "Gougar vs. Mandler, Mrs. Gougar's Case," *Lafayette Daily Courier*, 8 Feb. 1883.
7. "The Verdict," *Lafayette Morning Journal*, 12 Apr. 1883.
8. "Mrs. Gougar's Triumph," *Indianapolis Journal*, 12 Apr. 1883.
9. "Verdict of the Verdict," *Our Herald*, 14 Apr. 1883.
10. "Gougar-Mandler," *Lafayette Daily Courier*, 23 Feb. 1883.
11. Ibid.
12. Ibid.

V. Gaining Strength and Money

CHAPTER 11. **Travel and the Lecturing Life**

1. "Mrs. Gougar's Latest," *Lafayette Morning Journal*, 18 July 1883.
2. Ibid.
3. *Lafayette Daily Courier*, 27 Mar. 1884.
4. "George Sand on the Woman Question," *Lafayette Daily Courier*, 22 July 1884.
5. "The State Editorial Association," *Lafayette Daily Courier*, 6 Sept. 1884.
6. "Blackburn," *Lafayette Morning Journal*, 16 Oct. 1886.
7. "Green Isle," *Lafayette Morning Journal*, 12 Nov. 1886.

CHAPTER 12. **Talking for Fun and Profit**

1. "Mrs. Helen M. Gougar in Kansas," *Lafayette Morning Journal*, 1 Feb. 1887.
2. "Mrs. Gougar Memorialized," *Lafayette Morning Journal*, 5 May 1887.
3. Harper, 2: 622.
4. Ibid., 623.
5. Ibid.
6. "A Great Compliment," *Lafayette Morning Journal*, 21 May 1887.
7. "Sunny Skies," *Lafayette Morning Journal*, 8 Aug. 1887.
8. Harper, 2: 626.
9. Ibid.

CHAPTER 13. **Third Party Politics**

1. "Woman's Woes," *Lafayette Morning Journal*, 17 May 1888.
2. "Party Politics," *Lafayette Morning Journal*, 6 Aug. 1888.
3. "Mrs. Gougar's Views," *Lafayette Morning Journal*, 9 Aug. 1888.
4. "Prohibition at Hebron," *Lafayette Morning Journal*, 13 Aug. 1888.
5. "Two Views," *Lafayette Morning Journal*, 31 Aug. 1888.
6. Ibid.
7. "Mrs. Gougar Talks," *Lafayette Morning Journal*, 26 Sept. 1888.
8. "Mrs. Gougar Talks," *Lafayette Morning Journal*, 2 Nov. 1888.

CHAPTER 14. **Preaching Prohibition**

1. "Republican Compliments to Mrs. Gougar," *Lafayette Morning Journal*, 13 Nov. 1888.
2. "Personal Mention," *Lafayette Morning Journal*, 12 Dec. 1888.
3. "Monster Meeting," *Lafayette Morning Journal*, 22 July 1889.
4. "Prohibitionists at Frankfort," *Lafayette Morning Journal*, 13 Sept. 1889.
5. "Mrs. Gougar in Nebraska," *Lafayette Morning Journal*, 22 Oct. 1889.
6. Ibid.
7. "Mrs. Gougar in Chicago," *Lafayette Morning Journal*, 13 Nov. 1889.
8. "Money Monopoly," *Lafayette Morning Journal*, 2 Dec. 1889.

VI. NOT-ALWAYS-GAY NINETIES

CHAPTER 15. **Backing Losers and Losing Backers**

1. "Post Office Muddle," *Lafayette Morning Journal*, 3 Jan. 1890.
2. "Prohibition Convention," *Lafayette Morning Journal*, 22 Feb. 1890.
3. Ibid.
4. "Sunday Service," *Lafayette Morning Journal*, 21 Apr. 1890.
5. "Mrs. Gougar in Nebraska," *Lafayette Morning Journal*, 9 Sept. 1890.
6. "Local Nuggets," *Lafayette Morning Journal*, 17 Feb. 1891.
7. "Women in the Legislature," *Lafayette Morning Journal*, 27 Feb. 1891.
8. "Balmy Mexico," *Lafayette Morning Journal*, 11 Mar. 1891.
9. "Mexican Curios," *Lafayette Morning Journal*, 30 Mar. 1891.
10. "Baby is Born," *Lafayette Morning Journal*, 21 May 1891.

11. "A Talk on Tariff," *Lafayette Morning Journal*, 7 Aug. 1891.

12. "Caught by Cunning," *Lafayette Morning Journal*, 12 Aug. 1891.

13. "A Knotty Problem," *Lafayette Morning Journal*, 18 Dec. 1891.

14. "Mrs. Gougar Defends Dr. Parkhurst," *Lafayette Weekly Journal*, 22 Apr. 1892.

15. "Views of Leaders," *Voice* (New York), 12 Dec. 1895.

16. "How Can Women Make Money?" *Lafayette Weekly Journal*, 16 Dec. 1892.

CHAPTER 16. **Writing, Speaking, and Suing**

1. *Arena*, March 1893, 7: 461–70.

2. "Women at War," *Lafayette Morning Journal*, 24 May 1893.

3. Henry F. Buswell, lawyer, Boston, letter dated 15 Sept. 1893, to Wilson B. Smith, Lafayette postmaster. Photocopy from the collection of Mary E. Anthrop, Lafayette.

4. "Mrs. Gougar in Kansas," *Lafayette Morning Journal*, 11 Sept. 1893.

5. "Purely Personal," *Lafayette Morning Journal*, 11 Oct. 1893.

6. "Reception to Mrs. Gougar," *Lever* (Chicago), 26 Oct. 1893.

CHAPTER 17. **Fighting the Tariff and the Courthouse Club**

1. "Those Apples," *Lafayette Morning Journal*, 23 Jan. 1894.

2. "Mrs. Lease's Lecture," *Lafayette Morning Journal*, 1 May 1894.

3. "Mrs. Gougar at Chicago," *Lafayette Morning Journal*, 8 May 1894.

4. "Mrs. Gougar Talks," *Lafayette Morning Journal*, 9 May 1894.

5. "Woman Suffrage in New York," *Voice*, 31 May 1894.

6. "Mr. Gougar vs. Congressman Morse," *Voice*, 28 June 1894.

7. "Mrs. Gougar Home from Colorado," *Lafayette Morning Journal*, 24 July 1894.

8. "The Failure of Populism," *Lafayette Morning Journal*, 10 Aug. 1894.

9. "Newer Politics," *Lafayette Morning Journal*, 30 Aug. 1894.

10. "Local Nuggets," *Lafayette Morning Journal*, 12 Sept. 1894.

11. "Mrs. Gougar's Test Vote," *Lafayette Morning Journal*, 7 Nov. 1894.

12. "The Test Vote Case," *Lafayette Morning Journal*, 11 Jan. 1895.

13. Helen M. Gougar, *The Constitutional Rights of the Women of Indiana*, (Lafayette: Journal Printing Co., 1895), Appendix.

14. Ibid.

CHAPTER 18. **Crusade: From Holy Land to Bryan**

1. "Mrs. Gougar in Chicago," *Lafayette Morning Journal*, 19 Jan. 1895.

2. "In Historical Lands," *Lafayette Morning Journal*, 16 Apr. 1895.

3. "They Cannot Vote," *Lafayette Morning Journal*, 20 Apr. 1895.

4. The *Lafayette Morning Journal* reported the reform conference under the following titles and dates: "The Reform Conference," 18 and 19 Nov. 1895; "Well Under Way," 20 Nov. 1895; "Harvey on Silver," 21 Nov. 1895; "Woman's Day," 22 Nov. 1895; "Organized Labor," 23 Nov. 1895; and "Reform Conference," 25 Nov. 1895.

5. "Prohibition Meeting," *Lafayette Morning Journal*, 20 Feb. 1896.

6. "Indiana Prohibitionists Name a State Ticket Yesterday," *Lafayette Morning Journal*, 28 Feb. 1896.

7. "The National Party," *Lafayette Morning Journal*, 12 Aug. 1896.

8. "Mrs. Gougar at the Grand," *Lafayette Morning Journal*, 3 Nov. 1896.

9. "Mrs. Gougar's Withdrawal," *Lafayette Morning Journal*, 7 Jan. 1897.

10. "Mr. Bryan to Mrs. Gougar," *Lafayette Morning Journal*, 8 Jan. 1897.

11. Mrs. Gougar's Case," *Lafayette Morning Journal*, 20 Feb. 1897, and "Gougar Election Case," *Lafayette Morning Journal*, 25 Feb. 1897.

CHAPTER 19. **Castle Cottage and Cuba**

1. "From the Bahama Islands," *Lafayette Morning Journal*, 8 Apr. 1897.

2. "On Behalf of the Rescue Mission," *Lafayette Morning Journal*, 21 July 1897.

3. "Pictures from Cuban Life," *Lafayette Morning Journal*, 22 Feb. 1898.

VII. CHANGING SCENES

CHAPTER 20. **Riling Republicans; Writing a Book**

1. "Memorial Services," *Lafayette Morning Journal*, 28 Feb. 1898.

2. "The Home Established," *Lafayette Morning Journal*, 17 Mar. 1898.

3. Helen M. Gougar, *Wall Street's Bold Threat*. (Typewritten manuscript, date and publication status unknown. In the collection of

the Alameda McCollough Library, Tippecanoe County Historical Association, Tenth and South streets, Lafayette.)

4. "Mrs. Gougar on the Republican 'Key Notes,'" *Lafayette Morning Journal*, 22 Sept. 1898.

5. Gougar, *Matthew Peters*.

6. Dunn, 4: 1706.

7. "The Young Woman's Home," *Lafayette Morning Journal*, 9 Jan. 1899.

CHAPTER 21. **Viewing Money, Labor, and Nationalization**

1. "Government Ownership, Control of Railways," *Lafayette Morning Journal*, 20 Apr. 1899.

2. "A High-Handed Outrage," *Lafayette Morning Journal*, 10 June 1899.

3. "Labor Day in Lafayette," *Lafayette Morning Journal*, 5 Sept. 1899.

VIII. THE TURN OF THE CENTURY

CHAPTER 22. **Training the Modern Girl; Turning Democrat**

1. "Home-Makers Meet," *Lafayette Morning Journal*, 30 Jan. 1900.

2. "Helen M. Gougar on Industrial Training for Women," *Lafayette Evening Call*, 3 Feb. 1900.

3. "The City in Brief," *Lafayette Morning Journal*, 14 May 1900.

4. "Mrs. Gougar in Knightstown," *Lafayette Morning Journal*, 23 May 1900.

CHAPTER 23. **Women in Church: A Merciless Missive**

1. "The City in Brief," *Lafayette Daily Courier*, 12 June 1901.

2. "Thinks Men Will Go to Heaven," *Lafayette Morning Journal*, 29 July 1901.

CHAPTER 24. **World Tour; Time to Chat**

1. "Ex.-Gov. Shaw's List of Criminals," *Lafayette Morning Journal*, 14 Feb. 1902.

2. "Lafayette Woman Abroad," *Lafayette Morning Journal*, 25 Feb. 1903.

3. "Mrs. Gougar on Russia," *Lafayette Evening Call*, 15 July 1903.

4. "Will Write a Book," *Lafayette Evening Call*, 13 July 1903.

5. "Weekly Chat with the Call Readers," *Lafayette Evening Call*, 30 Nov. 1903.

CHAPTER 25. **What the World Needs Now**

1. "Answers Mrs. Gougar," *Lafayette Evening Call*, 15 Jan. 1904.

2. "Mrs. Helen M. Gougar's Estimate of Hearst," *Lafayette Evening Call*, 23 Feb. 1904.

3. "Foreign Missions," *Lafayette Evening Call*, 5 May 1904.

4. "Temperance Rally," *Lafayette Evening Call*, 11 Aug. 1904.

5. "Mr. and Mrs. Gougar's Dinner," *Lafayette Evening Call*, 12 Dec. 1904.

6. Helen M. Gougar, *Forty Thousand Miles of World Wandering* (Chicago: Monarch Book Co., 1905). All further references to this work appear in the text of chapter 25.

IX. LIKE AN EVENING GONE

CHAPTER 26. **End of a Rocky Road**

1. From *Headline History of Lafayette*, 1979.

2. "Woman Suffrage," *Lafayette Daily Courier*, 20 Feb. 1907.

3. B. O. Flower, "Noble Type of Twentieth-Century American Womanhood," *Arena*, Apr. 1906, 384–85.

CHAPTER 27. **Old Times That Are Soon Forgotten**

1. "Helen M. Gougar Expires Suddenly," *Lafayette Daily Courier*, 6 June, 1907.

2. "Death Comes to Helen M. Gougar," *Lafayette Morning Journal*, 7 June 1907.

3. "Death of Mrs. Gougar," *Lafayette Leader*, 9 June 1907.

4. Ibid.

BIBLIOGRAPHY

Anthrop, Mary. Untitled study of Helen M. Gougar's role in the 1882 Indiana political campaign and her slander suit against Henry Mandler during 1882–83. Alameda McCollough Library, Tippecanoe County Historical Association, Lafayette. n.d. Typescript.

Biographical Record and Portrait Album of Tippecanoe County, 1888. A reproduction by Unigraphic Inc., Evansville, 1972.

Boruff, Blanch Foster. *Women of Indiana.* Indianapolis: Matthew Farson, 1941.

Cincinnati Enquirer. Articles pertaining to Helen M. Gougar during March and April 1883.

Cottman, George S., and Max R. Hyman. *Centennial History of Indiana.* Indianapolis: Hollenbeck Press, 1915.

Cox, Sandford C. *Recollections of the Early Settlement of the Wabash Valley.* Lafayette: Courier Press, 1860.

DeHart, Gen. Richard P. *Past and Present of Tippecanoe County, Indiana* Vols. 1 and 2. Indianapolis: B. F. Bowen Co., 1909.

Dunn, Jacob Piatt. *Indiana and Indianans.* Vols. 3 and 4. Chicago: American Historical Society, 1919.

Flexner, Eleanor. *Century of Struggle.* Cambridge: Belknap Press of Harvard University Press, 1959.

Gougar, Helen M. *The Constitutional Rights of the Women of Indiana.* Lafayette: Journal Printing Co., 1895.

    Forty Thousand Miles of World Wandering. Chicago: Monarch Book Co., 1905.

    Matthew Peters: A Foreign Immigrant. Lafayette: Browne, Murphy & Co., 1898.

Harper, Ida H., *The Life and Work of Susan B. Anthony* . Vols. 1 and 2. Indianapolis: Bowen-Merrill Co., 1899.

Indianapolis Journal. Articles pertaining to Helen M. Gougar during April 1883.

Kingman Brothers. *1878 Historical Atlas of Tippecanoe County, Indiana.* Reprint. Knightstown: The Book Mark, 1978.

Kriebel, Robert C. 1979. *"Headline History of Lafayette."* Alameda McCollough Library, Tippecanoe County Historical Association, Lafayette. Typescript.

    150 Years of Lafayette Newspapers. Lafayette: Tippecanoe County Historical Association, 1981.

Lafayette Daily Courier. Articles pertaining to Helen M. Gougar, temperature, woman suffrage, and related topics between 1860 and 1907.

Lafayette Evening Call. Articles pertaining to Helen M. Gougar between 1901 and 1905.

Lafayette Journal and Courier. Articles pertaining to Helen M. Gougar between 1966 and 1983.

Lafayette Morning Journal. Articles pertaining to Helen M. Gougar, temperance, woman suffrage, and allied topics between 1860 and 1907.

Lafayette Sunday Times. Articles pertaining to Helen M. Gougar between 1879 and 1907.

Lafayette Weekly Courier. Articles pertaining to Helen M. Gougar from 1882.

Lafayette Weekly Journal. Articles pertaining to Helen M. Gougar from 1882 and 1892.

LaFlamme, Janice Marie. "The Strategy of Feminine Protest." Master's thesis, Indiana University, 1968.

Sanders, Ardis, and David McConnell. *Indiana History.* Wilkinsburg, Pa.: Hayes School Publishing Co., 1975.

Sutherland, James, comp. *Lafayette City Directory for 1858–1859.* Lafayette: G. W. Hawes Co.

Todd, Lewis Paul, and Merle Curti. *Rise of the American Nation.* New York: Harcourt Brace Jovanovich, Heritage Edition, 1977.

Webb, Cecil S. *Historical Growth of the Schools of Lafayette, Indiana.* Lafayette: Lafayette School Corp., 1972.

INDEX

231